"Howard Levine's fascinating volume of André Green's work offers anglophone access to previously untranslated papers that are missing pieces in Green's intellectual journey. The seven chapters along with Levine's introduction illuminate central metapsychological concepts that Green brings forward, along with their crucial clinical implications. Deeply rooted in Freud's oeuvre but acknowledging Bion and Winnicott's contributions, Green proposes here his key conceptions of the frame, 'the double-limit', death-drive, language and silence."
Marilia Aisenstein, author of *An Analytic Journey* and *Desire, Pain, Thought* (Routledge)

"Howard Levine collects valuable gold nuggets from the great mine that is the vast oeuvre of André Green and makes them available to the English-speaking reader. With these texts, he shines a powerful light on Green's indispensable contributions to contemporary psychoanalysis. It is evident in this volume how the French author, starting from his Freudian roots and influenced by Lacan, Winnicott and Bion, brings extremely original and at the same time fundamental contributions to the psychoanalyst of today. An indispensable read!"
Ruggero Levy, Full Member and Training Analyst of the Porto Alegre Psychoanalytic Society (SPPA – Brasil)

The Freudian Matrix
of André Green

The Freudian Matrix of André Green presents seven papers, never previously published in English, that will allow readers to more closely follow and more fully understand the development of Green's unique psychoanalytic thinking.

The chapters in this book provide valuable insight into Green's response to a perceived crisis in psychoanalysis. His thinking synthesizes the work of Lacan, Winnicott, Bion and other post-Freudian authors with his own extensive clinical experience, and results in a much needed extension of psychoanalytic theory and practice to non-neurotic patients. Green's focus on drives, affect and the work of the negative and his introduction and exploration of the Dead Mother complex, narcissism, negative hallucination and the death instinct constitute a vital expansion of Freudian metapsychology and its application to the clinical setting.

The Freudian Matrix of André Green will be essential reading for psychoanalysts in practice and in training, and for any reader looking to understand more about the enormity of his contribution.

Howard B. Levine is a private practitioner in Brookline, Massachusetts. He is editor-in-chief of the Routledge Wilfred R. Bion Studies Book Series, the author of *Affect, Representation and Language: Between the Silence and the Cry* and has edited and co-edited *André Green Revisited: Representation and the Work of the Negative, Unrepresented States and the Construction of Meaning* and *The Post-Bionian Field Theory of Antonino Ferro* (all Routledge).

Psychoanalytic Ideas and Applications Series
Series Editor: Silvia Flechner

IPA Publications Committee
Fred Busch, Natacha Delgado, Nergis Güleç, Thomas Marcacci, Carlos Moguillansky, Rafael Mondrzak, Angela M. Vuotto, Gabriela Legoretta (consultant)

Recent titles in the Series include

What Nazism Did to Psychoanalysis
Laurence Kahn

The Deconstruction of Narcissism and the Function of the Object
Explorations in Psychoanalysis
René Roussillon

The Infinite Infantile and the Psychoanalytic Task
Psychoanalysis with Children, Adolescents and their Families
Edited by Nilde Parada Franch, Christine Anzieu-Premmereur, Mónica Cardenal and Majlis Winberg Salomonsson

A Psychoanalytic Understanding of Trauma
Post-Traumatic Mental Functioning, the Zero Process, and the Construction of Reality
Joseph Fernando

The Poetry of the Word in Psychoanalysis
Selected Papers of Pere Folch Mateu
Edited by J.O. Esteve and Jordi Sala

The Freudian Matrix of André Green
Towards a Psychoanalysis for the Twenty-First Century
Edited by Howard B. Levine

Desire, Pain and Thought
Primal Masochism and Psychoanalytic Theory
Marilia Aisenstein

The Freudian Matrix of André Green

Towards a Psychoanalysis for the Twenty-First Century

Edited and Introduction
by Howard B. Levine

*Translated by Dorothée Bonnigal-Katz
and Andrew Weller*

Designed cover image: The Virgin and Child with Saint Anne and the Infant Saint John the Baptist ("The Burlington House Cartoon"), Leonardo da Vinci, c. 1499–1500. The National Gallery. Purchased with a special grant and contributions from the Art Fund, The Pilgrim Trust, and through a public appeal organized by the Art Fund, 1962.

Chapters 1, 2, 3 and 4 first published in French as
VI – "Après-coup, l'archaïque" (1982)
VIII – "La double limite" (1982)
IX – "Le silence du psychanalyste" (1979)
X – "La capacité de rêverie et le mythe étiologique" (1987)

La folie privée. Psychanalyse des cas-limites © Éditions Gallimard, Paris, 1990

Chapter 5, 6 and 7 first published in "Du signe au discours" pages 31 to 60, Les Editions d'Itaque, 2011, Paris; "La clinique psychanalytique contemporaine", pages 5 to 30, Les Editions d'Ithaque, 2012, Paris; "La clinique psychanalytique contemporaine", pages 79 to 105, Les Editions d'Ithaque, 2012, Paris.

First published in English 2023
by Routledge
4 Park Square, Milton Park, Abingdon, Oxon OX14 4RN

and by Routledge
605 Third Avenue, New York, NY 10158

Routledge is an imprint of the Taylor & Francis Group, an informa business

© 2023 selection and editorial matter, Howard B. Levine; individual chapters, the contributors

The right of Howard B. Levine to be identified as the author of the editorial material, and of the authors for their individual chapters, has been asserted in accordance with sections 77 and 78 of the Copyright, Designs and Patents Act 1988.

All rights reserved. No part of this book may be reprinted or reproduced or utilized in any form or by any electronic, mechanical or other means, now known or hereafter invented, including photocopying and recording, or in any information storage or retrieval system, without permission in writing from the publishers.

Trademark notice: Product or corporate names may be trademarks or registered trademarks, and are used only for identification and explanation without intent to infringe.

British Library Cataloguing-in-Publication Data
A catalogue record for this book is available from the British Library

Library of Congress Cataloging-in-Publication Data
A catalog record has been requested for this book

ISBN: 978-1-032-39524-1 (hbk)
ISBN: 978-1-032-39521-0 (pbk)
ISBN: 978-1-003-35013-2 (ebk)

DOI: 10.4324/9781003350132

Typeset in Palatino
by Apex CoVantage, LLC

Contents

Series editor's foreword viii
Acknowledgements x
Sources of the original texts xi

Introduction: Why Green? By Howard B. Levine 1

1 *Après-coup*, the archaic 15

2 The double limit 36

3 The silence of the psychoanalyst 53

4 The capacity for reverie and the etiological myth 75

5 Language within the general theory of representation 91

6 The psychoanalytic frame: Its internalization by the analyst and its application in practice 120

7 Dismembering the countertransference: What we have gained and lost with the extension of the countertransference 141

Index 165

Series editor's foreword

The Publications Committee of the International Psychoanalytic Association continues, with the present volume, the series "Psychoanalytic Ideas and Applications".

The aim of this series is to focus on the scientific production of significant authors whose works are outstanding contributions to the development of the psychoanalytic field and to set out relevant ideas and themes, generated during the history of psychoanalysis, that deserve to be known and discussed by present day psychoanalysts.

The relationship between psychoanalytic ideas and their applications needs to be put forward from the perspective of theory, clinical practice and research, in order to maintain their validity for contemporary psychoanalysis.

The Publication's Committee's objective is to share these ideas with the psychoanalytic community and with professionals in other related disciplines, in order to expand their knowledge and generate a productive interchange between the text and the reader. The IPA Publications Committee is pleased to publish *The Freudian Matrix of André Green: Towards a Psychoanalysis for the 21st Century*, edited by Howard Levine.

This book grew out of the editor's awareness that there were several important papers by André Green that had not been translated into English. Dr Levine and Fernando Urribari (who worked closely with André Green for many years) selected seven of these untranslated essays based on what they considered would be most relevant to an English-speaking readership. With the support of the IPA Publications Committee, excellent English translations were produced by Dorothée Bonnigal-Katz and Andrew Weller. The seven translated chapters reflect this work, offering readers access to ground-breaking, previously untranslated papers of André Green.

What is extraordinarily valuable about the work of André Green and about this book in particular is that it provides a unique opportunity to go back to Freud's ground-breaking contributions which form the pillars of psychoanalysis. During his career, André Green brilliantly unearthed Freud's genius, highlighting its fundamental importance in contemporary psychoanalysis while proposing numerous important concepts, such as the work of the negative, that emanate from Freud's metapsychology. André Green carefully interweaves his clinical and theoretical contributions with those of Freud. With this in mind, the editor, Howard Levine, rightly proposes that Freud and Green provide the foundation for a contemporary psychoanalysis of the 21st century.

In his study of unrepresented states, André Green goes back to early contributions in Freud's thinking, in particular to the economic perspective proposed by Freud in his understanding of the workings of the psyche. In paying particular attention to this, he underlines the importance of unrepresentable forces such as the impulse, the drive, the discharge and the act. These forces have the capacity to disrupt the capacity to think, to symbolize and to communicate internal experiences.

In the introduction to this volume, "Why Green?", one can appreciate Dr Levine's deep understanding of Green's thinking and of those authors that influenced him such as Bion, Winnicott and Lacan. He brilliantly captures the essence of the ideas and contributions of each paper. In this manner, he gives the reader not only an overview of the content of the book, but a desire to discover these previously inaccessible papers.

Each of the seven chapters is one of Green's papers. One will find "*Après-coup*, the archaic"; "The double limit; The silence of the psychoanalyst"; "The capacity for reverie and the etiological myth"; "Language within the general theory of representation"; "The psychoanalytic frame: Its internalization by the analyst and its application in practice"; and "Dismembering the countertransference: What we have gained and lost with the extension of the countertransference".

This book is a remarkable addition to the English-speaking readership both for those who are already acquainted with Green's work as well as for those who want to discover and appreciate his ground-breaking contributions in the field of psychoanalysis. One should be thankful to Dr Levine for having had the initiative to take on this important project and for bringing it to fruition.

Gabriela Legorreta
Series Editor
Chair, IPA Publications Committee

Acknowledgements

Howard B. Levine

The idea of this book arose out of a series of conversations between myself and Fernando Urribarri at the 2019 André Green and Unrepresented States Conference held in Mexico City by the Antonio Santamaria Psychoanalytic Educational Association. I felt that in the warranted enthusiasm for the implications of Freud's work for the understanding and treatment of neurosis and neurotic structures, a great deal of what Freud had indicated or alluded to in regard to other states and conditions had been overlooked or remained underdeveloped in current psychoanalytic thinking. We both felt that Green's work was an exception to this neglect and that it had the potential of containing the roots of a new and powerful – pragmatically necessary – Freudian paradigm for contemporary psychoanalysis. Since Fernando had worked so closely with Green in the last dozen or so years of Andre's life and knew his work in the original French, I suggested that he select a set of previously untranslated essays by Green that would be of vital interest to an anglophone audience. He did so and with the support of Gabriela Legoretta and the Publications Committee of the IPA, I arranged with Dorothée Bonnigal-Katz and Andrew Weller for the excellent English translations that comprise the main chapters of this book. The IPA Committee and I are grateful to Gallimard and Les Editions d'Ithaque for permission to translate and reprint these chapters. It is my hope that what readers will find here will help them reappraise and even more deeply appreciate the brilliance and continued contemporary relevance of Freud's genius, as well as Green's vision and tenacity in wedding his own clinical experience to his careful, deep and generative reading of Freud's opus. Together, I believe, they present us with the foundations for a contemporary psychoanalysis for the 21st century.

Sources of the original texts

1 "Après-coup l'archaïque". In *La foliée privée*, pages 225 to 254. Gallimard, 1990, Paris.
2 "Le double limite". In *La foliée privée*, pages 293 to 316. Gallimard, 1990, Paris.
3 "Le silence du psychanalyste". In *La foliée privée*, pages 317 to 346. Gallimard, 1990, Paris.
4 "La capacité de rêverie et le mythe étiologique". In *La foliée privée*, pages 347 to 368. Gallimard, 1990, Paris.
5 "Le langage au sein de la théorie general de la représentation". In *Du signe au discours* pages 31 to 60. Les Editions d'Itaque, 2011, Paris.
6 "Le cadre et son intériorisation par l'analyste". In *La clinique psychanalytique contemporaine*, pages 5 to 30. Les Editions d'Ithaque, 2012, Paris.
7 "Démembrement du contre transfert". In *La clinique psychanalytique contemporaine*, pages 79 to 105. Les Editions d'Ithaque, 2012, Paris.

Introduction
Why Green?

Howard B. Levine

Looking back over the trajectory of André Green's work from the perspective of his 1974 London IPA Congress panel presentation (Green, 1975), we can see the extent to which he responded to what was then perceived to be a psychoanalysis in crisis by revisiting, reanimating and extending its Freudian foundations. A vital issue raised in the London Congress revolved around the question of whether or not – or to what extent – clinical psychoanalysis, as it was classically elaborated and understood, should be restricted to neurosis or could be successfully applied to the broader group of non-neurotic patients who comprised what was termed "the widening scope". Green recognized that neurosis and neurotic organizations did not offer the most effective templates on which to base a model of psychic functioning that would help analysts understand and treat patients whose psychic structures placed them at the boundaries of what was then considered analysable. While maintaining and defending the initial gains made by psychoanalysis in the study of neurosis, Green responded by placing borderline and other non-neurotic structures and organizations (*les cas-limites*) at the center of psychoanalytic study in order to bring forward and elaborate upon what was implied or hinted at, but not yet fully developed by, Freud.

In retrospect, part of the problem that psychoanalysis faced, at least in the US, was that the optimism and idealistic expectations that had flourished in the first half of the 20th century had, after Freud's death, begun to wear off in the face of the often disappointing and sometimes problematic attempts to extend analytic treatment beyond neurosis. Were contemporary patients somehow different than the classical neurotics on which psychoanalysis had been centred or were we now more sensitive to pre-genital conflicts and fixations? Would our outcomes improve if we abandoned the familiar, so-called Freudian classical approach in favour of one derived from Inter-Personalism, Self Psychology, Winnicott, Klein or Lacan? Should Freud, drive theory and metapsychology be removed from their central roles in our thinking in favour of models that were more congruent with the findings of neuroscience, infant development and other contemporary sciences?

2 Introduction: Why Green?

Green's response was powerful and direct. Having been influenced by Lacan, Winnicott and Bion, his close reading of Freud coupled with reflections on his own, extensive clinical experience produced an extraordinarily deep, synthetic and creative outpouring. The chapters in this book reflect that work, offering anglophone readers access to certain key, previously untranslated missing pieces in Green's intellectual journey.

Green recognized that Freud's move from the Topographic Theory to the Structural Theory necessitated a change that went far beyond the emphasis on ego defences, signal anxiety, adaptation and the question of a conflict-free sphere that was given to it by the North American Ego Psychologists. He felt that the theoretical revisions of the second topography, made necessary in the light of Freud's clinical experience with narcissism, trauma, unconscious guilt, negative therapeutic reactions and the savagery of war, compounded by the unmourned – perhaps unmournable! – enormity of the loss to our field imposed upon us by Freud's death, had produced a diffraction – even fragmentation – of the homogeneity of psychoanalytic thinking into a heterogeneous group of rivalrous, "post-Freudian" schools. Perhaps most important of all, death prevented Freud from fully working out the very significant implications of his second topography, Revised Drive Theory and his paper on constructions (Freud, 1937b).[1]

Initially, Freud had illuminated the understanding, psychic organization and treatment of *neurosis*, culminating in his Topographic Theory. The latter, based upon the dream, dreamwork and dream interpretation, described the conflicts and interactions of fully formed, unconscious representations. It is a model that still is and will probably always remain a cornerstone in the foundation of psychoanalysis. What Green's work has shown us, however, was that Freud's thinking and discoveries involved far more than this. Green took a careful reading of Freud's second topography – the Structural Theory (Freud, 1959 [1923]), *Beyond the Pleasure Principle* (Freud, 1920) and the introduction of the death instinct – and began to work out and fulfil Freud's intimations of a psychoanalysis modelled not only on established unconscious representations, but also on the negative and unrepresented and unrepresentable forces, such as the impulse, drive movements and the act.[2]

As Green convincingly describes it, Freud's transition from the first to the second topography (from the Topographic Theory to the Structural Theory) was a shift from a theory based predominantly, even exclusively, on representation – wish, desire and hope – to one that centred theoretical focus "upstream" of the vicissitudes of conflict between unconscious representations, onto the problem of the force of the drives and its various

---

1 For discussions of the latter see Levine (2011, 2022).
2 For extended discussions of unrepresented states and their clinical implications, see Levine et al. (2013) and Levine (2022).

expressions: affect, impulse, action, and somatic discharge. The major development that this entailed was the change from:

> one model, at the centre of which one finds a form of thinking (desire, hope, wish), to another model based on the act (impulse as internal action, automatism, acting) . . . the analyst now not only has to deal with unconscious desire but with the drive itself, whose force (constant pressure) is undoubtedly its principal characteristic, capable of subverting both desire and thinking. (Green, 2005, p. 47)

The clinical implications of the disturbance and subversion of desire and thinking is at the heart of Green's contribution (e.g. Green, 2011). In an interview in 1984, Green put it this way: "neurosis is no longer at the centre of our preoccupations, not that it has disappeared, but the interest of the borderline cases is that they constitute the ideal promontory from which one may observe both the side of neurosis and the side of psychosis" (1987 [1984], p. 125). In the light of more contemporary developments, many of which follow from Green's (1999) explications of the work of the negative, we might amend his statement to contrast not only neurosis and psychosis, but represented and unrepresented states.[3]

For Green, "desire" – which implies motivation and a specificity of intent; "I want to do this to or get that from you" – is not an inherent, in-borne characteristic of the drives in the same way that it is for Klein. It is a later evolution, a developmental achievement, a product of transformation that can come into being only after the drive produces a derivative that achieves the status of becoming psychic. This means that certain drive-related "movements" of what we might call the primordial mind (Green, 1998) may not deserve to be designated as "wish" or "desire", but should be seen instead as non-specific "forces, tensions or accretions of stimuli" in search of reduction or discharge and a suitable form within which to contain and direct them. Thus, Green (2005) says that it can be misleading to "speak of desire . . . [when] it is legitimate to ask . . . if this category is really present, . . . [R]aw and barely nuanced forms [of action], expressions of imperious instinctual demands, throw a doubt over the relevance of this qualification" (p. 102).

Prior to containment, the sensations ("feelings") associated with not-yet-qualified drive movements and perceptions[4] may be seen as the product of a raw, undifferentiated "something" that we might call *angst* or *anguish*, rather than a specific, qualified emotion, such as terror, fright,

---

3 See Levine (2022).
4 Bion (1962) categorized the sensations of raw existential Experience as beta elements. In doing so, he articulated a model of perception implicit in Freud (1911, 1925) in which the first registrations of perception of external reality were not quite available for psychic work until they were transformed and registered and therefore made available for psychic processing and recall.

fear, etc. To put it succinctly, while sexuality is common to all patients and is essential in the structuring of the mind, "desire" is the provenance of neurotic patients or the neurotic sectors of the mind. Desire differs in both quality and quantity from the blind, instinctual, action-oriented discharge and demands of the drives and the not-yet-represented forms of raw perception in the non-neurotic parts of the psyche.

What Green's work amounts to is not another "school", but the building blocks of an expanded, *deeply Freudian paradigm* for psychoanalysis, one that encompasses something that can be seen in language and discourse as an unending oscillation and shifting dynamic balance and conflict between language and thought, speech and action, communication and discharge. That is, between represented and unrepresented states (represented states <-> unrepresented states).

As Green (1977) poetically put it: "Language without affect is a dead language: and affect without language is uncommunicable. Language is situated between the cry and the silence" (p. 205). And: "The aim of analytic interpretation is to make language say what it does not say". (Chapter 5). It is the vicissitudes of the continual oscillation between the silence of what we cannot find words for and the inchoate cry that may indicate that failure that is the problematic of the two poles of the work of the negative (Green, 1999) and is at the heart of Green's clinical contribution.

Bion, who classified emotions as beta elements and therefore not yet "psychic", had emphasized that "what takes place in the consulting-room is an *emotional* situation" (Bion, 1970: 118, italics added) and noted the "lack of any adequate terminology to describe" it (Bion, 1962: 67–68). He also cautioned that "Sometimes the function of speech is to communicate experience to another; sometimes it is to miscommunicate experience to another" and that "Reason is emotion's slave and exists to rationalize emotional experience" (Bion, 1970: 1).

The problem for the analyst is how to decide the degree to which that miscommunication or rationalization is in the service of some psychological motivation, wish or need or when it reflects the root inadequacy of thought or language to encompass or convey some aspect of psychic life. In regard to the latter, Bion (1965) analogized that attempting to use words to talk about psychic experience was like trying to solve certain math problems before the calculus had been invented, or studying the stars with a high-powered telescope – while the latter may prove useful as a powerful means of observing stellar and inter-planetary light in the *visible* spectrum, it cannot discern infra-red and ultra violet emanations.

In "Memory and desire" (Bion 2018 [1965]) said:

> as analysts we do know – and I think it is borne in on us more and more as experience builds up – that we really do deal with *something*; that the psychoanalytic experience, however skeptical we may be, is

> really an emotional experience and it really exists, even if we shall never know or shall be in a position to give an approximately correct description of what takes place. (p. 3)

There is an enigmatic and ineffable epistemological status to experience, especially emotional or psychic experience, that inevitably leads to a series of problems and paradoxes: the very subject of psychoanalytic investigation and interest consists of things that can be *felt* but not fully or directly *known*, made sense of or put into a meaningful relation with our identity and personal idiom and are certainly not fully amenable to being spoken of by language. "Psycho-analytical events cannot be stated directly" (Bion, 1970: 26). A good deal of what is most relevant to psychoanalytic investigation and discourse – affect, emotions, feelings, psychic states, etc. – while capable of being "felt" or in some way "sensed", are beyond the reach of being known empirically by our senses. Our words may indicate and refer to them, but they cannot fully describe them. "The realizations with which a psycho-analyst deals cannot be seen or touched; anxiety has no shape or colour, smell or sound" (Bion, 1970: 7).

Many of Freud's descriptions of drive movements, cathexes and the Id reflect this realization. For example, in the *New Introductory Lectures*, Freud (1933) described the Id as: ". . . the dark, inaccessible part of our personality" (p. 73) and said that:

> We approach the id with analogies: we call it chaos, a cauldron full of seething excitations . . . It is filled with energy reaching it from the instincts, but it has no organization, produces no collective will, but only a striving to bring about the satisfaction of the instinctual needs subject to the observance of the pleasure principle . . . Instinctual cathexes seeking discharge – that, in our view, is all there is in the id. (pp. 73–74)

Freud (1933) added that the quality of the cathexes of the id differ so completely from those of the ego that we cannot speak of or expect to find in the Id "what in the ego we should call an idea" (p. 75). Green drew upon Freud, Bion and Winnicott's (1971) descriptions of de-cathexis in his accounts of foreclosure (*Verwerfung*), negative hallucination and the progressive and disruptive poles of the work of the negative.

The line of reasoning that Green's theories leads us to applies to the analyst's psychic states as well as those of the patient. In trying to think about or put feelings and the psychic qualities of experience into words, analyst and patient are trying to make the best of a bad situation and are always, *per force*, falling short of full description, because:

> The psycho-analyst and his analysand are alike dependent upon the senses, but psychic qualities with which psycho-analysis deals, are

not perceived by the senses but, as Freud says, by some mental counterpart of the sense organs, a function that he [Freud] attributed to consciousness. (Bion, 1970: 28)

Green (1987 [1984]) makes a similar point when he describes a central enigma that is inherent to the psychoanalytic situation:

There was on Freud's part a deliberate choice that psychoanalysis should be a treatment that worked exclusively through speech, through verbal exchange, and that it should manage to deprive itself of any other means ... the crucial question of psychoanalysis remains: how is it that by means of speech we change something in the structure of the subject, whereas what we change does not belong to the field of speech? (p. 121)

Keeping all of this in mind, we might say that psychoanalytic theory and metapsychology are models and sets of concepts and descriptors that help us to utilize the phenomena that we *can* come to know via the senses to point to, indicate and talk about the noumena that we cannot come to know fully and directly. And if these theories and models are helpful to us in guiding our actions and interventions in the clinical setting, then their pragmatic value renders moot the question of whether they relate to what is actual or "real" in the external world.

Readers of this volume will come to see the extent to which Green's epistemology, similar to that of Freud, is firmly embedded in a European philosophical tradition descended from Kant and Hume, via Hegel to Husserl, Merleau-Ponty and Sartre. This stands in contrast to the more reality-based, positivist, anti-metapsychological stance of the Ego Psychologists.[5] The tension or conflict between the two views has often been miscast in debates about the supposed status of psychoanalysis as a science. No doubt aided by Bion's comparison of psychoanalytic theory to mathematics, Green's insistence upon and use of metapsychology reflected his recognition that like other sciences – e.g. quantum mechanics and mathematics – psychoanalysis consists of a series of interlocking, sometimes nested, interdependent models and theories, many of which are theoretically implied or made necessary by the others. In such a system, the crucial element is not whether they are literally or factually "true", but whether or not they prove useful in their clinical application. As Bion (1962: iii) said, what matters is not whether an interpretation is "right" or "wrong" but whether or not it leads to psychic development.

The title of our first chapter, "*Après-coup*, the archaic", may be read both as a content statement and as a play on words. For Freud, the archaic leaves

---

5 See Kahn (2018, 2022) for further discussion.

an unobservable imprint that cannot be directly known via experience, but may be inferred or conjectured beneath the superimpositions of later development. The latter overlays the primordial organization and forms of the archaic, as illustrated by the sequence infantile neurosis -> adult neurosis -> transference neurosis, with each a transformation and redeployment so to say of the forces and even the contents of the other. So in that sense, the archaic cannot be directly known, but only conjectured *après-coup*.

Our problem as psychoanalysts is that "the archaic persists, present in practice and theory alike, even though we remain benighted as far as its nature is concerned while having no choice but to take it on board, willingly or not" (Chapter 1). The very Freudian solution that Green proposes to this problem is to have us "read the archaic *après coup*, which is in fact the only way to talk about it; it will be surmised or inferred *a posteriori*, behind or beneath the walls that were erected against its threatening power" (Chapter 1, original italics). For those analysts who can discern its power and potency, the archaic, often in the form of a permanent excitation, tormenting the Ego, "is not only forever, it is also everywhere, hidden under the appearances of normality" (Chapter 1). It "is less a fixed archaism or one moving towards an evolution than one stopped in its tracks on the way to the recognition of maturity" (Chapter 1). Chapter 2, "The double limit", reflects Green's efforts to formulate a psychoanalytic metapsychology of thought and thinking, as he explores the internal space needed in which to hold together a sense of identity and a thinking mind. This project will always remain framed by "the relations between the unthinkable constituted by the drive and the elaboration it is subjected to by language, allowing thought to arise . . . Its theorization is always focused on the problem of the sources of thinking [i.e. absence, emotion and therefore the body] and its entrenchment in drive-related life" (Chapter 2).

The concept of "double limit" applies to the borders between outside and inside and the systems Conscious–Preconscious and Unconscious, and includes the links between them. In clinical terms, Green tells us that this is a "theoretical formulation of a clinical and technical problem pertaining to the modalities of transference in non-neurotic patients, from the perspective of the object's function" (Chapter 2). "The crux of the psychoanalytic action ultimately aims for the representation of psychic, intrasubjective and intersubjective processes . . . Adjustments of the frame have no other function than the facilitation of the function of representation" (Chapter 2). In regard to the latter, Green adds the important observation that "Representation implies binding but thinking implies re-binding the representation in a non-specular mode" (Chapter 2). The double limit reflects the very paradoxical structure of thought, which "must abide by the double task of establishing enough distance with drive derivatives where it originates while retaining contact with its affective roots through which it acquires its weight of truth" (Chapter 2).

In non-neurotic structures, instead of having to overcome the limitations imposed by reality on desire by providing it with roundabout satisfactions, the psychoanalytic investigation might come to learn, rather, that most of the psychic activity is directed towards the preservation of a relation with the object which is always facing the threat of mutual destruction . . . Concern with the preservation of identity is at the centre of these object relations. The autonomy of thought becomes the stake of a battle waged by the analysand to ensure his identity, i.e. to defend his Ego's territory as the only site where a continuity of being may be sustained. (Chapter 2)

In the third chapter, "The silence of the psychoanalyst", Green explores the metapsychological status of the analyst's silence from a position heavily influenced by the thinking of Bion and Winnicott. What will prove decisive is how that silence is experienced and interpreted by the patient and what that silence says of the analyst's receptivity. Will it be and be seen at any given moment as "a living space, inhabited by all the associations of analytic listening" indicative of "the intense work of elaboration undertaken by the analyst" or as "a herald of the void" and the threat of Ego disruption and fragmentation? (Chapter 3).

While this choice point can be crucial, the matter is not at all straightforward or simple. Green notes that while Freud advocated a stance of abstinence and neutrality, he never enshrined the analyst's silence as a "golden rule" of technique. In fact, with the exception of the group of English analysts, including Strachey, who were in analysis with Freud as reported by Kardiner (1977), Freud and the early Viennese analysts offered patients a rather active and vocal presence (see also Roazen, 1995). With an eye towards Winnicott (e.g. 1974, 1989 [1965]), Green "reminds us that, with some patients, we are used for our very deficiencies, which symbolize the initial deficiencies of the environment" (Chapter 3). That is, as disruptive and painful as its manifestations may be, we perforce rely upon the traumatophilic/traumatolytic power of the repetition compulsion to bring the necessary, often pre-verbal, disturbances into the analytic field. And that in regard to technique, "Bion's recommendation is not to be silent but to prove oneself to be as available as possible at the beginning of each session, so as to be able to hear whatever new material the patient might bring" (Chapter 3).

While the classical neurotic patient may be able to tolerate, accept and make use of the analyst's silence, "cases where narcissistic traits dominate, or the borderline cases, or those who present serious personality disorders, all show that the analyst's silence is not productive. Either patients do not tolerate it or they settle into a false self position in the analysis" (Chapter 3). In such instances, which unfortunately may predominate in today's consulting rooms, *"The analyst's silence can only be understood as part of the psychoanalytic frame. Its meaning can only be elucidated as embedded in the set of conditions that circumscribe this frame and constitute the a priori of psychoanalysis or of this application of the psychoanalytic method to the psychoanalytic treatment"* (Chapter 3, original italics).

Thus, Green describes the frame, an internal function of the analyst's mind as well as an external set of parameters, as a symbolic matrix, container and condition for the discovery, construction and creation of meanings related to other meanings, including those that have not yet been spoken, constructed or known. "The analyst is the guardian of the frame where silence is the main parameter . . . The frame is a symbolic matrix, a container that is itself contained, a condition for the meaning that pertains to another meaning" (Chapter 3).

His emphasis here is on the vital and necessary role of interpretation as a vector of psychoanalytic transformation, but with the following caveat: "the silent function of the analyst is independent of the quantity of words (or information) that he introduces in the analytic frame" (Chapter 3). "Interpretation is not the opposite of silence because silence can also be a form of interpretation. In the analytic frame, there are nothing but different models of interpretation" (Chapter 3). And a meaningful silence – preferable to "empty" or de-vitalized speech – can be a powerful "statement" in its own right!

The paradoxical nature of the analytic process is that *"the analytic frame induces the production of a speech that interpretation will subject to the silence of punctuation, followed by the resumption of associations"* (Chapter 3, original italics). In the optimal cases, this will be followed at times by the silence of elaboration, a shared silence, within which "the interpretation emerges from the work carried out in the gaps in speech, in the associative discontinuity" (Chapter 3). Thus, Green emphasizes that along with and beyond the manifest content of the analyst's words, there is the analyst's *being*, and an interpretive "speech", which may include the pause of the analyst's silence, that is "not cut off from its unconscious roots by way of preconscious elaboration" (Chapter 3). Green concludes that it is impossible to speak of the analyst's silence without speaking of the frame, the analyst's words, the analyst's being and the very nature and limitations of language. He reminds us that "what must be understood is that the unconscious structure is *reverberated-reverberating*, which means that the various positions resonate with one another" (Chapter 3, original italics). This underlines the crucial role of metaphor, myth and polysemy and leads to a final observation that *"silence is the site where the manifest is erased so that the latent may be unveiled"* (Chapter 3, original italics).

An important corrective to the emphasis of psychoanalytic thinking on the intrapsychic and constitutional offered by Bion, Winnicott and Green was the recognition that especially in regard to non-neurotic psychopathology, the quality of maternal participation, absence or reverie, proves crucial in determining developmental outcomes. In Chapter 4, "The capacity for reverie and the etiological myth", Green provocatively notes where

10 Introduction: Why Green?

Bion (1962, 1970), in his theory of thinking, goes beyond Klein: "even if the breast actually feeds the child, the preservation of the good breast is not enough to generate thought. It is a necessary condition but not a sufficient one" (Chapter 4). "Bion thus observes that the psychical cannot be elaborated on the basis of the physical experience of the breast, however good it might have been. *The psychical can only arise from the psyche, namely the mother's psyche*, which is another way of saying that thought can only arise from the thought of the object" (Chapter 4, original italics).

What is at stake in the analysis of the non-neurotic patient and structures of the mind is the transformation of "facts" or "sensations" into *emotions* belonging to and relevant to a sense of self (in line with one's personal idiom). The problem with the non-neurotic often rests with the psychic voids (traumatic disruptions) produced by the failure of maternal reverie and of psychic/emotional provision. But the traces of this early failure are often pre-verbal and not available to ideational representation. They therefore evade and direct recall or verbalization. This implicates the analyst's psychic functioning and construction in the process of the cure and leads to still another paradox of language:

> If language refuses to help us in the process of remembering, it still mediates the apprehension of the preverbal. And even though the analyst's intuition might relate to aspects of the material located outside language (bodily behaviour, emotional tension, anxiety, etc.), the fact remains that the analyst relies on the word representations to fill the gaps in speech towards the construction of what has been permanently forgotten. (Chapter 4)

Chapter 5, "Language within the general theory of representation", continues this examination of language and is a metapsychological *tour de force*, a deep dive into an exploration and explication of modern linguistics and its relevance for psychoanalysis, a rejoinder to Lacan and an extended examination of representation in the work of Freud and its implications for a contemporary psychoanalysis. While motivated by a strong theoretical bent, the chapter nevertheless includes a number of implications worth noting for their immediate clinical value.

In regard to dreams and their analysis, Green argues that:

> No dream can be analysed directly. The dream content, which often consists exclusively of visual images, sometimes sounds, or more rarely other sensations, is formed from thing-presentations that have welled up quite independently of perception and consciousness. As such, its manifest content can be translated into words with the help of secondary elaboration, but not analysed. Its analysis requires the dream narrative in word-presentations to trigger an associative process so that interpretation, which concerns the dream itself, becomes

possible, by means of deduction, thanks to the mechanism of the dreamwork. (Chapter 5)

In regard to unconscious representation, he concludes: "*the unconscious representation is constituted by a mixture, an association, an amalgam formed by the cathexis coming from the psychical representative, that is, originating from within the body, and from the object representative, that is originating in the external world*" (Chapter 5, original italics). Thus, he argues that drive and object constitute an ensemble and an indissoluble pair (Green, 2005). The drive discovers the object and the object elicits the drive. And as for the drives, going back to Freud, Green once again reminds us that while drives are anchored in the somatic, they may already be psychic in a form unknown to and unknowable by us. Thus, "the aim of analytic interpretation is to make language say what it does not [and cannot] say" (Chapter 5).

In Chapter 6, "The psychoanalytic frame: Its internalization by the analyst and its application in practice", Green returns to the question of epistemology, asserting the "singularity of psychoanalytic clinical experience and its independence with regard to medicine and psychiatry". He objects to the repudiation of metapsychology and the drives in favour of the relational, the developmental or other supposedly "more scientific" or "contemporary" perspectives and in a provocative but really quite brilliant move, Green looks at Freud's (1937a) *Analysis Terminable and Interminable* and suggests that "in Freud's work, the entire analytic theory is articulated around one and the same aim . . . why 'it doesn't work' and what we can do or think in order to create more favourable conditions for analysis to work well" (Chapter 6).

As far as Green is concerned:

> we cannot do without the notion of force: without it, a good many psychoanalytic concepts would become unthinkable, in particular, those of fixation, resistance, transference, repetition and the compulsion to repeat. No theory grounded in representations can account for it; this ensemble of concepts cannot be reduced to psychology and absolutely calls for the *energic* and *economic* notion of force as the vector of a signifying potentiality that can be characterized by quantitative power and the capacity for transformation. (Chapter 6, original italics)

This brings us back to the fundamental paradox:

> we are faced with the formidable paradox of having to find meaning and of elaborating it on the basis of formations that are *apparently* meaningless . . . Psychoanalysis cannot base its practice on intuitive meaning and logical meaning; it has to break with ordinary modes of understanding. We cannot be satisfied with a meaning that originates

> in the emitter and reaches the recipient intact, as the traditional theories of communication claim ... Another logic is necessary. (Chapter 6, original italics)

That "other logic" is that of the work of the negative, the internal framing structure of the analyst, the psychoanalytic frame as a field of forces and "the transference as a double act in two parts that take place within a single operation: "transference onto speech" and "transference onto the object" (Chapter 6).

> The act of verbalization translates all the psychic movements that carry within them something that is not in the nature of speech but that infiltrates it and carves out a path for itself through it. Affect finds a space for expression there. Speech, which is movement, is inhabited by force; thus it cannot be reduced to meaning. (Chapter 6)

Our final chapter (Chapter 7) examines the vicissitudes of the concept of countertransference, examining what we have gained and what we have lost as the concept has evolved over time. In Green's view, in order to understand the unknown that inhabits the analysand, the analyst "will have to give up his own subjectivity and allow himself to be possessed by the strangeness induced by the analysand that he will have to recognize while preserving his ability to communicate" (Chapter 7).

Green argues against a certain idealizing tendency of some intersubjective theses, which he feels attempt to deny or cover over the fact that "Psychoanalytic experience refers to an unknown that is even more elusive than that to which the critique of knowledge refers ... We must not confuse the certainty that the transference depends on the one who analyses it, and who therefore mingles his own subjectivity with it, with the idealism of intersubjective theses" (Chapter 7). He suggests that:

> It is perhaps because intrapsychic theories seek to circumscribe a hypothetical source material at the limits of what is thinkable, conceived as uncontrollable, that all profitable analytical work can only relate to its more readily available derivatives ... [I]t is easier to elucidate what is happening in the analytic session by turning to the exchange of relations between the two partners and their search for a consensus than to dwell on the fundamental darkness of the phenomena over which we have only an indirect and partial grasp. (Chapter 7)

Green, of course, like Freud, Bion and so many others, opts for the need to try to tolerate that darkness and face the ignorance of not knowing (negative capability). The danger and potential price we pay for failing to do so is a movement toward a more superficial understanding of analytic exchanges.

As we have seen earlier, Green offers a *Freudian* solution to this problem by returning to the drive as force, a force that:

> is not totally blind but nor can it be said that it possesses a quality of consciousness allowing us to attribute to it the properties of intentionality ... [W]hat Freud calls "wish" (*désir*) is the movement that drives the repetition of the experience, rather than the consciousness of its aim. It is a force that responds to a state of internal tension that can be of somatic or psychic origin but which, in any case, remains linked to its roots in the body, and therefore, is not aware of itself ... [O]nce set in motion, it progresses, most often through an object, towards a goal of which it has only a vague knowledge and which will only emerge when it is in the vicinity of the object ... [P]roximity of the object ... helps meaning to be born, to be constituted. But in any case, we cannot do without a conception of movement, in search of *both satisfaction and object* (to obtain it). (Chapter 7, original italics)

As we look back on Green's oeuvre, the articles presented here and the overall trajectory of his work, we can see the outline of a development that began with his careful study of borderline states and other non-neurotic structures, continued with his explication of the work of the negative and left us at his passing with the foundations for a new and expanded Freudian paradigm for psychoanalysis. An important component of this development is a shift in our attention to the force and potential of the unrepresented and the importance of processes that move *towards* representation. The result is the production of a *clinical* metapsychology, a theoretical development that has great relevance and immediacy for the treatment of non-neurotic patients, and promises to help reorient readers towards a psychoanalysis of the future.

References

Bion, W.R. (1962). *Learning from Experience*. London: Heinemann.
Bion, W.R. (1965). *Transformations*. London: Heinemann.
Bion, W.R. (1970). *Attention and Interpretation*. New York: Basic Books.
Bion, W.R. (2018 [1965]). Memory and desire. In: Mawson, C. (Ed.) *Three Papers of W.R. Bion*. London and New York: Routledge, pp. 1–10.
Freud, S. (1911). *Formulations on the Two Principles of Mental Functioning*. S.E. 12. London: Hogarth Press, pp. 213–226.
Freud, S. (1920). *Beyond the Pleasure Principle*. S.E. 18. London: Hogarth Press, pp. 3–64.
Freud, S. (1925). *On Negation*. S.E. 19. London: Hogarth Press, pp. 235–239.
Freud, S. (1933). *New Introductory Lectures on Psychoanalysis*. S.E. 12. London: Hogarth Press, pp. 1–182.
Freud, S. (1937a). *Analysis Terminable and Interminable*. S.E. 23. London: Hogarth Press, pp. 209–253.

14 Introduction: Why Green?

Freud, S. (1937b). *Constructions in Analysis. S.E.* 23. London: Hogarth Press, pp. 255–270.

Freud, S. (1959 [1923]). *The Ego and the Id. S.E.* 19. London: Hogarth Press, pp. 1–66.

Green, A. (1975). The analyst, symbolization and absence in the analytic setting (on changes in analytic practice and analytic experience) – In memory of D.W. Winnicott. *International Journal of Psychoanalysis*, 56: 1–22.

Green, A. (1977). Conceptions of affect. In: *On Private Madness*. London: Karnac, pp. 174–213.

Green, A. (1987 [1984]). Winnicott and the model of the environment: Interview with André Green. In: Clancier, A. and Kalmanovitch, J. (Eds.) *Winnicott and Paradox: From Birth to Creation*. London: Tavistock, pp. 119–126.

Green, A. (1998). The primordial mind and the work of the negative. *International Journal of Psychoanalysis*, 79: 649–665.

Green, A. (1999). *The Work of the Negative*. London: Free Association.

Green, A. (2005). *Key Ideas for a Contemporary Psychoanalysis: Misrecognition and Recognition of the Unconscious*. Trans. A. Weller. London and New York: Routledge.

Green, A. (2011). *Illusions and Disillusions of Psychoanalytic Work*. London: Karnac/IPA.

Kahn, L. (2018). *Psychoanalysis, Apathy and the Postmodern Patient*. Abingdon and New York: Routledge.

Kahn, L. (2022). *What Naziism Did to Psychoanalysis*. London and New York: Routledge.

Kardiner, A. (1977). *My Analysis with Freud*. New York: Norton.

Levine, H.B. (2011). Construction then and now. In: Lewkowicz, S., Bokanowski, T. with Pragier, G. (Eds.) *On Freud's "Constructions in Analysis"*. London: Karnac, pp. 87–100.

Levine, H.B. (2022). *Affect, Representation and Language: Between the Silence and the Cry*. London and New York: Routledge/IPA.

Levine, H.B., Reed, G. and Scarfone, D. (Eds.) (2013). *Unrepresented States and the Creation of Meaning*. London: Karnac/IPA.

Roazen, P. (1995). *How Freud Worked: First-Hand Accounts of Patients*. Northvale, NJ and London: Jason Aronson.

Winnicott, D.W. (1971). *Playing and Reality*. New York: Basic Books.

Winnicott, D.W. (1974). Fear of breakdown. *IRPA*, 1: 103–107.

Winnicott, D.W. (1989 [1965]). The psychology of madness. In: Winnicott, C., Shepherd, R. and Davis, M. (Eds.) *The Psychology of Madness*. Cambridge, MA: Harvard University Press, pp. 119–129.

1 *Après-coup*, the archaic[1]
(1982)

> There are three orders of things: the flesh, the spirit, and the will. The carnal are the rich and kings; they have the body as their object. Inquirers and scientists; they have the mind as their object. The wise; they have righteousness as their object.
> God must reign over all, and all men must be brought back to Him. In things of the flesh lust reigns specially; in intellectual matters, inquiry specially; in wisdom, pride specially. Not that a man cannot boast of wealth or knowledge, but it is not the place for pride; for in granting to a man that he is learned, it is easy to convince him that he is wrong to be proud. The proper place for pride is in wisdom, for it cannot be granted to a man that he has made himself wise, and that he is wrong to be proud; for that is right. Now God alone gives wisdom, and that is why *Qui gloriatur, in Domino glorietur*.
> Pascal, *Pensées* 460 (1908 [1660]: 74)

Prima and *Summa*

Thirty years ago already, George Dumézil demanded that more attention be paid to the distinction between *Prima* and *Summa* (1952: 95). The point was to avoid confusing what comes first with what counts most. Coming from a specialist in very ancient civilizations, from a scholar whose thinking influenced many researchers exploring areas quite distant from his, this observation must be relocated in the context of the controversies over the relations between structure and history. They once opposed Lévi-Strauss and Sartre, as well as Chomsky and Piaget more recently. Psychoanalysis entered the debate when Lacan, however Hegelian he might have been, converted to Saussurian linguistics. His reading of Freud led him, in 1953, to present a view of the unconscious that was closer to structuralism than any other, even though its author could not be classed among those referred to as structuralists in the 1960s.

In his famous "Rome discourse" (2007 [1953]), Lacan engaged in a merciless critique of some of the impasses besetting psychoanalysis when it gives in to the lure of the imaginary and misconstrues the role of the

---

1 Translated by Dorothée Bonnigal-Katz for this edition.

DOI: 10.4324/9781003350132-2

symbolic whose place is designated by language and the law. Freud is henceforth deciphered with the codes of Saussure, Jakobson, Lévi-Strauss and probably Moses too. Among the heretics Lacan railed against is Melanie Klein, the – at times brilliant – "tripe dealer", guilty of making the Freudian unconscious drift in the direction of the archaic. This reference to – or reverence for – "primary fantasies" turns the analysand into an *infans* and beguiles the analyst with the mirages of the genetic illusion.

Despite Lacan's efforts to summon as many lost sheep as possible and return them under his discipleship, many analysts – even in his own circles – could not, nevertheless – and still cannot – steer clear of the fascination with the archaic. By dint of usage, the word has made its way into the language of psychoanalysts. It is not likely to find its way out.

The fact that Lacan might not necessarily be right on this point does not prevent us from stating that this fascination, whose wish is to get closest to the psyche's unfathomable depths, is the same one as our fascination with myths. This does not imply that the psyche does not bear the indelible mark of its archaic period; yet, psychoanalytic practice, even when applied to very young children with severe disorders, never reveals the psyche's archaic foundations to the naked eye. The theory based on this practice does not give us one shred of evidence of its validity. No conviction can arise from a mere appeal to experience. What seems obvious to a Kleinian analyst remains highly objectionable to a psychoanalyst aligned with Winnicott, not to mention one inscribed in Hartmann's or Lacan's legacy.

By leaning on Freud's authority, psychoanalysts console themselves easily – too easily – of the inaccessibility of what relates to the archaic. Indeed, did Freud not relentlessly assert that nothing ever disappears from the primary experiences of psychic life, the unconscious preserving their traces and re-actualizing them on occasions? The archaic according to Freud is nonetheless not the same as his successors'. While they might have diverging opinions, they all share the fact that they differ from him. In short, in a variety of ways, Freud's view on the archaic is deemed archaic, i.e. obsolete, because it is not archaizing enough! The basic idea is that the clinical structures bespeaking fixations increasingly distant from those pertaining to the Oedipus complex have a tell-tale value, revealing what the psychic archaeology might be. This is a prized metaphor for Freud, with the proviso that the excavations always reveal the superimposition of civilizations, that is to say, still, of already highly elaborate cultures, which have hardly anything to do with the chaotic world predicated by the connoisseurs of "archaic objects". The latter, based on the traces that the clinical material of regressed analysands unveils, could elicit a reconstruction of the psyche's primal times, which usually remain buried under the sands of repression.

Numerous arguments have been pitted against such a shortcut. Anna Freud disputed the fact that the child reconstructed through the analysis of adults might be the "real" child. But is such realism the object of analysis? Along with Hartmann, she advised analysts to take more interest in direct observation (Spitz, Bowlby, M. Mahler) so as to better ensure the validity of their theories. But does analysis pertain to something observable or representable?

Kleinians, who claim to be the psyche's speleologists, have been accused of being misguided because they confuse the manifest and the latent; or because they translate verbally – sometimes in very flowery ways – their analysands' communications, which they hold as direct archaic communication, whereas they are in fact dealing with reshuffled material comprising defence mechanisms of an often very late type.

The archaized version of the manifest mistook the shadow for the prey. Claiming to be deep, Melanie Klein would have been superficial unknowingly, seemingly overlooking the role of primal repression, which obscures primordial times forever. Whatever we might gather from them through the return of the repressed, cannot convey, as such, any faithful idea of the most distant past, because it comes with all the layers of the periods of life that overlie it. What resurfaces is not the faithful witness of the prehistory but a highly suspicious product adulterated by the falsifiers of the preconscious, all of varying ages and each impressing its signature on the supposedly "primitive" psychic object. In other words, Freud's metaphor was inadequate because it naively held that the excavated past retained its primordial form. A similar argument dealt a blow to the hypothesis that pathological regressions had the merit of making archaic states visible. Psychotic regression, to stick to this example, is no mere backsliding in development in the direction of its point of fixation, because the predominance of disorganizing, destructive drives destroys at the same time as it progresses backwards. As Winnicott incidentally underlines, disintegration is not to be confused with non-integration.

All these arguments have remained devoid of impact, as efficient as advising realism and caution to someone in the throes of passion. But what is the passion at issue here?

The archaic illusion might well be buttressed by a voyeuristic passion that satisfies a very powerful fantasy: that of attending, via someone else, the origins of psychic life which the analyst – supposedly less regressed – can no longer access. This fantasy of origin – in which the analyst is always in the mother's place – is not unrelated to another one that operates in the opposite direction: the fantasy of crossing the border of death both ways after a very serious accident or a suicide attempt that comes very close to succeeding. To the "Great Game" with the beyond, we must adjoin the speculations on what dwells below, the archaic going in reverse, back to time immemorial.

Voyeurism is extended by epistemological sublimation, with a yearning for causality. It all happens "as if" (such a paradigmatic psychoanalytic phrase) the presumption to know the archaic (a presumption which often endows the psychoanalysts who refer to it with the condescending air of being in the know when they relate to those who dare not explore such abysms) rested on the idea that, if we could know about psychic life in the ovum, we could know everything about its vicissitudes. Consequently, in the course of the theoretical developments that came in succession throughout the history of psychoanalysis, the diversity of observable and analysable psychic structures dissolved into the reference to the same single aetiology, the oral fixation, sometimes even in utero.[2] Psychoses, retardations of all kinds, psychosomatic states, severe neuroses, all strictly pertain to the same plague, without any attempt to ever explain why such a variety of destinies might apply to a single evil.[3]

Ontogenetic myths, like many myths of origin, rarely avoid being cosmogonic.[4] And it is no inconsequential observation to point out – following Freud – that a society needs to have achieved a certain degree of development before it may concern itself with mythicizing. At any rate, the cosmogonic myths which vary depending on civilizations provide us with a rich variety of versions that relate to the birth of the universe and the conflict of powers to ensure supremacy. Despite a statement by Winnicott who distinguished between deep and early (1965 [1957]), the general trend in psychoanalysis remains based on the confusion between *Prima* and *Summa*.

The archaic according to Freud

The only one who really comprehends the archaic in psychoanalysis is Freud. He escapes the criticisms of the narrowly ontogenetic perspective. That is in fact what he is reproached with by his successors who have, quasi for the most part, repudiated the hypothesis of phylogenetic schemes. The Oedipus complex itself would belong to the same specific stockpile. Featured in the form of inherited mnemic traces, fantasies of origin – from which all other fantasies stem – signify psychic life. In other words, they decipher events according to their grid, they sort them, order them and, to put it bluntly, they organize the unconscious as so many pre-determinations or universals.

The two meanings of the archaic are thus brought together: not only the oldest term but also the *principal* term on which power is based. Freud's

---

2 It must be said that things are hardly better with Lacan: the foreclosure of the "Name of the Father" is a *pons asinorum* as loaded as the Kleinian "breast".
3 I except Pierre Marty's work on psychosomatics from this series of criticisms, despite the numerous obscurities that this work contains.
4 Cosmogenic is the adjective form of cosmogony: any model concerning the origin of the cosmos or universe.

conception complies with the *Prima/Summa* opposition insofar as the organizing power does not always appear at the outset. It must often first emerge from a prehistory before revealing itself in its activity. Numerous examples are evidence of such a historical and structural intersection in Freud.

The Oedipus complex is the core complex of neuroses, the term being understood here in its broadest sense. It is not featured from the outset. It appears in the wake of infantile sexuality during the stage that bears its name.[5] Its action is not limited to this stage however. And in this context, Lacan rightfully points out that the notion of pre-Oedipal stages is not a tenable one, strictly speaking. We should be referring to pre-genital stages instead, insofar as the structural dimension of the Oedipus complex is potentially present from the very start. It pre-exists in any case in the parents of the human child who is thus granted his human status.

A similar statement – one that is in fact closely related to the previous one – can be made regarding castration. Freud never denies that weaning or sphincter control are forerunners of castration but he adds that the "colossal narcissistic cathexis of the penis" endows castration anxiety with its referential and metaphorical value in ways that are incommensurate with the anxieties that precede it. However dreadful the latter might have been, they remain secondary nonetheless because their symbolic power over sexuality is less rich in consequences. They are not affected by the difference between the sexes and the generations. Some detailed development would be in order here, explaining why sexuality has been granted its conceptual rank in relation to the pleasure principle; but this would take us too far. Let us limit ourselves to recalling Freud's opinion on the impression felt by boys at the sight of female genitals during the phallic stage: he compares it to a fall from a throne or an altar.

Previously, this perception had only led to a variety of sexual theories (the penis will grow on the little girl's body, like her breasts; it is hidden inside; women do not have one except for the mother). But once the libido has invested the penis, the absence of the organ is a threat of breakdown for the phallic order, which founds an actual *Weltanschauung*.

My third comment relates to defence mechanisms. Freud alludes more than once to defences against castration before the inception of repression (reversal into its opposite, turning round upon the subject's own self) but, though their importance is far from negligible, such defences will never be granted the same metapsychological consideration as repression. The latter very much appears as the paradigm of defence, even though its outward unity must be broken up into foreclosure, disavowal, denial and

---

5 The onset of the Oedipal stage can be more or less early but the Oedipal period in its fullfledged form is an unquestionable fact.

repression proper. And it is not incidental to underline the links between repression and castration.

The ontogenetic inspiration of modern psychoanalysis – concerned as it is with scientific credibility and thereby honourability – therefore only gives half of its fair share to the archaic according to Freud because it overlooks the structural dimension inherent in its nature. Even if nothing confirms the phylogenetic hypothesis in contemporary science, the fact remains that it seems heuristically necessary, provided one resists the leniency of a pragmatic empirical position. Let us remember, however, that in certain disciplines (ethology, linguistics), the hypothesis of innate structures has been proven or upheld (IRM[6] in ethology, deep structure in linguistics), structures whose activity depends on stimulations arising from the environment. What has been conceded in one field is rejected in another, not on the grounds of the hypothesis itself but as a result of its content. For what is shocking to the scientific spirit is that fantasies – i.e. aberrations of the mind – and, what is more, *sexual* fantasies should be inscribed in the genetic inheritance. I do not know whether human imagination will find a better solution to substantiate the existence of such organizing terms in human sexuality. I remain convinced that a strictly developmental perspective will fail to account for the stereotypic character of fantasmatic structures featured in cultures that are very remote from ours.

Lacanian structuralism diverted the question while raising it. According to Lacan, the organizing axes of development consist in the structures of language and the law, both combined in the paternal metaphor. This change in direction must be noted. The content that Freud provided for primal fantasies (seduction, castration, primal scene) supplied a solid base for the idea of psycho-sexuality – i.e. for the close relations linking the psyche and sexuality. Sexuality is this aspect of human life that continues to tie humans to the animal kingdom. It anchors them in their body (and their object of desire), but it is also the *copula via* which they connect with the most cultural dimension they bear within, hence with their most human dimension. Sexuality grants man access to the status of psychic being – more than that of speaking being. Wondering about the difference between animals and men, Freud had to conclude that not the Ego but the Superego had to be signposted as a differential trait, by means of which the whole cultural development is inscribed. Repression, a psychic process (and not a biological one – Freud insists – as it could be envisioned for regression) is also an effect of cultural development. Freud's man is sociobiological, social because biologically founded, biologically destined for socialization. The threads of the former are closely interwoven with the threads of the latter, in such a tight weave that they sometimes cannot be

---

6 Innate releasing mechanisms.

taken apart. By locating *Arche* (in the sense of organizing principle) on the side of the signifier and the law, Lacan gets rid of any reference to biology in Freud. Unlike other forms of structuralism, Lacan's frees itself from all ties to the body: *Arche* has become the Ark of the Covenant.

However, in his late work, Lacan had to carry out a revealing reshuffle. On the one hand, he identified in *"lalangue"* the existence of *a* language ruled by mechanisms that have seemingly very little to do with the tropes of language. He nevertheless related it to the signifier – by way of an inconsistent and arbitrary use – even though the term had completely lost touch with its Saussurian sense.[7] At that point, the imaginary and the symbolic were closer than they ever were. Conversely, and probably as an indirect consequence, the signifier became overtaken by the matheme,[8] abstraction getting resounding revenge for what it had seemingly conceded to fantasy. It could be said that, in a way, the secret plan in this reading of Freud was to clear psychoanalysis from any allegiance to biology, by drawing it in the direction of the human sciences that have striven to approximate the exact sciences.

However, Lacan only had little sympathy for the human sciences. His theory's ambition was to go much farther than what linguists and anthropologists ever dared to achieve. In fact, such a view of psychoanalysis is torn between materialism – a highly disembodied form of materialism – which it aligns itself with and a kind of spiritualism that does not name itself but which Lacan tries to endow with the colours of the flesh.

Alternative strategy: The archaic *après-coup*

So this is the lay of the land, somewhere between a naive and improbable form of historicism and a rather arrogant kind of structuralism that pursues its taste for sophistication to the extent of becoming pure mind game. But the archaic persists, present in practice and theory alike, even though we remain benighted as far as its nature is concerned while having no choice but to take it on board, willingly or not.

The hope for some direct access to the psychic archaeology via the clinical and therapeutic experience of psychotic structures is too tentative, however rich its lessons may have been. There has to be room for another

---

7 Initially, the Lacanian signifier could sometimes be compatible with the Saussurian version but it was sometimes completely alien to it: e.g. "the phallus signifier of desire".

8 The matheme is a concept introduced by Lacan, a series of mathematical formulae used to represent his ideas in an attempt to create a more exact, albeit enigmatic, terminology than could be conveyed by language alone.

In Bion's terms, the matheme might be seen as Lacan's attempt to indicate his theory without the accompanying "penumbra of associations" that inevitably follows upon the usage of descriptive language.

theoretical strategy that is less trapped in the lure of a direct transposition of practice to theory.

Instead of hunting the archaic down in a backward quest for the improbable *arche*, why not try a reversed route? Why not seek the archaic where it is hiding but remains present nonetheless, among the latest agencies in libidinal development, where it has supposedly been overcome and replaced by much more differentiated psychic structures. If it is true that the unconscious is stamped by the inscription of the most primitive psychic mechanisms pertaining to the beginnings of psychic life, and that it is impervious to time, it makes sense to think that the structures that have arisen on top of the primal inscriptions were not merely superimposed on them. They were not formed *on* the archaic but *against* it. They attempted to modify its functioning through processes of binding, symbolization, differentiation, etc. In short, let us read the archaic *après-coup*, which is in fact the only way to talk about it; it will be surmised or inferred *a posteriori*, behind or beneath the walls that were erected against its threatening power.

Out of all the agencies that make up the psychic apparatus, the latest, the last one to appear, is the Superego. As a result, the qualifier archaic is often appended to it. How can we in fact talk about the archaic Id when the archaic *is* the Id and we know nothing about it? Conversely, it is not proscribed to talk about the archaic Ego and we do not deprive ourselves. But what does the phrase refer to? A drive-dominated, fragmented or fragmentable Ego incapable of circumscribing anxiety, giving in to despair, etc. The picture is a hackneyed one. But what are the powers presiding over it? The drive-related daemon, granted, but what about the question of reality? Is there such a thing as an archaic reality? Missing in this picture is the object, probably because, in this context, it is not supposed to have an autonomous existence, as a result of the assumed undifferentiation between Ego and object. This leads some objects to be qualified as "archaic". The archaic illustrates for us, in the material, the state of confusion supposedly prevailing among drive, object and Ego. The fact remains that this chaos is never completely formless: running through it are certain fundamental mechanisms, which Freud already described before being relayed by his successors' speculations.

A strange agency likely to be grasped by the least erudite intuition while remaining the hardest to comprehend all the same, the Superego results from a division of the Ego. Just as the Ego derives from a partition of the Id (under the influence of the external world), the Superego arises from the split of a part of the Ego. The schematic aspect suggested by such a view – as if development were but a series of budding processes elicited by time – is dismissed here in favour of a more dialectical theorization. The Superego results from a partition of the Ego indeed, but it is not constituted by an ascending process. To understand its genesis, a retroactive course or developmental loop must be set in motion, since the part of the

Ego that has acquired this new status is rooted in the Id. The Superego therefore carries weight in the Id and in the Ego alike and it feeds on the same supplies as the Ego. Consequently, in the normal state of affairs, it is legitimate to seek the archaic on the side of the Superego rather than the Id. In this instance, Freud is close to Nietzsche's views in *On the Genealogy of Morality*.

Even though it is tied to the Id, the Superego nonetheless remains the most metaphorical agency of all, not only from being the vector of values, but also because of its very constitution. In this context, let us recall the extremely important observation made by Freud: the child's Superego does not develop on the basis of the parents; it is modelled on the parents' own Superego. Tethered to the body by the Id, it is grafted onto the least carnal aspect of the child's relation with parental images. Its contradictory structure definitely provides us with the most favourable circumstances for an understanding of the permanence of the archaic, precisely where it seems to have completely disappeared.

The Superego's relation to the least carnal aspect of the relation tying the child's Ego to his parents is only possible via the function of the ideal. The latter is to the Superego what the drive is to the Id. So much so that Freud seemingly hesitates between Superego and Ego Ideal. Is the Ego Ideal a scotomized part of the Ego or only one of its sub-sets? The Superego-Ego Ideal pair has given rise to interesting distinctions. Without settling the nature of the links that tie the two, an agreement on their relations seems to exist as summed up by the formula: *the Superego is the heir to the Oedipus complex, whereas the Ego Ideal is the heir to primary narcissism.*

The Superego is therefore the direct product of the Oedipus complex, i.e. of the psychic conflict pertaining to the wishes targeting the parental objects. Let us recall quite rightly that the Ego's relation to the Superego stems from the internalization of the links between Ego and object. Conversely, the Ego Ideal has its roots in the form of identification for which Freud distinguishes three types: primary (narcissistic), secondary (or hysterical) and identification to the Ego Ideal.[9] Such a sequence speaks for itself: narcissism, hysteria, Ego Ideal. In other words, for the first type, the Ego is identified with the object in a fusional relation, with no differentiation between the merged terms. For the second type, the Ego is identified with the object's desire, it is distinct from it and inscribed in a triangular configuration. Finally, for the third type, the Ego is identified with a post-Oedipal agency, with the Ego Ideal replacing the object. This series of functions has in fact led Lacan to oppose the psychologizing views of

---

9 The resolution of the Oedipus conflict certainly leads to identification, but the Ego Ideal seems more directly related to it. Out of the three aforementioned types, two can be tied to narcissism, i.e. the first one and the last one. Such links between narcissism and identification can be direct, or indirect when identification is to the object.

an Ego valuing its relation to reality and to uphold that the fundamental function of the Ego consists in being ensnared in the subject's imaginary identifications.

The coupling of the Superego and the Ego Ideal shows that a single agency can take on two types of relation with the object: internalization and identification. The primary objects will possibly reveal to us what the archaic relation consists in. Among the functions of primary objects, we must include the function of authority – a fundamental one – but this term needs to be stripped of its moral connotation and be envisioned from the viewpoint of a ratio of power, which the child's dependence on his parents inevitably entails. Once the Superego has internalized the function of the love that the parent bears towards the child, along with the function of the object's authority, Freud is not afraid to qualify this agency in metaphorical terms: the Superego symbolizes "the protective powers of Destiny". Their love is so necessary that suicide would ensue in the event of their desertion. The exigencies of life expose the child to the inevitability of abandonment, whether temporarily or permanently as growth requires. According to Freud, identification is then the sole condition likely to make this loss of the object acceptable. Identification and narcissism are in league; both denote an emancipation from the dependence on the object, which, in its extreme form, leads the Ego to the giddy heights of proud self-sufficiency.

We are thus led to an initial conclusion: the archaic relation could be based on the alternation of compliance-arrogance between Ego and object. In fact, this condensed formula does not characterize one pair of opposites but two pairs of contrary opposites: *compliance-disobedience* and *pride-humiliation*. The first one pertains to the relation with the Superego and is essentially on the side of the object; the second one is tied to the Ego Ideal and thus concerns the side of narcissism. Along with others, I already opposed, in the past, the very different effects of *guilt* with regard to the Superego and those of *shame* with respect to the narcissistic dimension of the Ego Ideal.

If the archaic objects are characterized by the confusion that prevails within the psyche between drive, Ego and object, we must also add that the distinction is not any clearer between erotic drives and aggressive drives, between the drives likely to find auto-erotic satisfaction and the drives whose satisfaction requires the mediation of the object. But the confusion we suggest fails to quench our thirst for understanding: exonerating our ignorance does not improve our understanding. We cannot *tell* what the archaic is because it *is* archaic. There is confusion but to what end? The Ego is the seat of this confusion, not only because it is the theatre of the conflict, but because it seemingly engages in confusing the terms that are opposed in its midst: the drive-related demonism and the impossibility to make the object coincide with the Ego's wishes. The two functions, compliance and pride, operate in a different way. Compliance is the site of a dilemma: whether to comply with the drives or with the object? The question is further problematized owing to the projection that ascribes the characteristics of the drives to the object and animates or animizes the drives, making them take on the object's finery. As for pride, it is twofold as well, insofar as it relates to the victories achieved over the object, as much as to the negation of the latter.

The Superego-Ego Ideal relations have thus pointed us in the direction of the nature of the archaic relation. We can now, retrospectively, examine the archaism of the Ego. It is significantly in the context of his essay on "Negation" (1925) that Freud revisits the model of the psychic apparatus as he developed it in his *Metapsychology* and, more specifically, in "Instincts and their vicissitudes" (1915).

In the genetic myth elaborated by Freud as regards Negation, the Ego undergoes three sequential states: "original [or initial] reality-Ego", "purified pleasure-Ego" and "definitive reality-Ego". The initial reality-Ego is confined to identifying the sources of the excitations: external when it manages to evade their harmful effect, internal when action fails to lift the tension. This original distinction, prior to any discussion of the archaic, can only be understood from the perspective of a foundational division of space, the way many cosmogonies account for the initial divide between Earth and Heaven, then between Night and Day, etc. Each entity that is thus constituted is ruled by a power which is tied to it and attaches itself to it, which does not fail to generate conflicts over supremacy. The first task of the original Ego will have identified what is internal with the threat of irreducible danger.

The time that follows will perform a new division. The (purified) pleasure-Ego separates what is good, incorporable, identical to the Ego, from what is bad, excorporable, alien to the Ego.[10] The archaic is Manichean. If we complement this model with the model of the object relation, we then understand that what underlies the functioning of the purified pleasure-Ego is the compliance-pride relation. Evidence is that the purified pleasure-Ego will have to renounce the sole bipartition between inside and outside to then carry out, within, a new bipartition between what is pleasant to the Ego and the object (which will be retained because it is approved by the object) and what is unpleasant to the object first and then to the Ego (the Ego being contingent on the object) and which necessitates repression. Repression not only implies removal from consciousness, it also implies condemnation. The last stage, that of the "definitive reality-Ego", transfers the relation of compliance from the object to reality. Pride arises either from the success of repression or from a few secretly

---

10 Let us notice that in "Negation", Freud does not revisit a hypothesis he ventures in "Instincts and their vicissitudes" where a pleasure-Ego is opposed to an indifferent reality. At that point (1925), the pleasure-Ego is opposed, from the outset, to a non-Ego that must be rejected.

successful transgressions that elude the object's attention or, alternatively, and in extreme cases, from the negation of the object (Freud mentions in passing the negativism of schizophrenics).

Seemingly limited to speculation and devoid of any reference to experience, Freud's theoretical development is nonetheless substantiated by practice. The context in which he puts forward the idea of *Verwerfung* (Lacan's foreclosure) is the Wolfman case in which a part of the Wolfman's psyche "wants to know nothing" about castration – a fact that will be confirmed until the end of his life. At the height of psychological misery, hit by ageing, he will always remain avid for sexual experiences, failing to see the fundamentally masochistic nature of his object relations.[11]

The knowledge/non-knowledge of castration will occupy Freud's later thoughts from his essay on fetishism (1927) to "Splitting of the ego in the process of defence" (1938). And the same observation always returns: in splitting, the child disregards the threat of castration, even though he is very troubled by it.

The rejection of castration is a sin of pride on the part of the Ego, it is disobedience to the Superego. Castration anxiety is compliance with the Superego and subjugation of the Ego. The castration conflict is making us sail between Scylla and Charybdis. Where modern clinical practice has taught us to know the functioning of the archaic Ego better, we recognize the characteristics of the "Negation" model. What else do we say when we underline the role of projection or projective identification? That the analysand has a hard time distinguishing between what comes from him and what comes from the object, that he constantly struggles to exorcise the evil that haunts him. While the castration conflict is paradigmatic when it comes to exposing the stakes of authority, ahead of this we can see the conflict of authority preside over the relation to the object and the drives, in the analysand's relation with the analytic frame.

Should we then sound off about the admonishment of Freudian ideology and accuse Freud of authoritarianism as some are keen to underline? The question is more complicated.

At the time of his death, Oedipus is taken away from the sight of men and flies to the heavens, carried away by the gods, but we will never know what has earned him this glory, the text does not explain. Is it thanks to the punishment he imposed on himself when implicitly acknowledging sins he did not knowingly commit? Or is it because he dared challenge prohibitions and fulfil his most reprehensible wishes in the same state of knowledge/non-knowledge? There are numerous observations in Freud that seem to tally with the latter sense.

---

11 See Karin Obholzer, *Wolfman: Conversations with Freud's Patient, Thirty Years Later* (1982). It is significant to point out that, after having been fixated on the body image, this masochism is electively fixated on money (see my comments on anality below).

When it unfurls at the cultural level, the compliance-pride conflict leads Freud to paradoxical positions. He battles against the archaism of social and religious prejudices towards sexuality, which is subject, in men, to definite atrophy as a result of collective repression. Religion is combatted because it is incompatible with the freedom of thought. But such liberalism, which pleads for a softening of the Superego, aims to further ensure the proper functioning of the latter. And if *Analysis Terminable and Interminable* attributes the grip of the illness to the (biological) bedrock of castration, it is but the diversion of a question: how can we achieve equitable relations with our fellow men based on the fair recognition of our own rights and a form of self-appreciation that no longer sees the potential superiority of others as a reminder of the infantile conflict?

And yet, Freud only advocates submission to *Logos* and *Ananké* for the ordinary mortal. While he wishes for the triumph of the intellect over blind passions, on more than one occasion, he glorifies the hero who was able to brave prohibitions and carry out a great task. Alongside the liberal Freud is a Nietzschean Freud. This apparent paradox could be overcome: heroes override major prohibitions symbolically. No one repeats Oedipus's archaic gesture: parricide and incest, but every important conquest for humanity consists in the transference of transgression in the order of sublimation. Some make use of a superhumanity they credit themselves with, sometimes with the help of their zealots, so that the gap between the symbolic and the real may at times be very slim. Better still, in the name of the symbolic, they override the barriers of the law that only bind the common souls, which results in arousing the admiration of most; they merely repeat the archaic cloaked in the noble garb of their discourse.

Never bygone, the archaic breaks through maturity and it is still through this indirect approach that we can better get its measure. Its pressure, like the pressure of the drive, remains constant. Only the solutions that it opens onto differ. Why such permanence? The answer must be found on the side of the essence of the drive: the repetition compulsion that lies behind any resistance to change.

Interminable analysis and its causes

As early as 1937 – which is far away for us and late for Freud – Freud saw the drives' refusal to get domesticated, and the infantilism of the Ego bearing the after-effects of inevitable traumas of childhood, as hurdles to recovery: triumphant archaism of the Id, debilitating archaism of the Ego, either overly submissive or too proud to recognize its limits. Freud's formulations, when we read them again today, seem rather imprecise and mostly very partial.

They are not inaccurate strictly speaking. They have a flavour of abstraction, not because they are theoretical but because they are broad and vague; they hardly speak to us or they only speak to their author.

Let us not forget that, by his own admission, Freud had, for many years, lost any taste for practice, only theory mobilized his interest. The fact is, with age, he had also lost this fundamental quality in the analyst: patience, the daughter of persistence. Furthermore, he had the courage to admit that he was loath to take up the mother's position in the transference.

How surprised he is to discover the importance of the early relations with the mother in girls, the key to the fate of femininity! He compares his amazement with the one arising from the discovery of Minoan civilization in relation to classical Greece. He was a man of the 5th century, not of archaic Greece, more comfortable in the shadow of Pericles than in that of the kings whose palaces harbour Minotaurs. How can the archaic be theorized when you deliberately oppose first the assumption and then the analysis of the maternal transference?

And what is the weight of Freud's admission when the point is to revaluate the true weight of the "biological" rock of castration? A rebuttal of femininity or a rebuttal of the maternal, as the threat of the return of the archaic? In my view, the second answer is the right one, which is not in fact completely at odds with the first one.

It is effectively with Melanie Klein, who undertook the "transvaluation" of the values of psychoanalysis by making the Oedipus complex the *Mutterkomplex*, that we can date back the archaic's seizure of power in psychoanalysis. There is no need to deplore it – or to approve it – this was a fair swing of the pendulum which the founder of psychoanalysis had launched to the most extreme point of its course. And since Klein was more of an innovator than an actual genius, she was not as widely followed as her master. Yet Melanie Klein must be credited with new contributions that are incidentally connected:

1. The emphasis on the importance of the first stages of development characterized by archaic anxieties, primal fantasies and the first defence mechanisms.
2. The interest in patients with a psychotic structure and the reinterpretation of the neuroses – especially the severe ones.
3. A view of femininity that relativizes penis envy, in favour of the relation to the breast.

Whatever we might think about Melanie Klein's work and about her quasi-constant reference to the archaic, whatever criticism we might make of the weaknesses in her theory, her merit is to have opened psychoanalysis to a different unconscious, one that was unsuspected by Freud. We are not naïve enough to believe that psychotic structures or borderline cases might let the analyst observe the bottom of the psyche's seas or know about the farthest past, thanks to a kind of time-travelling machine. The archaic uncovered by psychotic structures could be accounted for by the ways in which it differs from the neurotic structures, which are supposedly more akin – so people say – to the analyst's structure. The archaic would then be the other.

How does this difference strike the analyst? It would be a mistake to seek it in clinical facts only.

Neurosis, the fundamental object of psychoanalysis, gave up its secrets thanks to the unrivalled eye that Freud brought to bear on it and did not deign to bear (or so little) on psychotic structures – not least because neurosis is more coherent, hence more intelligible and therefore analysable, *de jure* if not *de facto*. After Freud, it continues to hold an important place in analytic literature and has inspired ninety years of work. Analysts like neurotics because they make them intelligent (they understand them), efficient (they cure them sometimes), loveable (the positive transference always predominates). Borderline cases make them stupid (they cannot understand anything), guilty (they feel they do not deserve their fees), despicable (they are hated rather than loved by the analysand who is blind to their efforts and ungrateful as well).

But the major pitfall in the treatment of borderline cases is the uncertainty of the relevant axiological landmarks that might shed light on the hidden structure that determines the polymorphous nature of the symptoms, anxieties and defence mechanisms that strive to fight against it. In the absence of Freud's authority, we are given over to the diverging interpretations of his heirs.

What does Lacan say? That this population has a stiff neck, that they refuse their symbolic castration. In other words, you need to give them a hard time with short sessions, punctuating the symbolic, the analyst making the Law since the analysand perseveres diabolically. Once he has understood, the analysand will only make use of his desire to relay the message to others.

What does Bion say? That the fundamental dilemma is to elude frustration by evacuating it, or elaborating it. In other words, refusing the inevitable suffering by denying it or making it an object of transformation in the order of knowledge, love and hate.

What does Winnicott say? That the analyst is used to repeat the deficiencies of the environment. In other words, that the analysand cannot do otherwise but to show the analyst the full extent of his powerlessness and ill-will even, with a view to asserting the rights of the omnipotence bestowed upon him by his victim position, which he intends to take proud revenge for.

A consensus dispels this apparent disparity of views: it all pertains to the archaic. It is less a fixed archaism or one moving towards an evolution than one stopped in its tracks on the way to the recognition of maturity. This nuance must be recalled so as to avoid confusing borderline cases with the neuroses on the one hand, but also the psychoses on the other hand. [12]

In 1974, I put forward a theoretical model in the light of which we might understand the meaning of the structure of borderline cases.[13] The latter could be interpreted as a displacement of intrapsychic conflicts at the border of the psychic field marked out by the soma within and by action without. Let us notice that these are the very limits that frame the montage of the drives (source and aim). These two extra-psychic parameters are responsible for somatization and *passage à l'acte*. Within the psychic field, two other parameters define fundamental mechanisms: splitting and decathexis which form the basis of projective identification and primary depression (the blank). These four parameters guide the analyst on the dynamics unveiled by the borderline transference. In 1976, I suggested stepping out of clinical empiricism on borderline cases by envisioning the borderline as a concept,[14] which Freud's reading and practice both justify. The hypothesis that I presently uphold on the archaic is inscribed in the aftermath of this theoretical development.

Power and potency: Primary anality

Every time I was able to take the analysis of a borderline case far enough, I was struck by the fact that the transference was wholly pervaded by a misunderstanding that was detrimental to its analysis: namely the confusion between power and potency (*puissance*). The patient's projection ascribes to the analyst a potency, if not an omnipotence, which leaves the analysand with no other solution than to fight against the transference and divest the transferential object of any power. The difference between these two terms, however close they might be, is considerable. It deserves some clarification.

Power is always limited, fallible, questionable. Nobody is absolutely endowed with it despite appearances, just as no one is absolutely deprived of it, if only the power to love or not, the power to be loved or hated by the other. Power is inherited or conquered, it increases or decreases, it peters out more or less. Power is always offset by a counter-power. Power can be shared or divided. It can be spread out in the relationship with the other. Potency, conversely, in the sense I am using it here, bestows an absolute force upon the one who possesses it, in the eyes of the other. It is always more or less divine (or diabolical), superhuman in any case. Its opposite is impotence.

---

12 See "Passions and their vicissitudes" in *On Private Madness* (Green, 1997 [1980]).
13 See "The analyst, symbolisation and absence in the analytic frame" in *On Private Madness* (Green, 1997 [1974]).
14 See "The double limit", Chapter 2 in the present volume.

In the eyes of the borderline analysand, the analyst is endowed with such potency. He is the one who imposes the contract – the oversight being that the analyst submits to the contract as well. The obvious inequality in favour of the analyst becomes an iniquitous, despotic law in the present circumstances. Neutrality is taken as indifference stamped with cruelty. Silent, the analyst demonstrates his haughty contempt. Should he suspend his reserve to provide an interpretation, the latter is never received as an interesting suggestion likely to shed liberating clarity on the obscure chaos the analysand complains about being trapped in: it is a diktat, take it or leave it. Should the interpretation be true, it will rekindle the humiliation of resorting to the help of someone who might know what you want to say better than yourself. In fact, is the analysand not lying in this infantilizing position, while the analyst dominates him from the height of his sitting position? If the analyst displays solicitude, it is an apt demonstration of his unbearable paternalism. If he gives in to boredom, it is clear that he does not care much for your suffering. And if, loosening his control of the situation to let in a bit of fresh air, he reacts in a vaguely vivacious way that is because he is striving to seduce or punish, and to reject in any case. The fact that he claims a fee confirms that all he cares about is money. If he treats you for free or very little (e.g. in an institution), that is because he needs guinea pigs or because he heaps his well-endowed pity on the destitute analysand.

Whether it is caused by an unconscious affect of intrusion or abandonment, a permanent excitation seemingly torments the Ego at all times. The description we just gave pertains less to the conflicts' content – even though it is indicative of how the internal object is experienced – than to the analysand's position towards the analyst *in the analytic frame*. It is the very principle of the analysis that is put into question. The analyst is but the manifestation or, in the frame, the representative of the object – even though the term is inadequate because, as Winnicott noticed, the analyst does not represent the mother in this context, he *is* the mother. The analytic setting, supposedly facilitating for the neurotic, is, to the borderline case, if not an influencing machine, at least a manipulative machine to satisfy the analyst's omnipotence. How can we understand such an adulteration of the frame?

The issue of conflict over power is usually tied to anality. Is this what we are dealing with here? Yes and no. No, if what we have in mind are the classic traits of anality and its fixation in obsessional neurosis. Yes, if we think that the anal conflict is fundamental in the borderline case because, in anality, we have rightly distinguished a dividing line with psychosis. I will readily refer to a *primary* form of anality that cannot be solely characterized by the prevalence of evacuation processes, as Abraham argued, but which exceeds the erogenous zone by a long way and engulfs the Ego. It forces the analysand to experience the compliance-pride conflict, which at times reveals him as lenient and obsequious and at times as rejecting everything, even the breathing of the analyst. And the analysand will exclaim: "I know I give you shit!" It is uncertain whether the analyst's denial might be upsetting to the analysand but the analyst's admission will certainly be experienced as offensive.

Such anality condenses at once Oedipal regression and the blockade against a possible slippage towards orality.[15] In short, because it is tied to this compliance-pride opposition, the archaic is already a break point against a form of chaos where no relation with the other could be tenable. The projection of omnipotence onto the analyst has a meaning. It features the analyst as the one who has successfully fulfilled the wishes of this primary anality, as a means to ensure omnipotence over the object – the omnipotent object.

In the analysis, because it cannot be assumed in act, the compliance-pride conflict is the way to *say* the archaic, by experiencing it without any effective distinction of either the object or the Ego. This primary anal conflict is at once the archaic and the defence against the archaic, because it would be a mistake to envision this opposition from the perspective of a coherence, however systematic the opposition might seem. Quite conversely, disobedience is chaotic in this case, just like the threat of chaos, which it strives to avert. At a push, the compliance-pride conflict is not about the Superego or the Ego Ideal, it is directed at the wound created by the existence of the unconscious, as a threat to mastery.

Omnipotence and Oedipus

Omnipotence is the concept thanks to which we can bring together, under a single heading, the issues of compliance in relation to the Superego and the issues of pride tied to the Ego Ideal. The roots of omnipotence are far deeper than its anal or obsessional expressions; they go back to the hallucinatory fulfilment of desire. Omnipotence is here, germinating, unfurling freely in primary process. It will take on another status in psychosis, as evidenced by the Schreber case, which should be read wholly from the perspective of the relations between compliance and pride with regard to an untouchable God. Omnipotence is summoned in a variety of ways in today's psychoanalysis. To Freud, the impotence of the mind accounts for its omnipotence and for its projection onto the parents, who often return the sentiment to the advantage of their offspring. Yet, in some of the contemporary readings, the primary

---

15 It might seem paradoxical to defend a view of the archaic tied to a stage that is but the second stage in the evolution of the libido. We are led back to the *Prima-Summa* opposition. In fact, primary anality is the first attempt to master the archaic which is otherwise ungraspable and merely doomed to expulsion.

object is seemingly presented as strictly omnipotent, without taking account (whether voluntarily or involuntarily) of the infantile source of such omnipotence, most often bestowed upon the mother. This is an old debate featuring the deadlock of geneticism: which came first, the chicken or the egg?

Things should be envisioned differently, by declaring the object omnipotent in relation to reality (the child's survival depends on it and mothers are often experienced as such) whereas the child, conversely, is omnipotent in psychic reality. The mother-child dyad is commonly experienced as "symbiotic omnipotence" (Khan, 1974). There lies the danger of making the *Arche* perennial: ever thwarted in his ability to experience *his* omnipotence alone, the subject is always seeking an irreplaceable object for nothing could possibly compete with maternal omnipotence.

It is only when both partners in the dyad – mother and child – give up on their mutual and reflected omnipotence that they may each gain access to a capacity at last.

Winnicott demonstrated exceptional astuteness regarding borderline cases. He modulated the leitmotiv of the struggle against dependence and the need for dependence. I will revisit his observations in light of my present hypothesis. Granted, the analysand repeats, with the analyst, the archaic conflict of the relation with the object, caught up between compliance and pride. When the false self gives in as a result of the analysis, what ensues is a dissenting, hateful and merciless outpouring, interspersed with a few moments of grace. However, such moments of grace should never last because they threaten pride: this wellbeing is owed to someone else who will undoubtedly praise himself over it. The analysand reproaches himself for those moments when he forgets himself because, for a minute, he was able to stop accusing the object and to discover powerfully repressed feelings of love for the one he deems responsible for all his misfortune. Thus, through his hate, he carries on complying with the object because he reinstates its omnipotence. This relates to erotomania.

Retrospective compliance? No doubt, but also compliance that has never been renounced by the analysand. In his discussion of the negative therapeutic reaction, J.-B. Pontalis points out that some subjects need to believe in the mother's omnipotence (2014). The analyst's *words* cannot measure up to the (internal) *acts* of the object that relentlessly besiege the Ego. And we know that the mother's omnipotence is always at its height when she is not here, i.e. when a resort to omnipotence is the only way the Ego can envision to offset its distress. Omnipotence is always at its height when one is alone. The Ego proclaims its powerlessness, it berates itself but draws pride from being the never fully defeated opponent of the dreadful despot. It will never let the analyst prevail upon it and elicit its renunciation of the excitation inherent in this merciless battle against an enemy whose evil genius it marvels at. Such *"hatenamoration"* (Lacan's *"hainamoration"*)[16] is until death do you part.

The dead father founds the structure of the Superego. His omnipotence, however tremendous it might be, is mitigated by his love for his children; God of anger, of justice but also protective God. What about the mother? The omnipotent mother is the one who cannot die. Incest (for both sexes) might have it tougher than parricide. The incestuous maternal object – in the broadest sense – is always here, accusatory, demanding, humiliating and cruel. It requires the child's adherence to its ideals. The child can only draw pride from the fact that he is the mother's child or is inscribed in her lineage. The reference to the maternal grandfather or to the uncle on the same side of the family supersedes the reference to the father. It might be useful to recall that I am referring to an imago here.

While borderline cases force us to think this archaic, psychotic cases blind us with it by unfurling it in all its possible forms. The archaic is not only forever, it is also everywhere, hidden under the appearances of normality. It is taken in by political ideologies in the societies of so-called autocratic regimes. Pagan or revealed religions have long granted it asylum. It might be at its most eloquent in their midst.

Reading Pascal's *Pensées* is more than demonstrative in this regard. In my view, the author's dialectic seems more inspired by the devil than by God. With outstanding lyrical eloquence, Pascal has plunged us into the misery of Man without God and has saved us thanks to the greatness of Man with God; the more he proceeds in his work, the more merciless dogmatism he displays, almost as extreme as the silence of infinite spaces, if we imagined him in charge of a State. There is only one religion: the Christian religion because it was predicted and produced miracles. The Jewish religion had the sole function of announcing Jesus. The misfortune of the chosen people is here to provide evidence: it prophesied the coming of the Messiah and did not believe that Christ was its incarnation. Without it, we would know nothing about it; without its misfortunes, we would not doubt the mistake befalling us should we not believe in Christ. There is only one Church: the Roman Catholic Church. Pascal justifies everything: its hierarchy, its power, the infallibility of the supreme pontiff. For all this is contingent on a superior goal. To "belittle the great" so that man may place his pride "properly", i.e. in obedience to God.

Descartes? "Useless and uncertain". Pascal has little use for this mediocre philosophy that uses God only to give the Universe a flick and then step back straight after. The trust that Descartes puts in man – even if God comes to his rescue ultimately, when he stumbles over the distinction

---

16 Translator's note: *"Hainamoration"* is a term coined by Lacan in Seminar XX. It is a portmanteau of the French words *haine* (hate) and *'énamoration'* (falling in love), hence *hatenamoration* as my suggested translation.

between dream and reality, for example – is disgraceful to Pascal. And yet . . . in Pascal's *Pensées*, we can find pages that recognize the supreme power of the imagination, which prevails over reason. Pascal is caught in the paradox: reason alone is not enough to find the truth of God and yet, if God is not rationally justified, God is absurd. Pascal has it both ways. He wagers by showing that there could not be any other solution. This wager is a wager of obedience. The hidden God was undoubtedly the means by which Pascal could satisfy his need for submission and draw some pride that justified the omnipotence also hiding behind the invocation of his misery.

Is language not the ultimate haven of omnipotence?

If the archaic is indestructible, is it alterable at least?

Psychoanalysis would not be if it did not harbour this hope. It involves the eradication of the Oedipus complex. This wager has equally serious consequences, especially since this eradication only leads to the genesis of the Superego. Binding the archaic, in the Superego and the Ego Ideal, remains the best way to avoid being stuck between the devil of obedience and the deep blue sea of pride.

References

Dumézil, G. (1952). *Les Dieux des Indo-Européens*. Paris: PUF.

Khan, M. (1974). *The Privacy of the Self*. London: Routledge.

Lacan, J. (2007 [1953]). The function and field of speech and language in psychoanalysis. In: *Ecrits*, trans. Bruce Fink. New York: Norton, pp. 197–268.

Obholzer, Karin (1982) *Wolfman: Conversations with Freud's Patient, Thirty Years Later*. London: Continuum Intl Pub Group.

Pascal, B. (1908 [1660]). *Pensées*. Trans. W.F. Trotter. London: Dent.

Pontalis, J.-B. (2014). No, twice no: An attempt to define and dismantle the "negative therapeutic reaction". *International Journal of Psychoanalysis*, 95: 533–551.

Winnicott, D. (1965 [1957]). On the contribution of direct child observation to psychoanalysis. In: *The Maturational Processes and the Facilitating Environment*. London: The Hogarth Press and the Institute of Psychoanalysis, pp. 109–114.

2 The double limit[1]
(1982)

When Freud first introduces thought or thinking[2] in the theoretical field, he finds himself forced to address the question with definite reluctance, as if he preferred to dispense with it.[3] This is indeed how things happened. The late discovery of *An Outline of Psychoanalysis* (Freud, 1938) has revealed to us the considerable role played by thought in this first attempt at theoretical systematization – an attempt disavowed by its author.

It is probably the analysis of Schreber's *Memoirs* that compelled Freud to supplement the theory with a psychoanalytic reflection on thought. Not featured in the essay on Schreber, this reflection will find its place in a paper written at the same time: *Formulations on the Two Principles of Mental Functioning* (1911). This account, qualified as introductory, puzzled the psychoanalysts who heard it, and for good reason, insofar as they knew nothing about the place of the problem of thought in the long private germination initiated by Freud in 1895 and made public by him in 1911 only.

Thought and reality will go hand in hand in Freud's later developments and they will become preoccupations of growing significance in the final part of his work, where psychosis and psychotic mechanisms are increasingly on his mind. This does not imply that there should actually be any in-depth elaboration of the preliminary hypotheses. The advance might come, rather, from the conceptual frame in which thought is recast (Freud, 1925). Freud's comments on thought always remain incidental. Unable to circumvent the problem, he does not linger over it, which does not prevent his recurrent return to it.

Hence some deferral and reluctance, some avoidance and some unease, as if it were a matter of not letting oneself be led astray, in every sense of

---

1 Translated by Dorothée Bonnigal-Katz for this edition.
2 Translator's note: "*La pensée*", used in the French original can be translated as both *thought* or *thinking*. For the sake of clarity, I have alternated between the two options throughout this translation, sometimes suggesting both when it seemed helpful.
3 See the conclusion of Freud's essay *Formulations on the Two Principles of Mental Functioning* (1911).

DOI: 10.4324/9781003350132-3

the word, the core of the psychoanalytic enquiry residing elsewhere. In Freud's view, thought does not belong to the body of fundamental concepts of psychoanalysis – drives, the unconscious, repression, etc. – even though it stems from them, without being able to claim the status of these key hypotheses.

I doubt that what psychoanalysis might have to say about thought could exceed the frame of the relations between the unthinkable constituted by the drive and the elaboration it is subjected to by language, allowing thought to arise. Even though what compels the psychoanalyst to make allowance for it is occasioned by the relations with reality, its theorization is always focused on the problem of the sources of thinking and its entrenchment in drive-related life. It is therefore important not to be mistaken about this convergence between thought and reality which, for the psychoanalyst, is but a constraining yet secondary relation.

Bion instigates a true theory of thought arising from the psychoanalytic experience with psychotic subjects in whom thought disorders can be observed in the foreground. In truth, Bion's work implements a whole reformulation of psychoanalytic theory. While he re-ties the link with Freud's ideas which Melanie Klein had broken off, Bion redefines psychic activity from a viewpoint located at the extreme opposite end of the one chosen by the founder of psychoanalysis: the starting-point of the theoretical elaboration no longer consists in neurosis but in psychosis. Let us point out, however, that the attempt at rigour and the fantasy, pursued by Bion, of a mathematization of the theory (which also haunted Lacan) dissolves in the final part of his work, as if the author experienced some skepticism towards his earlier attempt at theorization.[4] Yet, this is the part of his work that readers remain most attached to.

It seems to me that today's analysts, who must increasingly deal with patients known as difficult, find themselves compelled to tackle the issue of thought due to practical considerations. Indeed, even when they are not psychotic, the patients composing the current analytic population are not more neurotic for all that. While thought disorders might not be foremost in their clinical presentation, they certainly impose a strain on the analyst's thinking and what we can fathom in them is the more or less latent existence of an issue of this kind. The resistance, the repetition compulsion, the rebellious nature of the drives do not account for everything in these analyses. Other concepts seem to be relevant.

As I was looking for the theoretical axes likely to be involved in a clinic and a theory of thought through the work of Freud, Melanie Klein, Bion and Winnicott, I got the impression that, more or less explicitly, they all refer to theoretical tools whose organizing scope these authors do not

---

4 See André Green, "Au-delà? En deçà? de la théorie" in the preface to W. Bion's *Entretiens psychanalytiques* (Green, 1980).

38 *The double limit*

always foreground. Such are the theoretical tools that I offer to consider in this paper.

I will confine myself to listing them for now:

1. *Limits*.[5] Without always being explicit about it, no theory of thought can avoid raising the issue of the border between the outside and the inside from the outset. This is implicit in the question of projection from Freud's classical perspective or from the perspective of Melanie Klein and Bion's projective identification, or from that of Lacanian foreclosure. The difficulty consists here in linking together the relations of this border between the inside and the outside with the border separating the Conscious-Preconscious and Unconscious systems. This is but the theoretical formulation of a clinical and technical problem pertaining to the modalities of transference in non-neurotic patients, from the perspective of the object's function; the border makes up a stake that is always put into question, within relations of reunion with, and separation from the object.

2. *Representation*. A dominant concept in Freudian theory, representation covers a twofold field at least: thing representation and word representation, which forces us to consider the process of abstraction that leads one to the other and its retroaction in the regressive process that leads words to be treated like things. Representation cannot sidestep the reference to the optical model of the psyche, even though the whole problem in this case consists in the shift from a reflecting – and necessarily distorting – structure to a world where representation represents nothing but relations. Ever since Jean-Luc Donnet and I suggested the concept of blank psychosis,[6] the function of representation has appeared to me as the referent of psychoanalytic work. Regardless of the modalities that impose an adjustment of the psychoanalytic frame, the crux of the psychoanalytic action ultimately aims for the representation of psychic, intrasubjective and intersubjective processes. The rest pertains to a reorganization that is proper to the

---

5 Editor's note: Here, Green uses the French term, *limite*, but includes this paper in a book on borderline patients, which in French are called *des cas-limites*. We have chosen to use either translation of the word *limite* – limit or border – depending upon the context to emphasize one or the other sets of connotations.
6 Donnet and Green (1973). This work includes a long development on thought, a few points of which are revisited in the present essay. However, the perspectives I develop now are more based on the analysis of borderline cases. I stress the fact that I use the term representation throughout this essay in the broadest conceptual sense, including the affect tied to the representative chain (affect representative); but it excludes those that cannot come with any representation, or even oppose representation. In fact, the paralysis of thought stems from the non-admission of representations in the preconscious or from the feeling of not succeeding in bestowing a representable form upon overwhelmingly distressing emotional states.

subject and does not involve the analyst. I would even suggest that the adjustments of the frame have no other function than the facilitation of the function of representation. The reference that is usually made to the transference in order to substantiate the technical amendments is not invalidated by my claim for all that. Indeed, the point is merely to bring the transference to the level of what is representable, of the initial elaboration and the starting point of further elaborations. For insight[7] to develop, some form of representable must be featured first.

3. *Binding* and its relation to unbinding might be the most general concept of psychoanalysis. Indeed, it applies to energies as well as contents and the various materials that convey them. The main question here consists in the orientation presiding over binding, i.e. its aim. Representing already implies binding but thinking implies re-binding the representations in a non-specular mode. While analysis remains the essential process through which the transformations of binding may occur in the psychic apparatus, let us not overlook the fact that analysis also stumbles over syntheses – more or less basic ones and more or less compact ones – which can obstruct the expected recombinations. I will link symbolization with the processes of binding as a special case of this function: internal symbolization in Lacan's structuralist-inspired psychoanalysis, which is distinct from the Kleinian view because it seemingly rests on innate foundations whereas it arises from a process of evolution for Melanie Klein; symbolization somewhere between the outside and the inside for Winnicott in the potential space where a new reunion presides over separation.

To the problem of binding, we must link not only the regimes in which it functions differently (primary or secondary); we must also relate the processes that preside over communication between these various modes of functioning. Indeed, no theory of thought in psychoanalysis can limit itself to engaging with the end products of thoughts without connecting them with their forms of unconscious organization and their entrenchment in the rawer material from which thought arises.

4. *Abstraction*. It is probably the most specific aspect of thought. It implies a "purification" of drive derivatives and of the charge of affect through which they manifest themselves. It seems to me that we cannot envision the advent of abstraction without involving the "work of the negative" – from foreclosure to negation – whose consequences are at once economic and symbolic.[8] All the existing theories strive to account for this evolution of the drive representatives towards abstraction, in terms of a series of operations that are more or less inscribed

---

7 Translator's note: In English in the original text.
8 See Freud's reflections on this topic in his essay on "negation" (1925).

in continuity. However, careful examination reveals that abstraction is the fruit of a mutation with respect to representation, which can only be explained by a break instituting some discontinuity, with an obliteration of representation. This is where we must summon the conceptual part played by negative hallucination; failing that, we will always stumble on a mysterious "leap into the intellect" which will remain unexplained. But here again, the issue of the orientation, of the aim of abstraction will be raised: thought and abstraction go hand in hand with the exercise of a power of domination and mastery – as evidenced by the omnipotence of thought – which is granted proof of its full efficiency when their aims are limited to the exploration of the physical world. This power is infinitely more questionable when applied to the psychic world. Coupled with the knowledge of this universe, thought must abide by the double task of establishing enough distance with drive derivatives where it originates while retaining contact with its affective roots through which it acquires its weight of truth. There lies a paradoxical structure of thought in psychoanalysis which is unsurpassable.

These four parameters seemingly delineate, in my view, the minimum conditions required to fulfil a theory of thought in psychoanalysis. But I should add straight away that, among the four, the one pertaining to the border seems to prevail over the others. It is furthermore the pivot presiding over the organization of all the others. I highlight this point because it seems to have received less consideration in works devoted to thought, however implied it might always be.

The border is the parameter I will mainly tackle in this essay; the other parameters will be considered in relation to it. The psychoanalytic theory of thought is governed by the artifice that structures the psychoanalytic experience, i.e. the frame. It is certainly not incidental that patients who present difficulties with elaboration in relation to thinking or who, in some cases, deliberately refuse to think at all, should also be those who have trouble tolerating the frame. They exert pressure on it, ever tempted to smash it to bits when conflicts get reactivated. Even when they appear to accept it, they get around it in ways that far exceed the inner adjustments observable in neurotic patients. Far from being able to use it with the regressive benefits that stem from it, they battle with it as if they were tackling some invisible enemy taking advantage of the situation, either to launch an attack on their Ego or to surrender them to their sense of abandonment in some wasteland where they cannot hope for any help or where only monstrous presences dwell.

I showed elsewhere[9] that Freud's creation of the frame arose from the model of dreams. Under the usual circumstances, the frame aims to foster

---

9 See Chapter 3, "The silence of the psychoanalyst", in the present collection.

the production of *unthought thinking* which the dreamwork exemplifies. However, we now know that nothing is less assured than the dreamwork and that the other forms of nocturnal psychic life (insomnia, sleep walking, blank dreams, etc.) are evidence of its disablement or failure. And even when it seemingly occurs, its outcome depends on the dreamer's mental organization.[10] Yet, this mental organization remains structured by the double relation between the outside and the inside on the one hand, and by the double relation that presides over the Cs-Pcs and Ucs agencies on the other hand.

The frame not only determines the conditions of a work space, it also modifies the economy of borders. The closure it institutes strains, in its midst, the borders between analysand and analyst. It forces the analysand to restructure his identity which is imperilled by the intensity of the exchanges and to keep a close watch, at all times, on the borders of his psyche, to guard against the possibility of invasion – whether internal (by the drives) or external (by the object) – both being sometimes confused by him.

In non-neurotic structures, instead of having to overcome the limitations imposed by reality on desire by providing it with roundabout satisfactions, the psychoanalytic investigation might come to learn, rather, that most of the psychic activity is directed towards the preservation of a relation with the object which is always facing the threat of mutual destruction. Only some special attention to borders is supposed to safeguard an autonomy secured at a high price, especially as this autonomy comes with the sacrifice of the drive-related satisfactions tied to the object, in favour of narcissistic satisfactions. Yet, the term satisfaction is in fact objectionable in this context, insofar as we are mainly dealing with reassurances in which the mobility warranting the subject's independence or the subject's engagement with action constitutes one of the modalities of this autonomy. At the other extreme, intellectual overinvestment, stemming from sublimation achieved by dint of hard work, often signals a pointless and transient triumph over drive-related life. The latter storms in periodically, in especially wild fashion, triggering narcissistic anxieties, at the level of the Ego, against the internal intrusion of an object that one believed to be freed from through solitary withdrawal, which is itself exclusively sustained by sublimation. Sexuality and aggression converge in the idea of a violence imposed from within – the very violence ascribed to the internal object which prohibits thought. Concern with the preservation of identity is at the centre of these object relations. The autonomy of thought becomes the stake of a battle waged by the analysand to ensure his identity, i.e.

---

10 In this sense, the Wolfman's dream, which evidences some work at play, does not tell us anything about his mental organization, about the role played by splitting and disavowal in a case where they remain the masters of the psychic play.

to defend his Ego's territory as the only site where a continuity of being may be sustained, fighting against the impingements of an object that can never entirely tally with the Ego in question, past a certain level of limited or partial investment. This necessarily entails great difficulties in the transference and in the analysand's openness to the interpretations of the analyst. It is no longer a search for an identity in the sense of a coincidence between a representation and a perception but an unremitting struggle to uphold an identity subject to the constant threat of an external object that is always alien to the Ego, and cannot be assimilated by it. This is indeed where the supposedly acquired border between the inside and the outside is far from secured, hence the withdrawal predicated on a question of internal identity, so as to ensure the difference with the object.

The object is frequently experienced as hostile or harmful – more often than not, it consists in the mother who must be defended against because she is invasive and cannot be trusted. But the analysis then reveals that, despite all the attempts to put the object at a distance in reality, the Ego is drawn to this object like a magnet because of the excitation generated by such intrusion. This excitation is put to good use, offering the Ego the opportunity to pull itself together as it battles and to strengthen its coherence, as if surrendering to pleasure might entail some dissolution of identity: the danger then consists in the loss of any oppositional power.

But in other cases, the opposite situation is featured: union with the maternal object is what supposedly ensures the Ego's harmony, the Ego's agreement with itself. Analysis will have long upheld that this agreement could only be elicited by what came from the mother; any other object will present markers of strangeness that makes it threatening and likely to break the link with the mother. But as the analysis unfolds, the idealization of the maternal imago reveals its defensive nature. In fact, it is the maternal imago indeed that is itself perceived as this threatening and intrusive object against which identity must be preserved. Does this imply that we are dealing with two distinct moments in the development process? Does the analysand thus strive to safeguard a hard-earned asset which has led to the separation with the mother, a psychic space – one that has been successfully conquered against her impingement – he now seeks to keep out of the range of her intrusion? This could be an over-simplified view. The existence of a primal idealization might conversely tend to show that the mother will have always been foreign. Only a false self could make do with her by creating this identity of denial which was the prerequisite for the establishment of an object relation.

This is the point at which we can surmise the existence of an extremely subtle form of thinking, relying on double negation rather than on negation tied to repression, to safeguard the secrets of an Ego that is foreign to the object. The Ego must constantly ensure that there is no disclosure of any of the thoughts directed at an object whose intuitive capacities evidence the upholding of a tight, quasi symbiotic link. On the other hand, the excess of this intuition could reveal a wish for a break with a view to acquiring freedom.

Is there something lacking in this thought founded on the categorical preservation of psychic autonomy in order to exist as thought? It is so protective of its property that it exhausts itself in its self-assertion not so much as thinking than as *my* thinking. The defence against the intrusive voracity seeking to seize and control the object manifests itself as its opposite: the withdrawal into *"its"* thinking. This only pertains to close relations with the transferential object or its lateral equivalents. The subject can besides be fully cooperative in the ebb and flow of communication and exchange, as long as they are devoid of any subjective implication. Should this be regarded as a variant of narcissism? We could think so but I am afraid we might be misinterpreting the meaning of this functioning. Indeed, even though narcissism is always featured in this type of organization, it seems to me that the subject's investment is more directed at the control of the subject's borders which are experienced as under threat at all times, even in the absence of delusional projections. In fact, it is conversely the adhesion to reality which preoccupies the subject and the need to have others share and recognize an actual vision that is unobjectionable as it stands; this coincides with the analyst's perception that the so-called reality has been invested delusionally even though no "delusional idea" is ever exposed. For the rest, the interpretation, which is then directed at whatever may refer to the endangered borders in this reality, whether metaphorically or symbolically, can be recognized without altering the lived experience. In these structures, the aggression must always come from without – the intrusion into the Ego, into sex or into thought all resonate with one another. The interpretation in terms of projective identification – certainly the most accurate one in this case – encounters staunch resistance because it might lead the subject to recognize that the movement starts with him, which would contradict the seemingly inconvertible reference to external reality. All the initiatives start with reality. The Other is real and, if a psychic functioning is to be investigated, the Other's it must be. These patients are very skilled at detecting the counter transferential dynamics they induce and which the analyst sometimes has to yield to, because he is led to a projective counter-identification to relieve his own psychic apparatus from extreme tension. This confirms the need to consolidate the narcissistic defences against some hostile otherness, insofar as the other does not confine himself to validating the manifest content of the analysand's speech. In that case, the outside-inside border has come to eclipse the conflicts playing out from within. They resurface when, once alone, the analysand becomes prey to destructive anxieties, in the absence of the object, and requires the verification of his integrity and evidence of his survival. In contrast with the "delusion" of intrusion, the depressive lived experience of loss is what then incapacitates thought.

It seems as if there were a paradoxical aim in the experience of a scrambled, vague, uncertain and fragmented relation – the haze of thoughts – with associative sequences suggesting unrelated images in the analyst's mind. A form of fusional relationship is established, on the one hand, one in which it is seemingly understood that the analyst will not need the mediations required for intelligibility to grasp what is being transmitted at that particular moment. On the other hand, this apparently fusional relationship is the means found by the patient to ensure that his thoughts remain inaccessible to the analyst. This might be when it is key not to understand too much of what is being communicated. This also explains how the representational process of this thinking outside language might set in in the analyst in the opposite case – when the sophistication of thought generating confusion pursues the same goal: to be heard beyond the multiple contradictions in what is said and to think of oneself as indecipherable, protected by the wall of language and the accomplishments it can achieve in accordance with an unfathomable logic.

The omnipotence of thought is not that of wish fulfilment here; it would pertain, rather, to a negative measure: that of thinking that can never be thought out by the other. This is why the reference with which to approach this issue is not desire but the object, the thinking of the object insofar as it should never absorb the subject's thinking, for want of entrapping it in its midst. The idea of a container, developed by Bion, initially led to an improvement in our understanding – even though it needs to be supplemented by what experience brings to it. To the borderline case, a container can only be acceptable provided it is perfectly adapted to the patient's contained, as if it were its very own. In other words, it is as if what could be upheld is the illusion that the patient may find his own container in the analyst, thus disregarding the analyst's function as other. The patient's triumph then consists in feeling that he succeeded in making the other another him; that, in other words, he reversed the danger of intrusion by the object, the consequence of an interpretation of a part of him by someone who is not him, via an – unconscious – intrusion into the other, his representatives or his productions, whom he succeeded in making identical with himself.

Yet, the state of separation is not more tolerable than the state of intrusion. The silence of the analyst wishing to be respectful of the patient's dread of securing his own separation and identity lead to the familiar injunction: "Say something!", "Show me you have an opinion about it and that the state of separation has not led to your death". It all takes place in the back and forth of a kind of thinking that must make sure not to ever lose its link with its inviolable sanctuary; at the same time, it must give itself evidence of the other's existence in an indefinitely renewed way, in the context of a relationship within which the other's closeness and distance are constantly put into question. Anxiety is probably what justifies such alternations, which take the place of what would otherwise be investments truly on the side of life. But such investments are threatening to narcissism. Life is dangerous, death is dangerous. The quest for a state between life and death is often what is being sought in the experience of thought. By this, I mean that any experience of thought presupposes a distancing of the body and the object, leading to a suspension of life and stamping any thought, however exhilarating it might be, with the impression that only a renunciation akin to the beginning of a death can beget it. The analytic situation exacerbates this task. Indeed, in the analysis, thinking at once demands separation from the body and constant reunification with it. Yet, for these patients, the body never is the present-absent one that it should be. It is either excluded or overwhelming in the form of anxiety. This anxiety of the body merges with the object. It is experienced as if it came from the analyst, from the analyst's body-thought that must either be annihilated or endured in an annihilating relationship. The patient struggles to recognize the projection, because all his efforts are devoted to the establishment of a border with the other. And this border can only be secured by this expulsion of the object, leaving but little psychic activity left to make sense of the whole process. Yet, we must also factor in the border delineating the inside, whose function of counter-cathexis is often defective. Arising from this border, therefore, are not primary processes infiltrating secondary processes, as it was claimed, but processes that resemble primary processes but differ from them because of their subornation, i.e. because of the fact that they do not seek the satisfaction of erotic wishes as much as their destruction, destructiveness targeting the expressed contents as much as the thought that expresses them. These patients would not be understood at all without the awareness that, to them, it is a vital question. All their social and sublimatory achievements have aimed to set up this *double border* which the analysis puts into question. The exhausting struggle resumes in this setting despite the fact that reality seemingly provided enough evidence that this effort was in fact successful.

A reading of Freud's "Negation" from our present perspective is probably the most enlightening guide to pursue our reflection. Freud's familiar formulations on thought are revisited in this text but they are inscribed in a broader frame. A prehistory of thought is outlined and it should be granted the status of origin myth. It is this primal border indeed that Freud draws with the inaugural judgment of attribution operation. The decision that bestows its good or bad quality upon an object coincides with a process through which an inside and an outside are constituted. In the latter case, however, it is more accurate to refer to a process of *excorporation* – a radical expulsion that divides the world into two and constitutes an Ego split from what is alien and bad to it. But when Freud revisits the question at the level of the judgment of existence – a judgment which, thanks to the reality-Ego that arises from the primary pleasure-Ego, must decide whether the inside-outside division overlaps with the division between the subjective and the objective – the issue of the differentiation between representation and perception is raised once again. The reference to representation completes the Freudian theory of thought: "The antithesis between subjective and objective does not exist from the first. It only comes into being from the fact that thinking possesses the capacity to bring before the mind, once more, something that has once been perceived, by reproducing it as a presentation without the external object having to be there still (1925: 237). The active work of thought, its motor palpation thanks to the small quantities, aims to recapture the object, to confirm its reality, finally sanctioning the discharge that sets the process of satisfaction in motion. The logic at work in the *Project for a Scientific Psychology* (1966 [1895]) still pervades this text even though it was written thirty years later.

But Freud leaves out the fact that, between the establishment of the primary border and the implementation of thought, a second border separating the inside has been established. For the act of exorcism that expelled what is bad from the body has not solved anything. The return of these original impressions as memories of this painful experience remains to be mastered, which justifies the operation of repression; except for one major difference: repression comes to pass in the name of the Ego. The primal border stems from an original reality-Ego that merely locates the internal or external source of the excitation. Such an Ego is always tempted to tackle internal sources as if they were external, which is why it implements the supposedly emancipatory process of expulsion. It can only sustain the illusion that its mechanism is efficient insofar as the mother still delivers the expected satisfaction, but the mother-object is then one with the primary pleasure-Ego that comes to be at that very time and is the likely cradle of the omnipotent Ego Ideal. Yet, the psychic work is instituted according to various norms. The selection of excitations is then established following the modality of what is pleasant or unpleasant to the Ego when its good object is no longer conflated with the Ego. The Ego's pleasure is no longer tied to the feeling of self-sufficiency arising from the Ego's merger with the object likely to sanction the process of expulsion through the advent of an experience of satisfaction that may result from it. How is the object constituted on the outside; in other words, how is it lost? A descriptive approach accounts for the process as gradual. A metapsychological approach only retains the *fait accompli* of its external constitution. The constitution of a good internal object elicits the correlative constitution of an Ego sufficiently invested by binding capacities that allows for the thinking of the absent object beyond it. Such an Ego can work on hallucinatory wish fulfilment because it replaced the primal discontinuity that compelled it to the expulsion process with a feeling of continuity that authorizes wait, delay. It is not a final reality-Ego, it is just an Ego able to form representations of a certain duration and to play with these representations. The constitution of a preconscious requires the establishment of this internal border which can concede some representations of the unconscious, avoid others and implement processes on either side of this internal border.

The hypothesis I am venturing is that, between this play of representation and the advent of thought proper, a *negative hallucination* of the object (mother or breast) must be instituted. This is the condition for the emergence, not of a more or less realistic representation as Freud contends, but of a representation of the relations within a representation and between various representations.[11] For, if representation is a prerequisite for thought, thought will never derive directly from representation. The primary discontinuity that led to the bad object's exclusion did not free the psyche. A hole developed within it, like an empty space, a blank which, in the best of cases, will have been fulfilled partially by the experience of satisfaction. Whatever is left of it will have to be subject to the work of thought.

Psychosis offers us the hyperbolic version of the subject's experience of this ever-menacing disinvestment of reality by the void. In psychosis, the experience of satisfaction has been replaced by the delusion. The latter consists in a frantic attempt to bestow meaning upon the Id's anarchical invasion, thanks to links that remain tethered to drive-related impulses. It can take on the more limited form of a momentary experience such as the hallucination of the cut finger in such a borderline case as the Wolfman.[12] From these clinical facts, we can draw the normal prototype in which the experience of inaugural discontinuity is represented by the negative hallucination – a representation of the absence of representation. On its basis, discontinuous thoughts to be joined together by non-material links will develop. Such operations are then taken up by language, whose units are discontinuous and exclusive, following Freud's observation. Language becomes a privileged activity of investment because it can produce representations and representations of relations. All this therefore confers consciousness on a part of thought.

Yet language imposes its constraints so that its consistency may be ensured. Consequently, the way it relays thought leaves out whatever passes through the mesh of its net. It is a limitation of theory to have to use language only to account for unconscious thought which, for the most part, cannot be contained by linguistic processes.

In the analysis of borderline cases, the blank of thought emerges. The analysands who say "I have a blank" and those who say "I am not thinking

---

11 Hence the idea – which Freud always defended – of some unconscious thinking operating at a distance from primal perceptive residues. It seems to me that distance is not enough to create the conditions for this operation; instead, we must suggest an obliteration of representation.

12 See "L'hallucination négative" (Green, 1977). In this essay, I underline the fact that the Wolfman's hallucination of the cut finger, which begets terror, includes a negativization of the blood that should flow from the wound. The anxiety caused by the wound only stems from the gap that separates the finger from the hand, both finger and hand being held together by a mere fragment of skin.

about anything" are not the same ones. The blank that is being communicated does not refer to repression. Even if a transference thought is thus expressed negatively, as in the case of repression, what these analysands show the analyst is a thought that has no content but must be communicated; silence is not enough for it, it must be transmitted as a representation of the absence of representation. This blank was required for the establishment of thought. But, in the aforementioned analytic situations, what is represented is an inability to think that is a constant threat because this inability to think, or to represent, leaves the field clear for drives where the body will take advantage of this vacuity in the mind to seize upon the Ego. The blank could not be integrated into the binding of thoughts and representations: in other words, the negative no longer is the source of work, it is a result in itself, a suspension of psychic activity, a temporary death of the mind.

For the neurotic and, at times, even the borderline case, a suspension of speech paired with "I don't know" can suffice. For the psychotic, a reply is mandatory. For the borderline case, this suspension is neither a pause nor a sigh, it is an urgent request directed at the Ego or the analyst to fill the psychic space threatened by the void or by the intrusion of a drive more than by an undesirable representation. Unlike the obsessional, for whom doubt is the flip side of a compulsion that does without any decision on the part of the Ego, dictates the thought and the act to be carried out, the phobic, conversely, forces himself not to ever undertake the associative synthesis. Does this qualify as a thought disorder, however? We can probably believe so, except that, unlike the obsessional whose thought is sexualized, the phobic places all the excitation in the final act of synthesis, which then amounts to an orgasm.

He shies away from it simply because such an orgasm is always incestuous and phobia always features the same fear of being engulfed by the other, a fear limited to the orgasm alone. The repetition of these experiences of frustration safeguards the phobic organization against the possibility of orgasmic satisfaction. The latter is likely to generate a sense of being engulfed by the other, including castration, featured here only as the first stage and as the impossibility to reclaim the imaginary penis. Fusion is only wished for when it cannot occur, namely when it involves an Oedipal object that has been wholly invested as such, as implying, in other words, all the fantasies tied to the coitus of a primal scene which must consist in a scene of conception. The synthesis of associations thus takes on this value of "conception", which is why it never takes place. There is no blank of thought in this case but an ever partial suspension to be completed according to auto-erotic modes. But the suspension is heir to the blank.

Let us go back to "Negation" and to this primal border. Freud ties it to the language of "the oldest – the oral – drive-related impulses" (1925: 237). What we can now grasp between the lines of this text – a key insight if we

The double limit 49

want to make sense of Klein's developments – is that this border does not really make up an outside.

What is being expelled is an abyss, the flip side of a primal mouth that expels itself through a process of psychic vomiting and strives to seize the subject from without. Hate is thus expelled (or something that does not even have such an overly differentiated name), the activity of a boundless cavity intent on drawing the whole psyche to itself in deadly annihilation. Psychotic subjects are not the best illustration of this because they are sometimes beyond this – in inertia or, conversely, in the filling-in of this void through the multiplicity of meanings which the range of delusional floridity provides. Ever exposed to the abyss, the pit, the void into which the wish to seize them and drag them down to unfathomable depths is projected, the borderline cases are those who, in truth, make us experience – more than represent them for us – the depths where thought becomes lost.

From the primal expulsion that divides the subject's world into two to negation in language, the same operation is always repeated, the same psychic act endowed with the same meaning: expelling in order to purify, purifying in order to bind. Yet, even when the justification involves the worst annihilation or death anxieties, it is always a fragment of life that is thus eradicated in the psyche. A work of death is therefore always accomplished – from the negativism of acute psychosis to the negation necessary for the principle of non-contradiction. This work of death safeguards life but a form of life that is always more or less impoverished, all the more so as the series of operations are always directed towards the inside. But each operation carried out to set up this inside is followed by a double threat: on the one hand, the expelled outside always tends to return to its original land; on the other hand, in the inside that is thus set up, a new division will occur, treating a part within as non "agreeable", a part to be banished from an inside which it constantly strives to reinvest. The work of the negative never leaves the subject, despite its repeated exorcisms. When word presentations free themselves from their ties to thing presentations, language reintegrates the act of repression through the use of negation.

It might seem paradoxical to ascribe to death what is so vital to survival. However, this may be asking the question the wrong way: we must understand that life processes are only viable through the integration of death forces. Taming death implies forcing it to unite with life. Repression repeats the radical act of expulsion in the psyche, except that it makes up a repressed which will draw, in turn, whatever was rejected via an operation that is seemingly akin to the primal expulsion: i.e. attraction within the pre-existing repressed. The negative hallucination breaks the link with the thing presentation but the discontinuity it entails in the psyche ultimately serves the links of language. Negation succeeds in suspending the cost entailed by repression but it is also a way to recognize what it denies. In the end, as opposed to the pure and simple link which Freud posits between drive and thought within a series of continuous operations, the work of the negative allows us to recognize the importance of a function that was overlooked by Freud. Indeed, just as the reality principle does not strive to find the object but to recapture it, thought does not consist in linking processes but in re-linking them after some obliteration had disjointed them.

Where can we then locate the work of thought from a modern psychoanalytic perspective? If we want to avoid a theoretical position that likens thought to the kind of operational thinking developed in the psychosomatic approach – which Freud's formulations compellingly suggest – thought must be located at a crossroads, within a metapsychological model: between inside and outside, on the one hand, and between the two distinct parts that divide the inside (border of the Cs-Pcs and Ucs systems), on the other hand. This is how the two main areas of psychopathology might be brought together: psychosis and neurosis with all the space available for non-neurotic and non-psychotic structures. For this purpose, *one must tackle the border as a concept.*[13]

If we put together such a model very schematically with a vertical partition – the border between the inside and the outside – and we divide the inside section into two with a horizontal border separating the Cs-Pcs and the Ucs, the thought processes will be located at the intersection of these two lines. This returns me to the hypothesis I once ventured of tertiary processes whose function consists in establishing a back and forth movement between primary and secondary processes. But, on top of this aforementioned function, communication between the inside and the outside can be added.[14]

A modern psychoanalytic theory of thought can no longer confine itself to entrusting thought with the sole task of exploring the external world. Indeed, the condition of the validity of such an exploration is now correlated with its prerequisite: the internal psychic work that leads to the formation of the system of unconscious representations and its communication with consciousness, via the mediation of the preconscious. How can venturing such a hypothesis be justified? Admittedly, the experience which borderline cases grant us regarding the relation with the transferential analytic object allows us to recognize the impossibility to dissociate – as is the case with neurosis – the intrapsychic work and the intersubjective work dominated by a constant concern with borders and optimum distance. But this remains a rather objectivist perspective, as if the analysand could think himself per se outside the work carried out

---

13 See "The borderline concept" (1976) in *On Private Madness* (Green, 1986: 60–83).
14 Let us notice that Freud never tied his ideas on unconscious thinking processes with what he theorizes as thought or thinking (restrictions to discharge, experimental sounding action thanks to small quantities, etc.).

by the analyst. The main source of these reflections is the analyst's work, which always involves thought. In truth, Freud's description of thought could be rehabilitated, if it were applied to the analyst's work. Through his personal analysis, the analyst might develop – except in critical situations – the capacity for this quantitative reduction, for the possibility to defer the (interpretative) discharge, to delve into the material periodically by returning to himself, to provide himself with a representation of the psychic processes at work in the patient, and to link them through language, through the work of representation. The negative hallucination is not absent from this work; it characterizes each moment when the analyst does not understand anything in the material and can neither represent it nor find any links within it. This is why, just as Lacan urges us to be wary of understanding things too quickly, Bion retains from Freud the necessity to blind oneself to let the "unthinkable" interpretation arise. It also operates in the discontinuity of the thoughts that carried out the dismantling of the linearity of speech.

The analyst then knows that thinking is painful for the analysand because he can gauge, in himself, the considerable effort in thought which his work requires. This does not only pertain to the most accomplished achievements of thought, those he implements when writing a paper that accounts for his experience; on the contrary, it refers to the inchoate and embryonic forms of a thought that fails to be spoken.

Bion's sophisticated theoretical developments – or Lacan's – have generated a feeling of failure (Bion became aware of it while Lacan just forged ahead, that was his only salvation). This probably stems from our residual inability to envision the developments of a "proto-thought" which persists in a psychic apparatus that seemingly had to turn away from it in order to pursue its own evolution and demonstrate its ability to perform at a high level. At the end of his paper on the Wolfman, Freud foresaw the problem in all its complexity. We have an excessive tendency to theorize thought as a process that extracts whatever content might be germinating in a data, as if it were just a matter of drawing the implication the data secretly holds. In his discussion of the effect of the primal scene on his patient, Freud writes:

> it is hard to dismiss the view that some sort of hardly definable knowledge, something, as it were, preparatory to an understanding, was at work in the child at the time. We can form no conception of what this may have consisted in; we have nothing at our disposal but the single analogy – and it is an excellent one – of the far-reaching *instinctive* knowledge of animals. (1918: 120)

The inchoate forms of thought are not only caught between projection and analytic elaboration, they are anticipatory. This is how children's psychotic productions, like the delusional constructions of adults, sometimes preempt intuitions of thought which we struggle to move forward to their full theoretical construction. Freud is thus led to justify finding a metaphorized vision of his own theory in Schreber's delusion.

The unamendable persistence of this proto-thought therefore constantly forces us to repeat this work of the negative via the double border. This prevents us from being engulfed by it so that acceptable relations with others and oneself may be instituted, by sacrificing an overly exuberant share of this excess life.

References

Donnet, J.-L. and Green, A. (1973). *L'enfant de ça: Psychanalyse d'un entretien, la psychose blanche*. Paris: Editions de Minuit.

Freud, S. (1911). *Formulations on the Two Principles of Mental Functioning*. S.E. 12. London: Hogarth, pp. 213–226.

Freud, S. (1918). *From the History of an Infantile Neurosis*. S.E. 17. London: Hogarth, pp. 1–124.

Freud, S. (1925). *Negation*. S.E. 19. London: Hogarth, pp. 233–240.

Freud, S. (1938). *An Outline of Psychoanalysis*. S.E. 23. London: Hogarth, pp. 139–208.

Freud, S. (1966 [1895]). *Project for a Scientific Psychology, Part II*. S.E. 1. London: Hogarth Press, pp. 347–387.

Green, A. (1977). L'hallucination négative [negative hallucination]. *L'Evolution Psychiatrique*, 42: 645–656.

Green, A. (1980). Préface. In W.B. Bion, *Entretiens psychanalytiques*. Paris: Gallimard.

Green, A. (1986). *On Private Madness*. London: Karnac.

3 The silence of the psychoanalyst[1]
(1979)

I.

Last autumn, with a group of peer psychoanalysts, we had exchanges about the silence of the psychoanalyst. The discussion highlighted the fact that silence met a variety of interpretations among us. Two questions stuck in my mind:

– Can the psychoanalyst's silence be granted a metapsychological status?
  Is there such a thing as the psychoanalyst's silence?

The first question was a hard one to answer. As for the second question, it led to a questioning of the existence of silence, in view of the fact that, even though the psychoanalyst may be silent, if not even mute at times, this silence is nonetheless a living space, inhabited by all the associations of analytic listening. A distinction therefore had to be made between silence as a herald of the void and silence as pertaining to a strategy based on the virtues of not speaking. We know that Bion advised analysts to be without memory and desire, and to approximate an optimum state of internal emptiness, to elicit the emergence of the thoughts prompted by the patient's speech. This observation becomes fully meaningful when we know that it was made by a representative of an analytic group whose reputation was to be chatty. Besides, Bion's recommendation is not to be silent but to prove oneself to be as available as possible at the beginning of each session, so as to be able to hear whatever new material the patient might bring.

If silence has two meanings, one that refers to the void, the other to verbal abstinence, both must, in any case, be related to the intense work of elaboration undertaken by the analyst in the course of his silent listening. To be precise, to Bion, the void is but a mythical point of origin.

---

1 Translated by Dorothée Bonnigal-Katz for this edition.

In the group of colleagues taking part in the discussion, two trends were voiced. The first trend – clearly the prevailing one – stayed true to the golden rule of silence, for a variety of technical reasons, in keeping with the rules classically taught in psychoanalytic training. The analysts who upheld this position all shared some form of scepticism regarding the value of interpretation as the fundamental mainspring of analysis. Many insisted on the maternal side of the transference, the fusional relationship, the unlived experience, the unspeakable – in short, the "mother's silence" as the vehicle for change. Interpretation could close things off, according to them. Two of Freud's comments were brought to mind in this context, one referring to the silence-death equivalence in *The Theme of the Three Caskets* (1913), the other one relating to *The Uncanny* (1919) and suggesting that nothing can be said about silence.

The advocates of silence defended the technical value of a form of muteness covering a bulk of thoughts to be withheld from communication, so as to "let the analysand do his analysis", as the saying goes. It is as if the virtues of silence rested on the idea that the analyst's silence might signal tacit acceptance and infra-verbal communication, this pre-verbal operating as a catalyst invisibly, allowing the patient to understand the meaning of the conveyed material on his own. It was furthermore pointed out that, to mention but the best known examples, Lacan and Nacht (i.e. Nacht before the final period) both agreed to champion silence. Nacht's position seemed more coherent on this point insofar as he laid emphasis on the pre-verbal relationship and the restorative virtue of silence. As for Lacan, while defending the "cadaverization" of the analyst, he nonetheless centred his theory on language, as if the work on language in the subject's relation to the signifier occurred exclusively in and through the enunciative process in the transference. Naturally, the silent analyst does not dispense with interpretation. But it is evident then that the economy of the interpretation, which should be rare, concise and short, pertains to an oracular stance. This locates us at odds with Winnicott who reminds us that, with some patients, we are used for our very deficiencies, which symbolize the initial deficiencies of the environment. Things are not so simple as, conversely, there was once an insistence on the need to frustrate the patient. Actually, we need to phrase the question differently: before which analysand, which session and which stage of the analysis must the silence of the analyst befall?

Another trend was voiced in the group and put this golden rule into question by relying on the following arguments:

1. Such a rule has never been put forward by Freud in his papers on technique. What we know of his practice shows that he generally was not very silent at all, even though he was silent with some patients: e.g. the group of English analysts who were in analysis with him, along with the informer who tells us about it, namely Kardiner (1977).

Furthermore, those who worked with the Viennese analysts can testify to the fact that they were neither very silent nor very neutral.
2. We cannot claim that such a rule was the object of a consensus; the meetings with the English analysts show us, for example, that they often intervene, regardless of the tradition they are affiliated to (Anna Freudian, Kleinian or independent).
3. In contemporary psychoanalytic practice, classic neuroses are rare. When we are lucky enough to have one among our analysands, they prove very difficult to analyse. Conversely, the cases where narcissistic traits dominate, or the borderline cases, or those who present serious personality disorders, all show that that analyst's silence is not productive. Either patients do not tolerate it or they settle into a false self position in the analysis. The problem then boils down to a few alternatives: either we reject these candidates for analysis as unanalysable when we recognize them as such before the start of the analysis; or, if the analyst has agreed to the analysis, the treatment is interrupted; or else, the analyst can agree to the continuation of the treatment in a more or less conscious collusion, with the knowledge that this is a pseudo-analysis. The remaining possibility is to amend the technique. In the latter case, the question will then be: what do we do? Is it psychoanalysis? Is it psychotherapy? Tinkerer's improvisation? Manipulation?

What are the implications for the metapsychological status of silence?

II.

The theoretical and axiomatic position I have chosen can be defined as followed: *The analyst's silence can only be understood as part of the psychoanalytic frame.*[2] *Its meaning can only be elucidated as embedded in the set of conditions that circumscribe this frame and constitute the a priori of psychoanalysis or of this application of the psychoanalytic method to the psychoanalytic treatment.*

Let us point out at the outset that the analyst's silence is connected to the other parameters that define the analytic situation. Thus visible at the beginning of the session, the analyst ceases to be so during the session until he becomes visible again at the end; the patient in analysis is subjected to this silence as he lies on the couch where his mobility is restricted. This set of conditions, in which silence is included, induces dynamics of thoughts that are directed at this inaccessible object and are returned to the analysand by linking up with other thoughts that are apparently

---

2 On the question of the analytic frame, one should refer to the work of Winnicott, Bleger, Jean-Luc Donnet along with myself (see "The analyst, symbolization and the absence in the analytic frame", Green, 1975).

unrelated to the previous ones; this silence therefore becomes like the backdrop against which some associative thinking unfurls, miming the flowing regime of free energy; if the patient's speech is a language indeed, it awakens, in the analyst, a swarm of representations for which, in many cases, there is no verbal translation. All these characteristics – which are the most familiar ones in the analyst's daily experience, so much so that the analyst no longer thinks about them – suggest a parallel with dreams: *just as dreams are the guardian of sleep, the analyst is the guardian of the frame where silence is the main parameter*. The theoretical formulations made by Winnicott on the frame are incomplete because there is much more to it than the metaphor of maternal care. The frame is akin to a symbolic matrix, a container that is itself contained, a condition for meaning that pertains to another meaning.

The first idea I would like to defend is that the silent function of the analyst is independent of the quantity of words (or information) that he introduces in the analytic frame. In fact, this function pertains to the silence that the analyst observes in his interpretative response in respect of the manifest content of speech. This is why, however loquacious an analyst might be, an analysand almost always feels that he is not saying enough and, most importantly, that he does not answer the questions he is asked so that they remain unanswered with regard to the manifest content. When the analysand feels that the analyst said too much, this always means that the analyst said what the analysand does not want to hear. Just as it applies to the analysand, we must oppose full speech and empty speech on the side of the analyst (Lacan). An analyst who speaks very little can open his mouth only to utter empty speech. Full speech is always interpretative (directly or indirectly) and silence is one of the forms it can take.

Because the referent of the analysis is the relation of the drives to the unconscious, the aim of the analysand's unconscious speech is to provoke the "specific action" (Freud). The analyst's speech is a metaphor of action but it is and it must only be a metaphor, which implies that the manifest content should be deviated, subverted. This accounts for the dissatisfaction of some analysands who react to this deviation imposed on the "specific action", i.e. the action that is likely to provide the drive with its satisfaction: "But what do I have to do then?" This question is often included in the content of what I call the "counter-interpretation" (a phrase modelled after the term "countertransference") to refer to the analysand's reply – whatever it might be – to the analyst's interpretation.

Furthermore, interpretation is not the opposite of silence because silence can also be a form of interpretation. In the analytic frame, there are nothing but different models of interpretation. As a patient of mine once remarked: "In the presence of the analyst, you can't trip on the carpet without it meaning something". You will not be surprised to hear that a few sessions later, she tripped (or had a good trip[3]) on my carpet. Whether I speak or remain quiet, it always means something. The question is, for the analyst as well as the analysand: "Since it necessarily means some*thing* and I have to choose between several possible meanings, which is the right one?" For the analysand, silence can thus mean consecutively and depending on the moments of an analysis or a session: fusion, attentive interest, benevolence, complicity, respect of the analysand's speech, agreement ("silence gives consent"), indifference, sleep, rejection and even a wish to evacuate the analyst. The question is to determine whether it is more beneficial to let the thread or the film of the projection go or to show *why* this or that affect, this or that representation rather than another, is experienced by the analysand: Who is addressing who, to say what, when and where?

Economy in the analyst's speech has been advocated. What does economy mean? It means saving, undeniably (yet, who is being saved?) but also, and most importantly, it means transformation, as indicated by the words of work production according to *"oïkos nomia"* – household law. If the law is not the oracle – saving seems to be of the low risk kind: the risk of making a blatant mistake. Bion was telling me that a patient who cannot make a fool of his analyst must be very ill. Economy is also championed in the sense of an economy of means, which an elegant solution always comprises. T. Reik pointed out the positive role of the element of surprise that always stamps the mutative interpretation. If, against the economical interpretation, I oppose an *interpretative process* during the course of a session, surprise then precisely arises when three apparently trivial and perfectly assimilable interventions are followed by a surprise interpretation; this has a knack for prompting silence, one that must always be respected because it signals a process of mute elaboration. A paradox – which will be contested by many, I am sure – consists in asserting that *the analytic frame induces the production of a speech that interpretation will subject to the silence of punctuation, followed by the resumption of associations*. The silence of elaboration will be a shared silence, one that the analyst should in no case break; according to Winnicott, the true self is silent and never communicates with the analyst. Similarly, the analyst's silence always protects the analyst's silent self for, however loquacious the analyst might be, he must never speak about himself as such; when it is impossible for the analyst to avoid self-disclosure, this disclosure can nevertheless always be the object of a projection.

---

3 Translator's note: In the French original, Green is playing with two expressions; "se prendre le pied" which means to trip or stumble and "prendre son pied" which means to experience a high or an orgasm. To keep the play on words, I used the term "trip" (to trip on / to have a good trip) which can imply both ideas even though it does not fully capture the sexual dimension included in the original.

The silent function is complex. It dwells in the hollow of the patient's speech, it is the shadow of this speech, its negativity. In the context of free association, this function is delegated to the analyst when this delegation is carried out completely. But this function is also fragmented in the gaps of speech, the articular discontinuities, the blanks that the associative process requires. When the analyst speaks, he only knows the line of what he has to say: the interpretation emerges from the work carried out in the gaps in speech, in the associative discontinuity. It develops extemporaneously in the binding of the act of enunciation that reincorporates and brings together what the gaps erased and dissociated. An analyst formulating his interpretations clearly to himself before saying them would be beset by a form of obsessionalization that denies the message of the unconscious (his unconscious) *including the risks of slips without any chance of putting it right*. I noticed that some of my interpretations were not grammatically correct and so much the better: I thus provided my patient with material on my countertransference, sustaining a live speech that was not cut off from its unconscious roots by way of preconscious elaboration. Every interpretation pertains to the preconscious because the interpretation is the twofold result of a process of thought formation and putting into words, just as the unconscious is a process of linking representations and affects.

The structuring function of the analyst's silence is unquestionable. Silence makes up the backdrop against which the patient's projective figures will move (or be moved), be delineated, written, formed. It could be seen as a forerunner of interpretation. However, from time immemorial, analysts have had to recognize that there are patients "who cannot bear silence". The conclusions that were drawn from this are highly questionable. Indeed, on account of the inadequacy of the technique known as classic, these patients have been relegated to the outer shadows of psychotherapy. The British school has a completely different take on them, it created its own analytic technique. Melanie Klein had a lot to do with this change. But Winnicott was the first one to denounce the collusion between analyst and patient, where both feel that the analysis is hobbling along, until the day when they come to the conclusion that the analysis has rolled off the analysand like water off a duck's back. As Winnicott suggests, not everyone can afford a psychotic breakdown. I was struck by this comment on collusion – which I myself was complicit with for a long time. Like children, the analysand has an immense capacity for adaptation, even when he is very troubled. Like children, he is also able to develop his neurosis or psychosis silently over the course of many years, while seemingly abiding by the rules of life and even appearing to take part, until a sudden process of decompensation occurs. Like the child with his parents, his play involves making use of the defences of the analyst whom he successfully turns into an unwitting acolyte towards the non-development of a transference neurosis. That is perhaps, precisely, because there is no neurosis to transfer but a "transference" psychosis, pre-psychosis, depression or borderline state.

Are such structures transferable and analysable? Many analysts answer negatively.[4] What seems undeniable to me is that they put the analyst's countertransference to the test, specifically regarding the question of silence. The analyst's silence can absorb these states in the treatment, i.e. finish the analysis on a *non liquet* likely to leave a pathogenic potential in the analysand. This will expose the analysand to further decompensation, hence these cases that involve "n" parts with the same analyst or another.

The triangular coherence (infantile neurosis, adult neurosis, transference neurosis) is satisfying for the mind that observes the course of operations from without: the non-structured or destructuring psychotic chaos, the objectual void, narcissistic duplications, the temperamental carapace, the borderline dynamics; none of these are likely to emerge on the backdrop of the analyst's silence. The links (according to Bion) are not self-evident, the relation between free energy and bound energy, for which language is the site of transformation, tends to lead, rather, to volcano or desert metaphors; the emphasis weighing on the signifier is likely to yield instances of semantic nuclear fission. Such apocalyptic images can give us an idea of what the analyst shields himself against to safeguard his quiet life. After all, the patient attends his sessions, he pays regularly and commits suicide rather infrequently; he rarely ends up in a mental institution. This is what I refer to as *private madness*, which only the frame reveals, at times when it may become cracked, fissured, split like the Ego discussed by Freud in his 1924 essay *Neurosis and Psychosis* (1951 [1924]).

In cases when the patient does not interrupt the analysis through flight or through some acting out that is damaging to the *analysis*, this capacity for adaptation is such that the patient becomes *organized* within the analyst's silence by way of a retaliating silence couched in the play of what Lacan calls empty speech. The analyst thus remains dead letter and the analytic pair is bored. There is nothing more deadly than the silent boredom of the analyst. Value judgments then arise: "the patient doesn't deserve the analysis". "He or she doesn't understand anything!" But what does the analyst understand for his part?

In these cases, the analyst's silence no longer is the opportune condition for the emergence of the transference neurosis; it is the statement of its dismissal. Refusing this deadly situation for myself and my patient is what led me to the decision to put the golden rule of the analyst's silence into question.

---

4 On the subject, see my discussion of Anna Freud in the paper I gave in London: "The analyst, symbolization and absence in the analytic setting" (Green, 1975).

III.

It is surprising to read the following in Freud's *Constructions in the Analysis* – a text that seemingly pertains to *esprit d'escalier* compared to *Analysis Terminable and Interminable*:

> the work of analysis consists of two quite different portions, that it is carried on in two separate localities, that it involves two people, to each of whom a distinct task is assigned. It may for a moment seem strange that such a fundamental fact should not have been pointed out long ago; but it will immediately be perceived that there was nothing being kept back in this, that it is a fact which is universally known and, as it were, self-evident and is merely being brought into relief here and separately examined for a particular purpose. (1937b: 258)

Such stylistic precautions are hardly in keeping with Freud's style. They might suggest, rather, that they defectively veil a very late realization – better late than never. For an understanding of the long delay that this statement of the obvious required, we must take a backwards step.

A fundamental question of psychoanalysis concerns the relation between theoretical models and clinical practice. These relations are not always clear in Freud's corpus. Four periods can be distinguished. The first one is a period of trial and error. It spans from the *Studies on Hysteria* to the *Interpretation of Dreams*. Clinical work drives Freud to develop his first purely theoretical model. This results in the 1895 *Project* and its failure.

The *Interpretation of Dreams* inaugurates the second period in the formation of a theoretical and clinical model. Four axes are defined over the course of five years: dreams (*Interpretation of Dreams*), the transference of transference psychoneuroses (Dora), infantile sexuality (*Three Essays on the Theory of Sexuality*) and language (*Jokes and their Relation to the Unconscious*).

The important thing about the break between the *Project* and the *Interpretation of Dreams* is that with this work, implicitly, *Freud provides a model not only of the psychic apparatus, but also of the analytic frame*. What is commonly pointed out is that the analytic situation, which is Freud's discovery – just as the unconscious is his discovery – has only been the subject of pragmatic justifications, whereas it institutes an unequivocally original and entirely new relation between two human beings. I will therefore venture the following hypothesis: the model put forward in the *Project* was abandoned because it was a model open to the elements. It comprises the peripheral and the central nervous system, the whole of which characterizes the somatic nervous system with its two levels – primary and secondary. To this – and there lies Freud's originality, featured at the outset – Freud adds the drive-related system, which I understand as a metaphorization of the vegetative or autonomic nervous system in the neurological references of his time into a signifying system of the drive-related body and, finally, the language system which he examines in relation to aphasia (1953 [1891]). Each of these systems is based on the reflex arc which Freud still refers to in the *Interpretation of Dreams*, with a receptor pole and an effector pole: sensibility and motricity for the peripheral system, perception and action for the central system, drive and affect for the precursory system of drive-related life, emission and reception for language. The science of the time views consciousness as the supreme stage of integration because it only considers the two systems of the somatic nervous system, centring psychic activity on the relations between organism and surrounding environment. Freud understands then that this perspective is too broad to grasp the fundamental reference it is searching for: the one presiding over internal psychic activity.

This decentring of the psyche towards the specific drive-representation-action system compels Freud to implement a reduction of the *Project*'s model, sacrifice the relational system pertaining to the external world, concede the cutting off of consciousness and language and agree to a strictly retrospective and indirect perspective on the internal world once all these parameters have been neutralized, if not removed. This is what the model in Chapter VII of the *Interpretation of Dreams* theorizes. Freud (1900) closes down the perceptual pole (the subject closes his eyes and "hallucinates" during sleep), shuts down the motor pole (the subject is paralysed when he sleeps) and allows for the unfurling of the psychic events reorganized by the dreamwork. I will skip the details that are known to all. In the process, Freud shuts himself up in the black box of sleep but, unlike the behaviourists, and more in keeping with the Platonists (myth of the cave), he recognizes the "true" psychic life at its core. Caught in the confines of dreams as protagonist and witness, he *experiences* dreams without understanding them; then, when awake, he remembers, associates, makes links between day residues, latent thoughts, dream wish, from a conjectural interpretative perspective. It all occurs in the *après-coup* of what has already been dreamed, in a process of indirect understanding with the aim of returning to the place where "it was" (or *id* was), just as the analysand seeks to recapture the lost past.

But the essential fact lies in the implicit homology of the model of the dream and the model of the frame. In the session, there is no shutting down of the perceptual pole, but the analyst is constantly perceptible to the analysand (the kind of perception available from the couch), though this constant perception is quickly annulled by its repetitive monotony, and he locates himself out of the analysand's sight. There is no closing down of the motor pole either but the motor function is restricted by the lying position. Associative speech unfolds between these two poles while consciousness is maintained; but moral and intellectual censorship is supposed to lift just as it is lowered in dreams. The concurrence of the two models underlies the intersection of theory and practice. A close reading of the *Interpretation of Dreams* already points to the lineaments of the other components of the full model, namely transference, infantile sexuality and language, which will be subsequently developed by Freud in the work we cited. The third period opens with *Beyond the Pleasure Principle*, where the reshuffling of the latest drive theory is a mere prelude to the second topography and is inseparable from the life drive / death drive dualism, which is often overlooked. But what strikes me most is the parallel re-evaluation of transference and dreams. The first one is explicit (repetition compulsion), the second one is implicit by means of the nightmares of traumatic neurosis. Finally, Freud prefigures Winnicott by introducing the importance of play and he foreshadows Lacan by referring to the theory of language that the "ôôô-da" phonetic opposition illustrates. Melanie Klein might already be on the horizon if we understand play in terms of destruction-reparation, i.e. as a mourning process. But I believe it is especially useful to underline the introduction of silence in the theory – the death drives act in silence, all the noise comes from Eros.

In the linking between Chapters II and III of *The Ego and the Id*, a decisive theoretical moment can be noticed. Whereas in Chapter II Freud closely considers the Cs-Pcs-Ucs relations from the perspective of the links between thing *representations* and word *representations* – relying on the observable processes in the analysis – he closes this chapter on the Ego as surface or projection of a surface, the Ego as body Ego. When he approaches the following chapter, he breaks this line of thought to enter a new theoretical field that introduces the reference to the *object*. On the basis of an eminently affective structure – melancholia – he describes the relations between incorporation and identification and it is not by chance that he should turn to this affliction – a pure culture of the death drive. We can then infer that the processes described occur against a backdrop of silence.

The last period consists, in my view, in an acknowledgement of failure – or, at least, in an invitation to humility. I am alluding here to the final texts – which are, as it were, his legacy to psychoanalysis and Western thought: *Analysis Terminable and Interminable, Moses and Monotheism, An Outline of Psychoanalysis*. While the outcome is decisive from a theoretical point of view, when it comes to practice, the results tend to call for modesty. The model evolves in the direction of drive-related constitutionalism, early traumas and their defences, and the Ego's quasi irreversible distortions. Attention shifts from repression to splitting. Psychosis is a more frequent threat than one would think. The psychoanalytic field is seemingly scaled down on the basis of sounder foundations. And yet, Freud rejects any compromise of principles in the area of technique, as evidenced by his disputes with Ferenczi and Rank.

We know what happens next: Anna Freud, backed by Hartmann, Melanie Klein (descended from Ferenczi and Abraham), the neo-Kleinianism of Bion (who strives to bring Melanie Klein and Freud together without going through Anna Freud), Winnicott's mediation and Lacan's logico-linguistic neo-Freudianism.

If the hypothesis of linking dreams and frame is correct, as I believe it is, it seems to me, actually, that, out of concern for coherence, Freud should have been urged to understand that the heuristically fruitful opposition involves *diurnal and nocturnal psychic life*. This is a view upheld by Denise Braunschweig and Michel Fain in *La nuit, le jour*, from a perspective that differs from mine. Their essay centred on mental functioning probably puts us on the right track.

In my view, dreams are not the sleeper's only psychic activity as Freud could lead us to think, following Aristotle on this point. The psychic night is more immense and varied because it includes, besides dreams and nightmares, stage IV dreams,[5] the mental ruminations of insomnia, sleep walking and, finally, B. Lewin's blank dream which I understand from the perspective of the negative hallucination.

The consequence is the emergence of a new model of relations between waking and sleeping, which brings Heraclitus to mind, and, simultaneously, of a new model of relations between neurosis and psychosis (the latter term being understood broadly). Similarly, sexuality no longer is the fundamental reference of the child. It must be re-evaluated with regard to the pair it makes up with the drives of destruction and, naturally, with regard to the object and the Ego. In any case, if we wish to theorize the clinic with a view to linking theory and practice, it seems key to substitute a dyadic logic for a unitary one. The analytic couple in the frame is the counterpart of the couple combining the infans-child and the speaking parent. It can be referred to the mother-child dyad, provided we locate the father in the absence of this relation. As Lacan reminded us, the Oedipus complex remains the structuring-structured condition of theory and practice alike.[6] The notion of the pre-Oedipal is theoretically untenable.

IV.

In the psychoanalytic situation, we can distinguish different types of exchange between patient and analyst within the frame:

1. What the patient says.
2. What the patient keeps silent, does not say and knows.
3. What the patient keeps silent, does not say and does not know.
4. What the patient cannot hear or conceive of.
5. What the analyst says.

---

5 See Furst (1978).
6 What a shame Lacan later disavowed his opinion.

6. What the analyst keeps silent, does not say and knows.
7. What the analyst keeps silent, does not say and does not know.
8. What cannot be heard or is unheard of for the analyst.

There are several heuristic advantages to accounting for things in this way:

1. Silence and speech are interdependent and conjoined in each partner.
2. If speech unknowingly conveys unconscious meaning, silence is very ambiguous because it overlies what the patient and the analyst hide (reluctance), do not know and what each cannot hear or hear of.

Silence not only consists in a strategy. It can indeed be filled with silent words that bear conscious and unconscious meaning. It can also be filled with other things besides words but it can equally consist in the inaudible of the unheard-of. We are no longer dealing with misunderstandings in this case but with an auditive blackout (or blank). This can lead to either nonsense, or some unspeakable meaning, which must be operative, albeit in a form in which meaning takes on the appearance of nonsense, i.e. not of incoherence but of a meaning that the laws of meaning do not *comprehend* in all the senses of the phrase.

While we have wished to link silence and words (and non-verbal signifiers), we must add that the quality and the function of silence varies depending on the type of uttered speech, from the double viewpoint of the analysand and the analyst. In other words, there is a tight relation between the characteristics of mental functioning and of the themes it is the analyst's task to elaborate and what the analyst experiences in response to the patient's speech, either as a kind of silence that is fertile, structuring, generative (the way we speak of a generative grammar) or, conversely, as heavy silence, overinvested in drive-related terms, highly projective or fusional or, lastly, as inert silence, degenerative, dead silence. Similarly, the analysand may experience the analyst's silence in a matching way depending on his interpretative attitude.

In borderline situations,[7] the patient's speech *imposes* emotional turmoil on the analyst, in a non-representational mode at first, leading to the emergence (in the sense given to this term by biologists) of a representation or a complex of representations in the analyst's mind, as the fruit of some labour, some work "exigency" imposed on the psyche as a result of its link with the body. I think we could compare this work with the one at the root of infantile sexual theories. Can sexuality not be "theoretical"? This is an interesting question, worthy of deliberation. Silence is, in any case, the *a priori* condition for the establishment of links between the various types

---

7 See "The analyst, symbolization and absence in the analytic setting" (Green, 1975).

of signifiers, or between signifiers of the same type. What I mean is that silence is the analyst's potential work space but it is useless to prescribe it forcedly and it does not disappear when the sum of words uttered by the analyst exceeds the codified dose. "He is trying to make me speak" is the view of a supervisee reciting his lesson; it is laughable. And when I am told: "I spoke too much, or not enough", I wonder rather "did he speak on or off key?" which is the only pertinent question. Or else, I wonder "Wouldn't it have been better to say this differently?" There is a logic of interpretation that involves giving it a form first, rather than mobilizing scarcity as an economic reference. Silence can be very costly if not to the analyst – who gets paid anyway – to the analysis at least which will unfold as an unsigned yet imperative contract: "please do not say anything, I promise you I won't say anything and we won't tell anyone". The point is to file some unanalysed material under seal.

The analyst's silence is not a form of meditation, it is a listening process but this is not enough. Evenly suspended attention bestows but a very partial dimension upon the attitude of the psychoanalyst. We say that silence is the wakeful equivalent of the analyst's sleep: he listens to himself listening while, in this locality where speech is heard, echoing the locality of dreams, the listener's associations arise, just as the dreamwork strives to bring figurative fragments together; this precedes the formation and then the formulation of the interpretation, the counterpoint of the secondary revision of manifest content in the production of dreams. This should urge us to have a better understanding of the analyst's inner discourse.

Because the necessary condition for this inner discourse to develop is the analysand's speech, the discursive work of the analysand is what presides over the analyst's silence. The latter depends on the former in other words, except when the analysand's speech fails to be heard by its recipient, whether this silence, which frames the analyst's inner discourse, is fruitless or fertile, the source of new or repetitive meaning, revelation or paraphrase, when the analyst fails to set up the semantic bridges that elicit a move away from the manifest content in the direction of the latent content. The question here is whether the singular is more appropriate than the plural because a polysemy, a plurality of meanings is available at all times – a multiplicity of meanings amid which the analyst can make choices depending on his theoretical options, on whether he implements the rule of superficiality or prefers to understand and interpret directly in the "depths" of the patient's fundamental language. He can then find himself facing the hysteric's associative fragmentation, the obsessional's constant speech breaks and emotional isolation, the monotony of the depressive, the reinforced rationalization of the paranoid, the incoherence of the schizophrenic, all of which requires the choice of appropriate interpretative strategies. In cases where communication betrays the presence of attacks on linking (Bion), it is advantageous to strive to form a *discursive thread together in a thread by thread dialogue in which the analysand's speech and the analyst's speech weave the fabric of a reticulated speech*. The danger of this interpretative attitude is the introduction of terms that are foreign to the patient's contents. This is where the analyst must demonstrate some psychoanalytic imagination and, most importantly, rather than translate contents, strive to use the *residues* of the patient's speech, the scraps that were left out of the session – the words meant to fall on deaf ears – in order to bring them together in a new potential space (Winnicott) whose form is often paradoxical. Therefore the analyst's silence is a laborious silence in which his psychic apparatus is made use of.

I must specify here that the criticisms I levelled against a kind of Lacanizing practice of analysis (by reason of an unsatisfying theory of language to which I just proposed an alternative – a theory that is more suitable to psychoanalysis, in my view[8]) lead me, nonetheless, to recall that attention to the patients' *words* must be extremely rigorous. Words indeed point to the limit of what the verbalizable may hold and make up another form of complexity in relation to fantasy.

This approach strives to collect everything that is verbalizable in unconscious discourse, no more, no less. This requires an interpretative production in which the exploration of language must be taken very far. This is only acceptable provided we put forward a model of the *psychoanalyst's* language. The transformations of the antilinguistic code of the unconscious into the linguistic code of the preconscious require a silent work where the self-referential function of language is at play. Such an attitude should in fact not be systematic; it varies depending on the patient's possibilities – as well as the analyst's, naturally. In my view, there is only one rule as regards interpretation. Applying it is easy and difficult: it consists in determining conjecturally what the patient can *hear* from the analyst. Hearing does not mean understanding or consenting tacitly; getting confirmation or negation of the analyst's interpretation on the part of the analysand matters very little indeed, as Freud points out. Conversely, observing the counter-interpretation, i.e. the analysand's immediate response to the analyst's interpretation is of utmost interest.

The positive effect of the interpretation can be summed up in four sentences:

- I thought about it (but kept it to myself).
- I was just thinking about it.
- I had never thought about it (I have always known it).
- It makes me think about . . .

---

8 I am referring here to the paper published in issue no. 381 of *Critique* (1979), the arguments of which were later developed in *Le langage dans la psychanalyse* (Paris: Belles Lettres) (see also Chapter 7, this volume).

The first two replies are when analyst and analysand converge. They only mean one thing, that analyst and analysand are on the same wavelength, without implying any lifting *of* repression. Similarly, the fourth reply implies that there is a lifting of *one* repression in the development of associative processes towards a repressed semantic core. Only "I had never thought about it" denotes the lifting *of* repression in relation to the past ("never" denoting the timelessness of the unconscious). The latter sentence can mean a lot of things – one of its possible meanings being the following: it was overlain by your silence, which your interpretation uncovered in the two senses of the word, laid bare and found. It must be added that, when the interpretation is correct, the analyst himself "had never thought about it", even though he was faced with this material on numerous occasions. One of my patients gave me the following counter-interpretation: "Fuck! And you're only telling me this now?" Much like when a daughter has been sleeping with a guy for some months and just tells her mother who replies "And you're only telling me this now!" In short, she had known all along.

As for the question of polysemy, we know by experience that any material can be interpreted according to various sub-referential categories (the referent being the unconscious). Far from necessarily having to choose one of the sub-references over another (a "dialect" of the unconscious as Freud would put it), what must be understood is that the unconscious structure is *reverberated-reverberating*, which means that the various positions resonate with one another. This is what allows us to speak of phallic, anal and oral castration or to say that the fantasy of the phallic mother implies, in some cases, the need to deny castration thanks to the fantasy of the maternal phallus(es) (see Medusa's Head); in other cases, this phallic mother is in fact a penetrating entity for the subject (using any orifice or all of them at once). This is why we can interpret the same material from the perspective of the paternal imago or the maternal imago. The reverberation is expressed even more fully when desire is only conveyed through identification, the Oedipus complex constructing relations of inverted symmetry between desire and identification. Yet, the Oedipus complex has been destroyed, reduced to silence, and only silence elicits the mapping out, among its vestiges, of the play of mirrors it once gave rise to.

We must be done with genetic realism or with the realism arising from a chronicle of phantasmatic figures buttressed by a form of historicism that is not only naive but furthermore unsupported by any viable evidence. The image of a spiralling temporality springs to mind here, where the illusion of continuity is less important than the pictures you can draw by crossing spirals belonging to different levels. One thing for sure: there is no way manifest content and latent content can be collapsed together. This self-evident truth is nonetheless overlooked in all the forms of simultaneous interpretations which merely paraphrase the patient's speech in psychoanalytic jargon. What remains to be established are the figures of the repression involved (repression, denial, disavowal, foreclosure) and the specific aspects of the latter.

It is in this sense that I consider silence as a potential space for the analyst. What I mean is that the sequencing of the patient's unconscious universe according to the various specified sub-references implies their non-communication; splitting is the acutest form, leading silence to circulate between two positions via a disjunctive gap devoid of generativity. Such disjunction (which still presupposes their negative metaphorical conjunction), such separation, that is, calls for their reunion in the form of a new interpretation – which is nothing but a symbolization. Silence is the time that precedes the conversion of successiveness into simultaneity. The completed reverberation allows the reverberated to be translated into another form of successiveness. In other words, *silence is the site where the manifest is erased so that the latent may be unveiled*. Silence is the absence through which the manifest falls into the void and then resurfaces in the form of the latent. Silence is condition, time in the conditional mode, ruled by implicative thought: if . . . then, in other words "if I could hear the desire of the discourse, then this is what the discourse of desire would be". "If" is a suspensive condition, an analytic silence where the guilty desire expects the analyst not to fail it. A patient once told me during a session: "to think that there's only one analyst who speaks in Paris and I have to end up with that one!" But at the end of the session, he said before leaving: "I thank you". Perhaps he was thus giving me my marching orders but it was up to him to recognize that such masochistic delights veiled a conflict of identification with a sadistic and seductive father (whom he hated for having forced his mother to abandon him six months after his birth by sending him to the countryside where the air was purer) and a good and generous grandfather (towards whom he had discovered experiencing guilty unconscious death wishes). In the transference, he availed himself of the alternated projection of these two images onto me without, naturally, having the slightest idea about this conflict. My silence buttressed the resistance of the "exception" in him: his sado-masochism – which went very far – appeared to him as legitimate retaliation for the harm that had been done to him.

This shows us the extent to which the analyst's silence, a silence hosting his own associations, a silence of anticipation, a populated silence, is mostly the silence of some work exigency imposed on the psyche as a result of its link with the body.

The idea that must prevail from this point forward is that of *the logic of the analytic couple represented by the connecting together of two psychic apparatuses, each separated by a difference of significant potential.*

I only give here the fruitful version of the analytic work. We must also add the associative blocks due to the countertransference (in the classical sense of the term) and, most importantly in my view, the analysand's "maddest" aspects. By *private madness*, I do not necessarily mean the analysand's *fantastic* psychosis, the image of a world in the style of Hieronymus Bosch where the picturesque quality is often forthright. This madness can be a mad language, a mad body, a mad sexuality, etc. The success of the analysis is contingent and depends mainly on the analyst's tolerance for this private madness. In such cases, the analyst's silence can be a silence of defence, of refusal or of refuge to safeguard his psychic health. Nothing forces the analyst to experience these ordeals and if he feels disconcerted by these drive-related excesses, he may remain a classic analyst. It is best to be a good analyst of classic neuroses rather than a bad analyst of borderline states. I would like to add, finally, that being the analyst of "borderline" patients should not imply being blind to the Oedipal resonances inherent in *all* material. For the Oedipus complex is everywhere and forever, ever since the subject's conception.

V.

Why do neuroses lend themselves to analytic technique whereas non-neurotic structures seem resistant to it? The reference to regression appears to me as a theoretical pretence. The adequacy of neuroses to analysis might be explained by their relation to perversions. Neurosis seen as the negative of perversion could be compatible with the demands that preside over the analytic frame; this stems from the fact that perversions involve partial drives within an Ego circumscribed by the borders of a frame (or framing structure) that might have managed to uphold its narcissistic unity via the eroticization of the drives of destruction. All and all, the perverse subject possibly carried out the narcissicization of his Ego to ward off a danger of fragmentation, in the face of the intolerable fact of sexual difference, by sacrificing the integration of drives under the primacy of genitality. In a nutshell, the perverse subject might have "opted for" the unifying narcissism of the Ego against the fusion of the drives in relation to the object. Under the threat of the drives of destruction, he could have succeeded in binding the latter thanks to the erotic libido (hence the sadomasochism), by instituting the primacy of the (narcissistic) phallus against the primacy of (objectal) genitality. Neurosis, the negative of perversion, achieves a symmetrical and inverted unity, i.e. it denarcissicizes the Ego by carrying out the fusion of the drives under the primacy of genitality. But as a result of the recognition of sexual difference, castration anxiety in other words, the phallic fixation becomes a refuge in the face of the vaginal abyss. Jouhandeau, in a squabble with Roger Peyrefitte, reportedly told him: "the phallus loves silence" – as if silence were a required condition for its election or its erection.

However, if Freud is right, if, in other words, neurosis is the negative of perversion, the retreat to the phallic fixation is the first step towards the process of regression that elicits the emergence of perverse partial drives (repressed in neurosis). But this emergence then takes place in the context of an Ego that is narcissicized enough to chance such a regression of the drives. This means that, in the analysis, we could establish a relationship of correspondence between the Ego and the partial drives on the one hand, and between the frame and associative speech on the other.

The tolerance to associative speech – a simulacrum of fragmentation – might then be under the sway of an Ego beset by the partial drives of perversion but secure enough in its borders and consistency to risk the lifting of moral and intellectual (or rational) censorship. In other words, the drives of destruction, bound by narcissism and limited in their expression by the sadism directed at the object, could not be a dangerous threat to either the Ego or the object: the analyst is serene as to what might happen to the patient between sessions. He lets the psychoanalytic process unfold and the transference runs its course.

In cases located outside the scope of neurosis, the conditions are different. The situation is less dominated by the perversion-neurosis relations than by the relations linking psychosis and borderline. Repression is the prevailing defence in the former case, splitting in the latter. In structures pertaining to the psychosis-borderline relations, the "partiality" of the drives is either not totalizable or it cannot be contained when it emerges. The partial drives go hand in hand with partial objects that expose the Ego to the threat of fragmentation.

All in all, in the case of the perversion-neurosis couple, Ego and objects are totalized and the price to pay is repression, which much relativizes their unification – possibly just a form of restraint – whereas, with psychosis and borderline cases, the solution involves a prior narcissization of the Ego in order to set up a relationship with the object. The neurotics dream and the borderlines strive to dream but they are, in fact, prone to nightmares, sleep walking, even when they seemingly succeed in having a "semblance" of a dream! The important thing to understand, in my view, is that the fragmented Ego, the partial drives, the partial objects, do not always go together and some limited grouping is possible. In this fashion, perversion, the expression of partial drives, is compatible with a unified Ego and a relatively unified object as well, with the exclusion of the vagina, however. Similarly, the borderline case has a less unified Ego than the perverse subject, along with more unified partial drives (superficially speaking, at least).

The distinction between drive and object is important because it can be the origin of essential conflicts. One must know how to differentiate between what pertains to one or to the other in the course of the session.

How does a non-silent technique face up to the situation? How can the narcissicization of the Ego be carried out? It can be carried out through a binding operation, the Freudian *Bindung*. Instead of letting the film or the associative thread unfold, the analyst will punctuate the analysand's speech with interventions – which do not all consist in interpretations – and tie together the various shreds of speech. This is a trap because the analyst could be tempted to think that the associative scraps included in the analysand's speech are contained by an Ego endowed with sufficient mental sheathing. In fact, splitting occurs *between each associative fragment*, each juxtaposed to the next without any relations between them. Symbolization is at issue, in other words. The binding carried out by the analyst therefore aims to re-connect the disconnected elements so as to be able to interpret at some point, and not only intervene. There are two stages in symbolization: the first one links together the terms from the conscious, the second one uses the established links to reconnect them with the split unconscious.

This work of binding and rebinding foils the work of the drives of destruction. In order to be effective, it must be *superficial*. Deep "bludgeoning" interpretations or systematic transference interpretations only have the power to exacerbate the splitting process. This *surface* work, level with associations, aims to set up a preconscious which, more often than not, fails to operate as mediator or filter, both ways, between conscious and unconscious.

A more in-depth reflection might lead to an acknowledgement of the solidarity between binding work —> eroticization, drives of destruction —> secondary narcissicization of the Ego, repression and preconscious. This implies a simultaneous understanding of borderline anxiety and neurotic anxiety where castration anxiety paired with penetration anxiety reverberates in the pair combining separation and intrusion anxiety. In this context, the concept of distance as theorized by Bouvet could be reconsidered. Suffice to say that the distance from the object is of interest to the analyst only insofar as it can be used to gauge what the analysand can hear in the message of the Other, reflected back to him in a reversed form, following Lacan's well-known formula.

The analyst's work is then located in the transitional field described by Winnicott and can be defined as a symbolic category. It is the symbol's intermediary section as "maybe", not what is or what is not, but what may be, while this hope of fulfilment is never realized for sure. But the worst is not always certain.

VI.

The analyst's work is *contentious*. It arises from a constant battle between hearing, mis-hearing, what is not-heard, unheard of, inaudible, either because it is not perceptible or because of the horror induced by the hearing process.

In the associative flow of the analysand's speech, the linearity of speech generates, as it progresses, retroactive effects (semantic feedback) that structure the progression of verbal formulation. Analytic listening is progredient-regredient. The unconscious is not segregative: it speaks itself however it can and pulls out all the stops. Any exclusive approach based on a single type of signifier – linguistic, representative, affective, bodily, active – is a drastic cut in *polysignificance* and deprives the psychoanalytic signifier of its proper functions. The analyst is multilingual, he can hear the language of dream, fantasy, slip of the tongue, parapraxis, or of anything the unconscious style may feed on. Silence is undoubtedly the backdrop against which the figures of signifying harmonies (and their dissonances) develop. Such encoding-decoding-recoding always refers to *another place* (other than the session) and *another time* (other than the analysis), to the timelessness of silence, to *time* in psychoanalysis and the fundamental heterochrony inherent in it.

The multilingualism of the analysis, the hearing of the idioms, of the dialects of the unconscious also impose a plurifunctional view of the formations of the unconscious. I just mentioned language, dream, fantasy, etc. But psychoanalytic clinical practice shows us that we can no longer agree uncritically to propositions as generally established as the following: dreams are *attempts* to fulfil a wish. This formula, which is Freud's and goes back to 1932 (the *Interpretation of Dreams* only mentions wish fulfilment and it does so in a more complex and nuanced way, without including the restrictive clause that the term "attempt" implies), however reflects a development in the thinking of the first psychoanalyst. Bion showed that dreams could have an evacuation function: getting rid of the wish through the dream rather than elaborating on the wishes that might seek fulfilment. Winnicott understood that hyperactive phantasization was the means by which one could wish to do nothing at all, while imagining oneself achieving a host of things. In publications that have been insufficiently read and mulled over, B. Lewin discusses the deep wish to sleep during the analytic session filled with words. All these revaluations force us to adopt a new perspective on the fundamental concepts. Yet, only silence, conducive to elaboration, unveils the masks of speech. Such silent unmasking is carried out by the analyst's affect, at odds with the messages embedded in speech. Luckily, the disguise is betrayed by minimal clues – sometimes of a strict stylistic kind – that help the analyst hear the inaudible.

In any case, the basis of silence in psychoanalysis is to elicit the emergence (hence the novelty) of *representation*. The analytic work consists in the analysis of the patient's representations (in the broadest conceptual sense) in order to replace them *with another representational system* apt to yield the advent of the subject. This is why the analyst's silence is but the means by which the analyst refuses to perceive the manifest, by absorbing himself in the spacing, to allow for the emergence of the psychic representation of the drive. A general model of psychic activity can then be put forward: organization, disorganization-deletion, reorganization. It can be applied to any form of psychic activity. This model reformulates notions we are familiar with: desire-repression-return of the repressed. In the session, silence coincides with the median stage, the interpretation bespeaking the third stage. It is important to bear the non-linearity of psychic work in mind, to remember its polyphony. This is the direction of psychoanalytic associativity. The broken line of associations matches the resistances awakened at each point of the associative tree, forcing facilitations to proceed elsewhere, to be displaced, condensed. *Interpretation consists in fathoming the barred, hidden pathway, through the examination of the relations between the various breaking points of the facilitations and what they let slip instead.*

In other words, deviation is the basic function of primary and secondary processes alike. Condensation means two (or more) in one, displacement means one in two. One never equals one in psychoanalytic thought, this is why it always takes two to undertake a psychoanalysis. Deviation demands two as a necessary and sufficient condition. It is time to adopt the logic of the couple; in order to do so, we must keep silent about the unitary logic of manifest discourse.

A conclusion ensues: the relation of resistance and association-dissociation to the intellect.

Indeed, since intelligence consists in the establishment of hidden, invisible relations, we can affirm that the joint-disjointed relations, as long as they stand together, are the fruit of resistance. In the *Project for a Scientific Psychology*, Freud writes that with thought, "every pathway must be cognized" (1950 [1895]: 383). But of course it never can. What needs to be uncovered must necessarily be commandeered.

Silence is this space of fluidity that accommodates the subterfuge to undo it and effect a *simulacrum* of truth, simulacrum as authors of models understand it: a *construct*.[9] Silence does not need to persist unduly because the risk that arises then is for the analysand to settle in it conveniently and to produce nothing but semblance (*semblant*; Lacan). In some cases, the analysis can look like a game of chess, putting in check the neurosis, the false self, the proton-pseudos. Let us not forget that these games of chess take place in silence, for the analyst's words do not abolish the backdrop of silence against which they are said.

The projected shadow of silence follows the luminous speech, appended in its footsteps. Kafka writes, in a metaphysical tale:

> Now the Sirens have a still more terrible weapon than their song, namely their silence. Though it has never happened, it is perhaps conceivable that someone might have escaped from their singing, but from their silence certainly not ... And in fact, when Odysseus came, these mighty singers did not sing, whether they believed that against this opponent only silence could achieve anything, or whether the look of bliss on the face of Odysseus, who was thinking of nothing but

---

9 Translator's note: "Construct" is in English in the original French text.

wax and chains, made them forget all about their singing . . . There is moreover a supplement to this, which has also come down to us. Odysseus, it is said, was so wily, was such a cunning fox, that even the goddess of fate could not see into his heart; perhaps, although this passes human comprehension, he really did notice that the Sirens were silent, and confronted them and the gods with the above mock episode merely as a kind of shield. (1991 [1917])

References

Freud, S. (1900). *The Interpretation of Dreams*. S.E. 4 and 5. London: Hogarth.
Freud, S. (1913). *The Theme of the Three Caskets*. S.E. 12. London: Hogarth, pp. 289–302.
Freud, S. (1919). *The Uncanny*. S.E. 17. London: Hogarth, pp. 217–256.
Freud, S. (1920). *Beyond the Pleasure Principle*. S.E. 18. London: Hogarth, pp. 1–64.
Freud, S. (1923). *The Ego and the Id*. S.E. 19. London: Hogarth, pp. 1–66.
Freud, S. (1937a). *Analysis Terminable and Interminable*. S.E. 23. London: Hogarth, pp. 209–253.
Freud, S. (1937b). *Constructions in Analysis*. S.E. 23. London: Hogarth, pp. 255–270.
Freud, S. (1939). *Moses and Monotheism*. S.E. 23. London: Hogarth, pp. 1–138.
Freud, S. (1940). *An Outline of Psychoanalysis*. S.E. 23. London: Hogarth, pp. 139–207.
Freud, S. (1950 [1895]). *Project for a Scientific Psychology*. S.E. 1. London: Hogarth, pp. 281–391.
Freud, S. (1951 [1924]). *Neurosis and Psychosis*. S.E. 21. London: Hogarth, pp. 149–158.
Freud, S. (1953 [1891]). *On Aphasia: A Critical Study*. New York: IUP.
Furst, S. (1978). The stimulus barrier and the pathogenicity of the trauma. *International Journal of Psychoanalysis*, 59: 345–352.
Green, A. (1975). The analyst, symbolization and absence in the analytic setting (on changes in analytic practice and analytic experience) – In memory of D.W. Winnicott. *International Journal of Psychoanalysis*, 56: 1–22.
Kafka, F. (1991 [1917]). *The Silence of the Sirens in The Great Wall of China*. Trans. M. Pasley. London: Penguin Books.
Kardiner, A. (1977). *My Analysis with Freud: Reminiscences*. New York: Norton.

4 The capacity for reverie and the etiological myth[1]
(1987)

Dreaming first meant wandering or raving, or else maundering[2] in both senses of the word. The reverie is a wandering of the mind, off the far-too-beaten track of reason. Even before Freud understood the benefits of free association, after the constrained research of hypnosis revealed their limitations, language intuitively grasped the kinship between such maundering of the normal psyche and pathological delusion. Is it not what some patients, for whom free associating implies risking madness, actually sense? With Bion's capacity for reverie, the emphasis shifts doubly: on the one hand, we shift from the side of the analysand to the side of the analyst as the mother's representative; on the other hand, what qualified as potential madness is conversely turned into a factor of psychic health.

Bion had not introduced the capacity for reverie in his theory yet when he alluded to the "penumbra of associations" that tends to obscure concepts (1962: vi). For my part, I would locate the capacity for reverie in the "penumbra of associations" of free association; this means that I will consider it, in the context of a session, as a replica or an analogue of free association – in the obscure and enigmatic aspects that it holds for the one who engages in it. Similarly, I will envision free association as a replica or an analogue of dreams and their primary processes.

Provided there exists a distinct division between secondary and primary process, this division can generate compromise formations. This precisely applies to the conscious fantasy – this "mixed blood", as Freud puts it – in other words, to "reverie". In all cases, the adjective *free* is what matters. In music (Schumann's *Reverie*) as in literature (Rousseau's *Reveries of the Solitary Walker*), the term "reverie" refers to an activity of the mind that has no specific goal, no methodical rigour, like a cork that lets itself be

---

1 Translated by Dorothée Bonnigal-Katz for this edition.
2 Editor's note: This is not a commonly used English word, but was chosen because it connotes both wandering/loitering (*vagabonder*) and raving (*délirer*) and so matches Green's French word, *divaguer*, which means both straying off course (for a river for example) and rambling (a psychological deviation).

DOI: 10.4324/9781003350132-5

carried along with the waves, following the streams that stir the sea. The freedom is tied to the fact of letting oneself go, by "freely" surrendering the exertion of control over the events.

Bion: The mother's reverie, the analyst's thought

Now, the starting point of Bion's reflection is his experience with psychotic subjects who present symptoms that pertain to thought: for them, unlike neurotics, free association is captive association rather. It takes place following the constraints of a projective activity that prevents every form of integration, every emergence of newness, as well as every form of learning – every form of maturation, in short. The mother's capacity for reverie can then be granted the role of a basic hypothesis inferred from experience where it might have been lacking. This presupposes a certain number of inferences:

1. The model of the analytic situation reproduces the situation of the mother-child relationship.
2. Such homology proves relevant and efficient with neurotic patients; it elicits the progress of the analytic process and some learning on the patient's part in the course of the analysis while it is jeopardized by psychosis. If anything, it requires interpretations of a different kind, drawn from hypotheses on the relations that might have existed at the beginning of life between the mother and the child and subject, at a very early stage, to distortions that were potentially harmful to thought processes.
3. Bion locates this disorder in the impossibility of a notation – i.e. of a preservative memory that is therefore potentially acquisitive and integrative. This deficiency results from a tendency to evacuate the frustrations tied to the presence of elements that cannot be assimilated by the subject's psyche: the β elements. However, and there lies Bion's originality with respect to Melanie Klein while making him closer to Winnicott, the key to this distortion is that the projected indigestible elements are not received and transformed by the mother's mental activity. In normal cases, the mother, thanks to her capacity for reverie, can return them to the child by carrying out the conversion of β elements into α elements, which make up the essential fabric of psychic activity.
4. Implicitly, Bion concedes that, at birth, the child is modelled by the predominance of the digestive system on the basis of the breast experience. However, this digestive model is paired with a psychic model that is *propped by* the digestive model. In other words, even if the breast actually feeds the child, the preservation of the good breast is not enough to generate thought. It is a necessary condition but not a sufficient one. The propping of the psyche on the digestive system allows

us to understand the need to predicate its recurrence at an intersubjective level. In other words, the mother psychically "digests" the projections of the child's mind (she chews them over, so to speak, thanks to her capacity for reverie) and feeds the child differently by returning this product that has been pre-digested by her. The child therefore receives food that is secondary, a metaphor of the primary version. He does not feed on the mother's bodily breast but on her psychic breast. The mother has accumulated the child's "vomit" inside her and carried out what he himself cannot carry out yet: she has "psychicized" it and turned this "concrete" food into psychic food. The child will be able to use it to construct his internal psychic object, by retaining this primary psychic breast which will elicit the gradual elaboration, on the basis of such inchoate thought, of an apparatus apt to think the thoughts – an apparatus endowed with the capacity for notation and *anticipation*. This apparatus is no longer subjected to events, it *anticipates them*. Bion's position is here most akin to Freud's in *Formulations on the Two Principles of Mental Functioning* (1911).

Contrary to what Melanie Klein contends – to Klein, everything seemingly takes place on the side of the infant, whatever comes from the mother being negligible (she is Freudian in this regard) – Bion, like Winnicott, uses the mother-child dyad as a starting point. Furthermore, he locates the genesis of the α function in the child on the side of the mother. In other words, a theory that confines itself to considering the effects of the good breast and the bad breast cannot provide any answer to the question of knowing how psychic *qualities* are in fact created. The contribution of the mother who dispenses not only milk but also love, understanding, tenderness, safety – so many psychic qualities, strictly speaking – is at the root of the translation of β elements into α elements, thanks to its *linking* function. Two kinds of links are at stake here: those that operate intrapsychically in the baby (thanks to the α function) and those that develop intersubjectively *between* mother and child (the transmitters of the α function) and presuppose that this function is available in the mother.

The originality of Bion's position consists in considering *the reverie as the buttress of the mother's love (or hate)* in her relationship to the child.

This is where some form of circularity emerges in Bion's thought, even though it is not always explicit. Bion's starting point is the analytic situation between a psychotic patient and an analyst. From that, *his reverie* urges him to seek a model of the mother-child relationship (elsewhere and in times past) likely to account for what occurs in the session (here and now). In fact, it is because the analyst, Bion, is indeed *driven by reveries towards his adult patient* that he ventures the causal hypothesis that the mother-child relationship is likely to comprise a reverie thus akin to what takes place in the analysis.

The analytic relationship allows one to observe that the analysand is in a state which Bion characterizes as neither sleep (dream activity) nor wakefulness (secondary activity). Such activity evidences the production of a (*language*) screen, one that is disjointed, incoherent and *not linked*, most importantly. However, what such communication yields is not unintelligible: the interpretative capacity (in terms of L = love and K = knowledge) is always at work in the analyst whose thought is theoretically unscathed as regards linking. But the response to interpretation reveals that the interpretative power remains unreciprocated in the psychotic subject. Far from concluding, as Melanie Klein already did, that the child's death drives are the only ones at play, Bion brings maternal participation to light via the absence of reverie in the mother, the reverie being the channel through which love is conveyed. What is therefore repeated in the analysis is the mother's deficiency: the analysand experiences the situation as if the analyst's interpretations remained without effect because the analyst-mother, *no matter what he does*, cannot feed the child psychically as it was the case in the past with the actual mother.

The analyst's capacity for reverie, which is reflected by his interpretations, is devoid of any incubating effect because it does not relay the mother's capacity for reverie which was, in fact, lacking in her. The interpretation does not awaken anything, it does not revive anything that might have been present but repressed. It leads to a void in the patient because the traces of the mother's capacity for reverie are lacking in him, it failed to leave any mark. This entails important conclusions: when an interpretation produces some effect, it stems from the fact that it successfully rekindles something that is already there. It could not generate meaning *ex nihilo* where there was no meaning in the first place. We gauge how crucially important the attunement between the two partners in the analytic dyad actually is, even though the dyad pursues a single object: the analysand's unconscious which the analyst's psychic apparatus dreams.

This inaugurates a reflection on the dyad – or the triad even – in both Bion and Winnicott. As is stated in *Learning from Experience*: "If the feeding mother cannot allow reverie or if the reverie is allowed but is not associated with love for the child or its father this fact will be communicated to the infant even though it is incomprehensible to the infant" (1962: 36).

In the Bionian model, the basic problem consists in transforming an impression of the senses into an emotional experience. This affective referent for the psyche is a good illustration of the difference between Bion's and Lacan's theories. Conversely, if Bion seemingly relativizes the place of representation with regard to Freud's reflection, thanks to this observation, he introduces a fact that is completely overlooked by Melanie Klein.

What does the mother dream of? Of the child *or* the father? The father's entry into the mother's reverie seems essential to me: it accounts – in the best possible way – for the early triangulation operating from the beginning of life. The love for the child is not exclusive of the love for the father and if, following Freud, the mother is the child's first seducer, a difference must be made between this seduction and the sharing of sexual pleasure as the acme of the love for the father. The drives maternity brings into play are inhibited in aim. While maternal tenderness may comprise many hidden pleasures, such as the eroticism of breastfeeding, for example, the mother's vagina does not reach orgasm with the child born out of her womb, even though giving birth granted her, in the midst of pain, a satisfaction no penis can ever contend with. Maternal erogeneity becomes the most diffuse and the most exclusive of genitality. The prohibition of incest is first operative in the mother, whatever the cost.

What does dreaming of the father imply? It means dreaming *of the link* that exists between the parents and the baby, the mother being its common place, if I dare say. The *Mutterkomplex*, as I understand it, consists in seeing, in the mother, the bodily space which both the child and the father inhabit. Dreaming of the father is therefore dreaming of the triangular (or more) reunion of what maternal care tends to separate in the intimate mother-child relationship. It thus already implies dreaming of the prospect of relating to a third, followed by the temporary side-lining of the baby through the reconstitution of the dual unit of the fully sexual relation. Mothers do not always manage the shift from one object to the other very easily.

Dreaming of the father is – already – remembering, for the mother, that the happiness of the mother-child relation is only temporary, that it must be experienced fully but that the child does not belong to her. The child belongs to itself just as the parental couple belongs to itself. The couple's happiness periodically demands that the child be "forgotten". If the child is loved and feels loved, it will accept this inevitable dispossession of the mother without too much damage. If this is not so, it will spend its whole life clinging to its object, to do away with an ever unsettled dispute. In other words, *clinging is the opposite of linking*. For clinging implies that one remains desperately fixated on the same object, whereas linking moves about and can become *the linking of linking*, i.e. not only relating but the relating of relating – in other words, thinking. However tempting analogies might be, I will set limits on the comparison between the mother's capacity for reverie and the analyst's interpretative listening. *The analyst is not the mother*, even if the patient might insist on wanting it to be the case. The analyst's love for his patient, without which no analysis can possibly be successful, excludes the physical contact that is the indispensable complement of the capacity for reverie in the mother. By introducing this concept, Bion wanted to establish the separation between the physical sphere (the senses) and the psychic sphere (the emotional experience endowed with meaning). He saw an equivalent of the physical aspect in the treatment in the conditions of material comfort in the analysis: the couch, the reserved space, the allocated time, etc., i.e. the material elements of the frame. The analyst's effective distance in the analysis necessarily turns the analyst into a paternal image *as well*. Communication via language further enhances this reference and there is no need to mobilize all the arguments of Lacan's development here – even though the latter is not unfounded.

In any case, how does the analyst "dream" of his analysand? It depends on the corpus that he starts from and on the reference myth that is supposed to account for it.

In this case, the corpus is the analysis of psychotic patients in which Bion detects the "fundamental disturbance" as it was referred to in psychiatry, or, alternatively, the signs denoting thought disorders. This change in corpus in relation to the classical model of analysis centred on the category of neurosis will serve as a psychopathological matrix. The *whole* clinical practice and the *whole* theory are reconsidered on the basis of the psychotic vertex. In this way, Bion is the continuator of Melanie Klein who presupposes an original psychosis *in every individual* – which only the luckiest will overcome. The change in basic corpus will entail a change in the reference myth. In fact, the Freudian reference myth no longer operates as an elaborative platform.

I call reference myth the historically articulated set of concepts presiding over the child's hypothetical development as can be reconstructed thanks to analysis. Bion's reference myth is a montage made up of Kleinian elements (the breast, projective identification, archaic anxieties, etc.), remodelled by their combination with Freudian elements (motor discharge of tension relief, the unconscious and the conscious, notation, attention, thought, reality, etc.). Such montage which also involves some of Bion's original creations (factors and functions, β and α elements, etc.) generates Bion's reference myths based on a few principles among which the distinction between the physical and the psychical is in the foreground.

The capacity for reverie arises in the aftermath of a long reflection on the relations between the good and the bad object, a reflection undertaken with a subtlety and a dialectical sense that are lacking in the thought of such a "lumberjack" of psychoanalysis as Melanie Klein. Equally, Freud's work finds itself being decentred in more than one way: the hallucinatory fulfilment of desire is a psychic event that presupposes that the disastrous effects of the bad object be neutralized prematurely, so to speak. Bion thus observes that the psychical cannot be elaborated on the basis of the physical experience of the breast, however good it might have been. *The psychical can only arise from the psyche, namely from the mother's psyche*, which is another way of saying that thought can only arise from the thought of the object. In this sense, Bion's theory breaks with Melanie Klein's.

It is absolutely essential to point out that Bion's theory and the reference myth it generates wholly stem from the elaboration of analytic exchanges in the context of sessions. In Freud, conversely, there is no avowed correspondence between the reference myth as "Drives and their vicissitudes" or "Negation" describe it and the analytic situation.

Freud: Construction, countertransference and representation

Let us therefore return to Freud and his triple characterization of the analytic situation: free association on the side of the patient, evenly suspended attention and benevolent neutrality on the side of the analyst. This classic description is highly vague and very deficient. We can see how it imposes itself: the analysand freely associates, the analyst's attention is evenly suspended. The second part of the comparison is symmetrical with the first: free associative activity on the part of the analysand, free floating receptivity on the side of the analyst. As for benevolent neutrality, it is the twin of what unfolds in the patient – because of the transference, the latter cannot possibly be neutral: he hates or he loves. In return, the analyst does not respond to the love or hate of the patient, in principle at least. Yet, his neutrality is benignant, which implies that he is led by a feeling of love towards the patient but this love is withheld and he steps back in relation to the analysand's loving or hateful projections. Love is limited here to an understanding of the patient. Such is the ideal situation.

According to Freud, the analyst does not associate, probably because the process of locating unconscious derivatives and primary process for the analyst in no way compares, in his view, to the frenzy raging in the patient. The analyst remains in control of his thinking so that he may put his art of interpretation into practice. If he associated, he would lose the distance that clear vision requires. To Freud, interpretation results from the analyst's deductions, not from some wandering in parallel with the patient's own meandering. This view of the analysis reproduces some of the flaws in Freud's reference myth. Today, there is ample criticism of the solipsistic character of his view on development which disregards the object's response. Similarly, for the analysis to be clear of all traces of suggestion, the analyst must refrain from introducing any subjective elements in the interpretation by summoning his own associations.

Yet, it is not until his last paper on technique that we hear Freud recall that the analysis takes two:

> What we are in search of is a picture of the patient's forgotten years that shall be alike trustworthy and in all essential respects complete. But at this point we are reminded that the work of analysis consists of two quite different portions, that it is carried on in two separate localities, that it involves two people, to each of whom a distinct task is assigned. It may for a moment seem strange that such a fundamental fact should not have been pointed out long ago; but it will immediately be perceived that there was nothing being kept back in this, that it is a fact which is universally known and, as it were, self-evident and is merely being brought into relief here and separately examined for a particular purpose. (1937: 258)

This leads Freud to stipulate these two tasks: it is up to the analysand to remember; it is up to the analyst to infer what has been forgotten based on the traces of repression, or to *construct* it, more accurately. However, it is clear that the division of labour is still firmly delineated and that there could not be any swapping or confusion of the roles. This very scientific ideality will not withstand the advances of the analysis. Freud's unease is manifest here and he who excuses himself accuses himself. Who does he have in mind when he reminds us of what is "still mysterious"? (260). I wonder whether he is not responding to Ferenczi here, in two respects at least: on the one hand, he finds himself in agreement with him on the double polarity of analysis which turns the latter into a coupling relation and, on the other hand, he limits the effects of a possible transferential-countertransferential collusion: "Do not love your patients beyond the prescribed rules of neutrality. Show your benevolence by listening to them and infer the repressed. And if the early traumas stupefied them to the point of abolishing all memory in them, or all traces of this catastrophe, express your love by *constructing* what happened to them, full stop".

What is important to stress here once again is the change in the reference corpus in both Freud and Bion. The end of *Constructions in Analysis* reveals that Freud envisions the possibility of analysable delusions (the delusional individual also suffers from reminiscences) in which traumatic events could be located *before* the establishment of language; subjects can therefore only rely on the memories and impressions of places without the capacity – in the absence of mnemic inscription owing to the preverbal fixation – to associate them with the recollections of events. *Constructions in Analysis* thus shows that, in some cases, the lifting of infantile amnesia must be relinquished without jeopardizing the analysis all the same. The interpretation's power of conviction can be acquired by erratic thing-representations lacking the linguistic connotation that used to endow them with coherence and form.

Once the path of preverbal fixation opened up, the whole of modern analysis was to dive into it. A paradox must however be underlined. If language refuses to help us in the process of remembering, it still mediates the apprehension of the preverbal. And even though the analyst's intuition might relate to aspects of the material located outside language (bodily behaviour, emotional tension, anxiety, etc.), the fact remains that the analyst relies on word representations to fill the gaps in speech towards the construction of what has been permanently forgotten. Basically, the question of the countertransference finds itself already raised. The response to the analysand's transference no longer seems limited to the mere interpretation of the latter, it also requires some thought activity: a construction. The countertransference stops having an inhibiting function and conversely becomes stimulative. All this is happening long before Paula Heimann's pronouncement around 1950. A question arises here however. What does thinking mean for an analyst and for an analysand? To Freud, thought activity fundamentally pertains to representation. Affects do not play an equal part in dignity to be precise, hence the direction opted for by Lacan and his banishment of affects in the theory.

Conversely, since Ferenczi and above all Melanie Klein, unconscious fantasies are the representative versions of what she refers to as memories in feelings, i.e. memories shaped as feelings, hence Bion's position in which the shift from the physical to the psychical coincides with the shift from the senses' raw data to emotional experience. It is not inconsequential that Bion's three factors, L, H, K [*or A, H, C in French*], should locate Knowledge on the side of the fundamental affects Love and Hate. Bionian paradox? The apex of the evolution of thought: algebraic calculus – not unrelated to the Lacanian matheme – is rooted in the emotional experience. Bion posits an equivalence between "I feel that" (i.e. "I sense that") and "I think that". In his theory, the affect is therefore elevated to the dignity of a principle of knowledge.

No matter how we tackle the problem, we are always left with the question of representation. The reason is, just as Melanie Klein provides her patients with representations, even though she thinks she is interpreting "memories in feelings", the counter-transferential affects conveyed to the patient in the form of verbal interpretations equally convert them into representations. I would say that we can *in no way* bypass the patient's speech (*parole*), i.e. the word representation associated with the affect (voice) and the thing representation (inseparable from the cathexis) that corresponds to it. The gap between the conscious thing representation and the unconscious thing representation is the core of psychic activity. However, as I have long argued, the thing or object representation far exceeds the frame of the ideational representative and includes what I have suggested we call the affect-representative, the states of the body proper (*corps propre*), the traces of the acts, etc. Conversely, any direct access to the (conscious and even more so unconscious) thing representation is an illusion. In other words, a verbal mediation is a requirement to access the thing or object representations.

The psychoanalytic experience and the history of the treatment

Let us leave the language of metapsychology and return to the experience. A patient speaks, interspersing his words with silences or sighs, he gesticulates or stands still, he crosses or uncrosses his legs, makes himself heard more or less clearly, more or less pathetically, he regulates his mood, implores, protests, declares his love or his hate, is barely intelligible or recites, says something incoherent or overly coherent, etc. What does the analyst's listening consist in? It first consists in understanding the manifest meaning of what is said, this is the necessary condition for everything that follows; then – and this is the fundamental stage – it consists in *imaginarizing* what is said, i.e. not only imagining it but also adding in the imaginary dimension through a different construction of the implicit in the patient's speech, in the staging of the understanding. The following stage will unravel the linear sequence of this chain, bringing to mind fragments of sessions: recent ones at times (from the previous session every so often), less recent ones as well (some that emerged a few months before) and much older ones lastly (e.g. a dream from the beginning of the analysis). Such is the stock on the basis of which the analyst's capacity for reverie develops. It will take shape during the final stage, that of the *relinking* which takes place through the selection and the rearrangement of the elements thus gleaned to produce the counter-transferential fantasy supposed to match the patient's transferential fantasy.

I must point out that the rearrangement brings together unrelated units of speech: a large associative section might educe but a single word or affect, which can become linked in turn with a single word characterized by a repetition, if not a rather unusual or slightly dissonant use, or with an important section of the material initially deemed trivial, casual or banal. The emotional tonality of the whole will then confer its colouration upon a causality link that emerges for the first time or is repetitive in familiar fashion. Everything will become precipitated or crystallized in an interpretation – the fruit of the reverie.

Such descriptions in which, I believe, every analyst will recognize his experience, lead to two points of disagreement on my part. The first one is with Bion when he contends that the analyst must be without memory or desire (even though it is worth mentioning that, as Bion specified himself, the proposition only applied to situations where the analyst's understanding was somewhat frozen, which has not always been taken into account). The second one is with Freud who asserts that the analyst, for his part, has nothing to remember. I think that, quite conversely, the analyst, who must be ready to welcome new material, can only do so provided he is the *custodian of the history of the analysis*. As regards the past, I used the notion of reference myth with a view to emphasizing the fact that myths and our developmental hypotheses share the characteristics of being explanations developed *après-coup – etiological* myths, in other words. But since we were not there and that, in respect of the phenomena at stake, nobody could have been there – this is especially true of the "direct observers" who can only record behaviour – it can only be a fictional construction. The term of interaction underlines this behavioural dimension well; which is why the phrase "phantasmatic interaction" seems self-contradictory to me and I prefer to refer to "phantasmatic interrelation".[3] Conversely, the analyst's task consists in being the archivist of the history of the analysis and in

---

3 Alternatively, we could use the term 'interinduction' if preferable.

drawing in the registers of his preconscious memory, summoning his associations at all times with this aim in mind.

The history of the analysis is not the reconstruction of the history that actually came to pass in reality (Anna Freud's famous real child). It is the *construction of the subject's psychic reality*. Let's just say that, in respect to Freud and his great concern with historicity (see the discussions on the Wolfman case and the hypotheses concerning the chronological dating of events), when dealing with psychosis or borderline cases, we find ourselves facing organizations which not only present us with patchy histories as in the case of neurosis, but often confront us with an ahistorical picture. The history of the illness is richer than the subject's history; it is not due to a lack of memories, but the link between the recalled memories and the psychopathological structure leaves an unintelligible gap. This does not account for that. The history of a subject's psychoanalysis will elicit, *before* the discovery of key events that had been kept secret for a very long time, the construction of the structure of the founding psychic processes that comprise the basal distortions shaping the development of the psychic organization. However, the question is sometimes more complex than it looks. After many years of analysis, after many periods of stasis and numerous unfruitful stages in the analytic process, one patient, who had seemingly destroyed or never constructed his official history – the history that the analysis will deconstruct, in a case of neurosis – brought up highly significant memories which were as many revelations for the analyst who rightfully saw them as crucial pieces in the analytic puzzle; they seemed underlain by fantasies of the most classic kind. The analysis of the prehistory, which, as we know, is much longer than the history, led to the unearthing of the latter. During the analysis of the prehistory, before the acquisition of language and the function of memories, the analyst's capacity for reverie turns out to be crucially essential, as if the analyst devoted a long time to the weaving of the canvas and the construction of the screen onto which the subject's film will be projected, telling a story or a tragedy at last.

Psychoanalytic theory's worst affliction stems from a deficient elaboration of the temporality that must link together the various concepts of development, maturation, chronology, foregoing and *après-coup*, repetition, the difference between the subject's time and the Other's time, retardation or acceleration, retrospection and anticipation, etc. In this case, the concepts must not only be discovered, they must be created. Rigour and imagination must help each other out rather than fight each other.

A fundamental question remains. If I fully subscribe to the function which Bion defines as constitutive of *links*, what are the principles presiding over *linking*? As concerns the patient, Freud's answer involves the pleasure principle and the reality principle. Granted, but every form of linked speech presupposes a causality and the analyst must apply this specific causality to his own thinking. By placing the imaginary in the foreground via the process of imaginarization under the guarantee of reality (the reality of the session safeguarded by the frame), what are the auspices under which the symbolic work is carried out? I suggest using the phrase *implicative thought* to refer to this work, which I sum up with the well-known formula "if . . . then". The "if" unlocks the extension of all the possibles. "If" implies the condition of possibility for the reverie . . . "then" represents the aim of the reverie itself: "if I carry out certain transformations on the manifest text and fill in its allusions with my associations on the patient's associations, I can then observe the preconscious or unconscious fantasy".

Each of the elements drawn from my listening will be a thought. The transformation resulting from their unlinking and their relinking will be *the* thought, the work of the thought-thinking apparatus. Bion's originality consists in having understood that the child could have thoughts but that, in order to have *a* thought, he had to be able to rely on, and lean on the mother's thought-thinking apparatus – the mother *making the link* between the father and the child. However, the mother and the analyst are different in respect to time. While both experience a regressive identification to the child, the mother addresses the present and future child.

The analyst's capacity for reverie, especially in the cases where the mother's capacity was lacking, is, conversely, *exclusively directed towards the past* even when it concerns the present; this is why it is important to remember the history of the analysis, just as a good mother remembers everything about her child's early infancy, even if the child might himself already be a father.

We must stress the fact that the *discontinuous* nature of the reverie eventually ensures the *continuity* of the patient's analytic history.

But this history is not raw, it is read according to the analyst's grids: one of them pertains to the channels of communication. In the *Project for a Scientific Psychology*, Freud states: "with theoretical [thought] every pathway must be cognized" (1950 [1895]: 383) – if it were not for resistance: the other grid pertains to the reference myth, as I previously said.

Interpretation and reference myth

Here are two examples in which interpretation depends on the reference myth. One of Bion's patients tells him "I was mad" in reference to his state of mind in the aftermath of what he calls a "bad" session; his analyst replies: "You seem to feel that you are mad when you are denying my interpretations by taking them in and getting rid of them at once. You must have felt that they have something to do with the peculiar dream" (a dream mentioned by the patient without saying anything further and which Bion regards as attempted evacuation following a digestive model). "Why are you moving like that?" Bion asks the question because he observes convulsive twitchings in his chest. The patient replies that he does not know and adds: "My thoughts go too quickly". In Bion's view, this confirms his reference to motor activity as a means, for the psychic apparatus, to get rid of an increase in excitation (1967: 78–79).

Let us take a similar situation in Winnicott. After listening to his patient, Winnicott says to him: "I am listening to a girl. I know perfectly well that you are a man but I am listening to a girl, and I am talking to a girl. I am telling this girl: 'You are talking about penis envy'". The patient replies: "If I were to tell someone about this girl I would be called mad". Winnicott retorts: "It was not that *you* told this to anyone; it is *I* who see the girl and hear a girl talking, when actually there is a man on my couch. The mad person is *myself*" (1971: 73–74).

Reading these two texts is enough – material and commentary – to realize that, in both cases, the authors hear, or digest, or dream of the communication of their patients based on their reference myth; the latter has not been created on the basis of their sole experience – i.e. the treatments of patients who are not classic indications for analysis – but is equally based on the transformations that they impose, each in their respective way, on the Freudian concepts (in Bion's case, the need to reduce tensions on the part of the psychic apparatus; bisexuality in Winnicott's case). The reference to Melanie Klein certainly had some bearing on both of them. In Bion's case, a return to Freud was implemented in order to construct his thought. In Winnicott's case, it is also a disagreement with her on the monopoly of internal objects that led him to rethink how to approach the role of the external object and highlight the deficiency of the latter in the full recognition of the reality of the child's gender; he also underlines the effect, on the subject's identity, of the suffusion, in the relationship, of the mother's unconscious fantasy. Where some might see a phantasmatic interaction, I would personally see a collusive relationship of mutual denials as a defence to safeguard and preserve the mother's protective love: a subjectal sacrifice.

I will now briefly discuss the case of someone engaged in a second analysis after a first silent treatment that lasted nine years and ended, after the end was set by the analyst, due to a somatic accident shortly before the scheduled end date. This extremely rich case, which would require a long presentation of its own, is that of a man suffering from quasi constant anxiety, after episodes of claustrophobia (especially in the Parisian underground (*Métro* and *RER*)) during which he is afraid of going mad. He is besides convinced that he is mad (he says "psychotic") and, following a two-month "honeymoon period" after which our idyll fell apart, he envisions the outcome of the second half of the analysis in very pessimistic terms. This aims to put my attachment to him to the test.

In the throes of his anxieties, whose lived experience he only describes in general terms, he experiences an intense feeling of persecution and he has the fantasy of being riddled with holes, adding that each of his pores feels penetrated. He then has but one idea on his mind: to escape, to get out of the underground, out in the open air. During a dramatic session when he asked to sit up but in fact remained on the couch, he had the fantasy of being like a whale washed up on the shore, a crazed look in his eyes, looking left and right, in a complete panic – a whale "without any arms or legs". I started seeking associations and thought: the whale is a mammal. The patient said: "But what I'm asking you for this whale is to toss it off back into the sea". I stressed his use of "toss off" and replied that he had stranded this whale on the shore, without any arms or legs, because a part of him wished to come out of this whale – which represented us both, merged, the way he and his mother were – in order to walk on dry land and make use of his arms. His reply to this interpretation was that his anxiety was extreme and that he lapped up my every word as if they were shards of glass that hurt him inside. I followed up by telling him that he felt so ill-nourished by me that his rage had led him to swallow not only the milk but also the bottle itself, which he had broken with his teeth. He replied that he often felt trapped in a glass bubble that he would like to break to get out. I said: "You just grew an arm". He associated on the fact that he once dodged the punch of a schoolmate whose arm went through the pane, rupturing his tendons.

Several months later (I mean after we analysed his primary identification with his anorexic, depressive and schizoid mother and his powerlessness at making her come out of this state), he returned to the whale and explained that it was the little whale that was washed ashore (it was the first time he distinguished between a big and a little whale). He associated on a recent reading he had made that had taught him that, as soon as they came out of their mother's womb, baby seals could barely walk and were attacked by birds that pecked at their eyes with their beaks. I told him then that he had a fantasy that I could still not understand very well but in which, freshly out of his mother's womb, he could walk and had to fend off attacks, something he did not want to relive. He confirmed this by telling me that he could not remember anything but had the feeling of a wrench.

During the following session, he told me he was riddled with debts and that, perhaps, he had to give up his analysis. "Riddled?" I asked. He then mentioned the previous session and told me he had spoken about his infancy a lot (long ago) with his father and his mother (who were divorced), each giving him a different version. The mother made an open apology: "I was so young, I didn't know anything, etc.". The father told him: "Your mother was completely unable to look after you, she was so helpless and anxious. She had an abscess on her breast and you soon became very ill. The paediatrician who was called prescribed injections of sea water. A nurse carried them out, after which point you were entrusted to a nanny".

Here is, therefore, how my reverie operated. I knew nothing of the separation with the mother or of the nanny's intervention when I told him that he was so ill-nourished that he had broken the bottle while drinking the milk. The punctured eyes of the little seals naturally made me think about castration by the father in an extremely early Oedipus complex. But it was in fact the nurse, at once merged with the mother and other than the mother (the object's other) that played a major role.

Anyhow, in this case, I did not apply the Freudian myth or the Bionian myth, or the Winnicottian myth, despite my admiration for all three. I did not apply the Lacanian myth either but I devoted all my attention to the language or the word-representations. I could supplement this clinical illustration with a hundred other examples of overdetermination of the signifier, of condensation between early experiences, of defence against oral penetration by the mother and anal penetration by the father, of sought-out repetitions of trauma and, finally, as it appeared in a dream, of the fear of breakdown. This led me to direct my reflection to the complexity of the psyche's temporal structures and their emergence in the transference. Indeed, our initial "honeymoon period" was marked by a kind of reunion akin to the reuniting of father and son in Kurosawa's *Ran*: "we have so much to say to each other", the father says. At that moment, an arrow is shot and hits the son, killing him. This arrow was my first absence in the analysis.

I have constructed such a myth by listening to the language of my patients, by reading my predecessors and by exchanging with my colleagues.[4] We see that language is of pivotal importance. In my view indeed, every reflection on language, every practice of language – and analysis is one of them – always refers to what is elsewhere, to that which does not pertain to language: to what we call the thing or the unconscious. This is what should surprise us most: the fact that, when tackling – in psychoanalysis at least – what is below or beyond language, language is always what we start from, it is thanks to language that we may gain some uncertain and difficult access to it. Language is what we must return to, for words mediate thinking, including thoughts that do not pertain to what is traditionally referred to as thought but still remain components of plural thinking or even anti-thinking.

Thanks to the reverie, the "science" of psychoanalysis – a qualification that summons many reservations – has discovered what the creators had always known. In 458 BC, exactly 2,454 years ago, in Aeschylus's *Choephori*, here are the words of Orestes's nurse upon hearing of the death of the child she once cared for:

> But now – alack, alack! – Orestes dear,
>
> The day and night-long travail of my soul

---

4 Let us add, obviously, the vestiges of my own analysis.

Whom from his mother's womb, a new-born child, I clasped and cherished! Many a time and oft Toilsome and profitless my service was,

When his shrill outcry called me from my couch! For the young child, before the sense is born, Hath but a dumb thing's life, must needs be nursed As its own nature bids. The swaddled thing

Hath nought of speech, whate'er discomfort come, –

Hunger or thirst or lower weakling need, – For the babe's stomach works its own relief. Which knowing well before, yet oft surprised

Twas mine to cleanse the swaddling clothes-poor, Was the nurse to tend and fuller to make white:

Two works in one, two handicrafts I took, When in my arms the father laid the boy.

(749–762)

"Whom from his mother's womb, a new-born child, I clasped and cherished . . . When in my arms the father laid the boy". The good enough mother, the locus and the link of the Oedipal triangle, is, like language, a mediating matrix.

References

Aeschylus (458 BC). *Choephori*, trans. E.D.A. Morshead. Cambridge, MA: The Internet Classics Archive. Bion, W. (1962). *Learning from Experience*. London: Tavistock.

Bion, W. (1967). *Second Thoughts: Selected Papers on Psychoanalysis*. London: Butterworth-Heinemann.

Freud, S. (1911). *Formulations on the Two Principles of Mental Functioning*. S.E. 12. London: Hogarth Press, pp. 213–226.

Freud, S. (1937). *Constructions in Analysis*. S.E. 23. London: Hogarth, pp. 255–269.

Freud, S. (1950 [1895]). *Project for a Scientific Psychology*. S.E. 1. London: Hogarth, pp. 281–391.

Winnicott, D. (1971). *Playing and Reality*. London: Tavistock.

5 Language within the general theory of representation[1]
(1997)

Trajectory

For the intelligibility of my remarks, I will begin by retracing a trajectory that above all harks back to the earlier stages of my reflections on the subject.

In 1956, I became aware of Jacques Lacan's Rome Report "The function and field of speech in psychoanalysis" (Lacan, 2006 [1953]), read in 1953, shortly after the split. In 1960, I discussed the work of Laplanche and Leclaire (1961 [1960]), heavily inspired by the ideas of Jacques Lacan and presented at the Bonneval Colloquium on the unconscious. I had already drawn attention there to the absence of affect. From 1961–1967, I attended and participated actively in Lacan's seminar at Saint Anne's Hospital in Paris and then at the École Normale Supérieure. At his request, I presented two papers, in 1965 and 1967, on the "objet *(a)*" (see Green, 1966) and on the Id. In 1970, I presented my Report on affect at the Congress for French-Speaking Psychoanalysts in Paris, a report that was published in 1973 under the title *Le discours vivant* (Green, 1973). In 1979, I published "Psychanalyse, langage: L'ancien et le nouveau" (Green, 1979), in which I mentioned the ideas of Charles Bally (1913, 1921, 1932) which had passed unnoticed by linguists; in it I present and offer a critique of the American theorizations of Marshall Edelson (1975) and Roy Shafer (1978), as well as the contributions of the students of Lacan, Jacques Alain Miller (1975) and Guy Rosolato (1964, 1977, 1978, 1984, 1985a, 1985b, 1989). In 1983, here, in this very room, on the occasion of the thirtieth anniversary of the Rome Report, I presented the paper that served as a point of departure for my long text published in 1984, "Le langage dans la psychanalyse" (Green, 1984). To the best of my knowledge, this text has never been refuted. In 1991, I pursued my reflections at a conference organized in Lyon on "Les

---

[1] Paper read at the invitation of Monique Pinõl-Douriez on behalf of the Groupes d'Etudes Cliniques et Pathologiques du Développement Psychique (GECP), and published in M. Pinõl-Douriez (Ed.) (1997) *Pulsions, représentations, langage.* Lausanne: Delachaux et Niestlé, pp. 23–66. Translated by Andrew Weller for this edition.

DOI: 10.4324/9781003350132-6

écarts du discours". The proceedings were never published. And here we are now in 1995. In this paper I will not be able to go into the detail of all these above-mentioned contributions, whether published or not. That would amount to standing still. If you have been curious enough to get acquainted with the text of 1984, it will serve as an introduction to my remarks today, if not, it's in God's hands . . .

Programme

I am going to deal with the following points: first, I will follow up this introduction with the necessarily short and schematic presentation of certain general ideas on the nature and structure of language, drawing on the opinions of Claude Hagège (1985), Antoine Culioli (1990), Michel Halliday (personal communication) and John Austin (1962); then, I will defend the specificity of the psychoanalytic position, while noting certain contradictions in it. Finally, I will try to show how only a generalized theory of representation can provide a response to the problems raised by practice and theory. I will make particular reference to the experience obtained from borderline cases, categories absent in Lacan's thought, which drives some Lacanians to deny their existence. As the saying goes: *"Ça n'empêche pas d'exister"*.

The language of linguists

I am perfectly aware that I could deal with my subject without making the slightest reference to contributions outside the field of psychoanalysis. The subject matter is sufficiently abundant to do without them. However, if I have chosen to speak about language considered from the angle of representation, it seems to me to be logical to begin with the picture I have formed of the language of linguists, regardless of its relationship to psychoanalytic theory: representation of the non-psychoanalytic as opposed to the representation of the psychoanalytic. My position on this point is no different from the one I adopt when I deal with sexuality or psychic causality. It is always useful to position oneself in relation to non-psychoanalytic knowledge before developing the reflections that arise from analysis. This indeed was how the problem presented itself to Freud (1953 [1891]) in his work *On Aphasia*, which preceded by a few years the *Studies on Hysteria* (Freud with Breuer, 1895), in which there were already differences of opinion with Breuer. This was also how Lacan (2006 [1953]) proceeded, by drawing on Saussure. I have already said that I will not return to my previous contributions. I will therefore simply recall in a few words some of the references that have nourished my reflections since my study of 1984.

L'homme de paroles, by Claude Hagège (1985) clarified the question in a remarkable way. He points out that linguistics is the only contemporary science whose object coincides with the discourse that it holds in relation to it. It is an advantage, but also a risk. The book carries the subtitle, *Contribution linguistique aux sciences humaines*. We already knew, thanks to Emile Benveniste (1956), that language was the interpretant of all the other systems of signs. This is what I am doing now, presenting in linguistic terms problems outside language, but with Hagège, the effect of closure is more pronounced. A fundamental ambiguity of reflection on language is that language speaks about something and about itself at the same time. But, to do this, I must express myself in keeping with the rules that govern verbal exchange if I want to be heard. Hagège considers three points of view:

1. *Morphosyntaxic*, which concerns morphology and syntax.
2. *Semantico-referential*, which concerns semantics and reference.
3. *Enunciative-hierarchical*, which concerns enunciation and the tiering of forms.

Six classes, then, grouped two by two. A few remarks in passing: syntax and semantics are different. In other words, the Chomskyan project of reducing semantics to syntax came to nothing. Benveniste had already seen this: grammar is not sufficient to exhaust meaning or the links of the signifier, and it can be concluded that:

1. The *signified* cannot be eclipsed. Meaning and signification involve referring to *reference*. While semantics is located between meaning and reference, for a psychoanalyst the consideration of reference is unquestionable, that is, the relation to external reality or to internal reality.
2. Novelty is even more pronounced due to the individualization of the *hierarchical enunciative level*. The former relationship – language = code, speech = message, which opposes a system of collective signs and its individual setting in motion (subjective speech which refers to the subjectivizable code) – makes way for a combined appropriation of language and meaning and implies the ordering of words. The concrete situation of enunciation refers to the speaker/co-speaker pair and highlights the role of interpretation at the level of form as well as of content.

Thus, if thought classifies by means of languages, languages themselves are made up of systems of classification that are spontaneously used by the user without his being aware of their existence. It is the formal unconscious that inhabits language, languages and speech. But let us be careful: languages, as Hagège tells us, can teach us something about systems of logic, about the methods used in the human sciences and about the ingenuity of those who shape them, but not about languages themselves as a manifestation of the faculty of language, nor about man whom they contribute to characterizing. This relativizes a great deal, in my opinion, the interest of a philosophy of language. Logic, Hagège says, is a product of reason, and languages are not necessarily the acknowledged and semi-conscious model of it. And here is the final blow: languages are not an instrument of the discovery of truth. Hagège concludes that the logic of languages cannot be superimposed on pure logic. Languages associate, he said in 1985, affective and drive *representations* (my emphasis) with *purely cognitive* processes. Charles Bally had already discovered this in 1913, on taking over from Saussure at the University of Geneva.

To this picture, I will add the profound reflections of Antoine Culioli (1990), disillusioned with the thinking of the 1950s, which also saw the birth of Lacan's Rome Report, and who attributed to linguistics the status of a "pilot science" – Lacan's expression – if not that of a queen of sciences. Culioli acknowledges that linguists no longer have exclusive rights of ownership over language.

The philosophy of language and of concepts, epistemology, as well as the history of sciences, are also recognized as having rights. Psychoanalysis – which Culioli is far from ignoring: he has worked with Laplanche and has Laurent Danon-Boileau, a member of the Paris Psychoanalytic Society, as his pupil – is the object of an elision. Culioli marks out his territory. He rejects neurobiological claims. To date, no one has made satisfactory links between studies on neuronal activity and what we know of the activity of representation at the level *one* of language (first level). He points out that it is not enough to be a speaker to be a linguist, any more than it suffices to trigger an associative process to know what language is. The strategy of this author consists, starting from oral or written texts, in identifying forms offered by natural languages. Culioli (1990) writes that "the activity of language is meaningful insofar as an enunciator produces forms that can be recognised by a co-enunciator as being produced in order to be recognised as interpretable".

You can see how far we have come since the thinking of the 1950s. It is clear that the perspective of enunciation gives full importance to *interpreting*. Speaking is thus a matter of giving the person to whom one is speaking material to interpret, and he or she will do the same. But, of course, everything depends on how one determines what is to be interpreted and the way it is interpreted.

There are three parameters here: *representation, referenciation* and *regulation*. Thus, giving language a place within the general theory of representation includes the fact that representation is conceived as one of the three major parameters of language by linguists. Referenciation raises a major problem. Culioli states an important truth when he admits that, in fact, the linguist is more interested in the dream narrative than the dream itself. There is a frontier here separating him from the psychoanalyst. I doubt that from the text/narrative of the dream alone one can deduce an interpretation in psychoanalysis. We only have to think of Michel Jouvet (1925–2017) who, having analysed some two thousand five hundred of them, came to no conclusions that are of interest to us.

Culioli's method is based on the manipulation of texts. It is a technique, and this is in no way a pejorative judgement, that makes it possible to define the forms of these languages of which language constitutes the necessary theoretical abstraction implied by the reference to translation, a term I will come back to, as an activity of representation, referenciation and regulation.

I will draw attention in passing to the activity of homogenization of these processes using abstraction while excluding the body and affect, and ignoring the disorders of reason which sometimes inhabit language, as Ruth Menahem (1986) showed in her thesis. She raises the question of the relations between linguistic acceptability and acceptability for consciousness or for the superego. The first obeys the requirements of form, while the second implies a censorship that is not just formal.

The body now made its entrance with Halliday, who considered that the ideas of Gerard Edelman (1992) on consciousness constitute a discovery of crucial importance for language. Edelman, like many theoreticians of the brain, distinguishes between two levels of activity of consciousness: the primary and higher levels. The second level is marked by the transformations effected by the acquisition of language and its potentialities. The idea of selective recognition, derived from the theory of the selection of neuronal groups, lent support to the hypothesis of a neural Darwinism contested by others (see Crick, 1989). Halliday found Edelman's ideas striking because the concept of complexity does not only concern the organism but also the relationship between the organism and the environment, which implies self-organization (von Foerster, 1960; Atlan, 1983). Moreover, Atlan proposes another differentiation at two levels: the relations between brain and language and those between language and thought.

In short, aphasia and delusion cannot be included in the same category. This problem was discussed at the end of the 1940s, if I am not mistaken, at the Bonneval conference on the relations between neurology and psychiatry.

Other concepts are important such as the difference between adult prototypical language and infantile protolanguage. The idea of genetic programming can no longer be defended. It is impossible to go into Halliday's ideas in detail here. Moreover, it is not my intention. Once again, epigenesis supplants the idea of programming. If meaning becomes the result of the "sharing of an experience", this reinforces all the theories on the enunciator/co-enunciator pair. Language is related to this pair but also to what happens outside this pair, to the environmental context. Language is a *semogenic* system. Language is increasingly considered as a theory of human experience and conceptualized using new concepts such as enactment.

This leads me to say a few words about the earlier tradition of linguistic pragmatics, namely, the theory of speech acts of Austin (1962) and of Searle (1969), based on the study of performative utterances. This corresponds to a reintroduction of the body; the subject speaks about his body in the act of saying: "I agree to speak on the 4th of November". Every statement contains an actantial aspect. We can see how the act of enunciating, the enunciation, becomes the new paradigm. Austin distinguishes three acts in the speech act: the locutionary, the illocutionary and the perlocutionary. Limitations of time prevent me from going into this in detail. The locutionary corresponds to the functioning of language; the illocutionary concerns the quality of language to perform an act in the relationship between the locator and the allocutor. The act is that of saying. The perlocutionary is a secondary derived effect that belongs to the strategies of discourse and is a matter of psychology and sociology.

In short, the more linguistics tried to evacuate psychology – and, of course, psychoanalysis, which is its most conjectural form – the more the theoreticians of language were obliged to reintroduce it in one way or another. Clearly, it was easier to reintroduce psychology than psychoanalysis, but with the notion of "speech acts" and that of "relations to speech acts", we move closer to the analytic situation. However, in my opinion, we need to resist this misleading seduction. It has driven more than one analyst, notably Daniel Widlöcher (1992), to defend theories with a cognitivist flavour which aim to replace the concept of the drive by that of "action scheme", a dangerous deviation that substitutes the fecundity of the point of view of the vicissitudes of unfulfilled desire (hallucinatory fulfilment, fantasy, return of the repressed . . .) with behaviourist themes; such a programme of action has its place more outside the psychoanalyst's consulting room than in it.

Before saying goodbye to linguistics, I would like to recall an observation I made in my text of 1984. Of all the branches of linguistics, that which speaks the most to the psychoanalyst is poetics. I do not have time here to explain why, particularly with regard to the relationship between the discourse of free association and that of poetry which is totally different from it. The usefulness of such an assessment of linguistics becomes clear retrospectively. It takes the measure of the distance separating us from the 1950s when Saussure (1972 [1916]), Hjelmslev (1970 [1943]) and Chomsky (1975) reigned unchallenged. The case of Jakobson (1962, 1963, 1968 [1941]) is more difficult to evaluate, precisely on account of poetics. Thus the positions that I have cited, those of Hagège, Culioli, Halliday and Austin, developed without any reference to psychoanalysis. And when Michel Arrivé (1994) tackles the subject head on, is it not at the risk of a possible misinterpretation? Michel Arrivé turns the spotlight on President Schreber, whom he considers as a distinguished linguist. He sees the "basic language" as the key to the problem. But is this not to confuse *Freud's verbal translation* of unconscious fantasies abolished within the author's (i.e. Schreber's) psyche and the text itself of the illustrious *Memoirs*? If there is a basic language, it is one that Schreber's unconscious does not speak; it is one that is made to speak in his place by Freud in order to address psychoanalysts; it is an imaginary language that is spoken by no one, because if it is what Schreber wants to say, there is no one to answer him. Not even Freud, who never communicated with him.

It is clear that the relations between linguistics and psychoanalysis remain laborious. The hopes that Lacan placed in them were disappointed. It was he himself who was to speak self-ironically about his "*linguisterie*".

This *linguisterie* did not want anything to do with psychoanalysis, any more than Chomsky (1975) was willing to listen to Lacan. But there is one question that cannot be avoided. Schreber's *Memoirs* fall much more within the domain of literature than of linguistics. It is clear that, although Freud never read Saussure, he frequently read Sophocles, Shakespeare, Goethe and other more minor authors, like Jensen. Myths form the bridge between poetry and the novel. It is clear that the analyst feels much more at home with them, hence the interest of theories of narrative and enunciation.

Reminder

I must recall, albeit reluctantly, some of my conclusions of 1984.

1. The distribution of the *effects of the unconscious on language* manifests itself at all levels without privileging any of them, from phonology to enunciation, including syntax.
2. The resonance between studies on poetics and theorizations about the unconscious is striking. In passing, let me recall the role of affect, of the *emotional function of language*, which was not forgotten by Jakobson.
3. The *three characteristics of language* according to me: double significance (of sign and meaning), double *representance*[2] (words and things), and double reference (psychic reality, material reality) are the minimal conditions for gaining acceptance by psychoanalysis.
4. The necessity of taking into account the *effects of the frame and of the fundamental rule*, to which linguists pay little attention.
5. The *linking up of the systems* of language with the system which includes representation.
6. The *conception of the subject*, which must include that of a playful subject, a crucial notion. It is simply a question of knowing, when we speak of a playful subject, whether we understand it in the sense of von Neuman or of Winnicott.
7. The *reference of the reference*, one can say, in the relations between drive and object and in the transformations to which they give rise, namely the transference.

---

2 Translator's note: *Représentance*: a general category including different types of representation (psychic representative, ideational representative, affect representative, representative of the drive, etc.) and which implies the *movement*, activity *of representation*.

Psychoanalysis – linguistics

Let us move on now to the specificity of the analytic position with regard to its relations with linguistics. Psychoanalysis intervened in the domain of language at the beginning of this century through two kinds of phenomena. One, which I shall refer to as under-significant, is the parapraxis; the other, which I shall refer to as over-significant, is the joke.

Before psychoanalytic interpretation imposed itself, to the point that a parapraxis at the French National Assembly made its august audience laugh, a parapraxis was considered as an error that turned the proposition into an absurdity that had to be corrected immediately. It is an excusable involuntary manifestation owing to a slip of the tongue in cases where it produces a scabrous effect.

On the contrary, the joke is voluntary, its effect is deliberately sought-after and it occurs by virtue of condensations and displacements. However, when we read Freud again on this subject, we can see that he distinguishes in jokes between the spirit of words and the spirit of what he calls the "purpose" (1905a: 90), a distinction that is absent from all Lacanian commentaries. The "purpose" is external to language and refers to eroticism or aggressiveness.

Jokes and their Relation to the Unconscious (the *Witz*) (Freud, 1905a) was written just after the *Three Essays on the Theory of Sexuality* (1905b), as if to show that sexuality, the theory of which was based on the sexual perversions of the adult and the polymorphous perversity of the child, can infiltrate, at its opposite pole, language, which is employed in the most valued activities of sublimation, in the mouths of the most civilized representatives of society, where the most polished language governs the exchanges between persons of quality. However, this only concerns "local" linguistic aspects, I would say, which only have an indirect relationship with analysis, at least where jokes are concerned. As for parapraxes, they can be observed both in analysis and outside it. Now Freud (1900) had already approached the problem more extensively in *The Interpretation of Dreams*. He considered the book on the *Witz* as nothing more than a diversion or a digression after the book on dreams. Fliess had already made the criticism that his dreamers seemed really too ingenious. Freud replied that all dreamers are necessarily incorrigible jokers because the direct path for expressing their wishes is closed to them.

The question of dreams is essential to my thesis. No dream can be analysed directly. The dream content, which often consists exclusively of visual images, sometimes sounds, or more rarely other sensations, is formed of thing-presentations that have welled up quite independently of perception and consciousness. As such, its manifest content can be translated into words with the help of secondary elaboration, but not analysed. Its analysis requires the dream narrative in word-presentations to trigger an associative process so that interpretation, which concerns the dream itself, becomes possible, by means of deduction, thanks to the mechanism of the dreamwork: mainly, condensation and displacement, as we know. There is thus a sequence: the dream during sleep – the dream narrative on waking addressed to the analyst – free associations to the narrative – interpretations.

Two systems are clearly identified here: that of thing-presentations which are remembered on waking up but without direct access, as this system is connected, for consciousness, only with the other system, word-presentations, which open out onto associations related to the present, the past and the future. Furthermore, two other systems connote the previous ones: the primary process at work in dreams and the secondary process that governs language. It must be understood that the case of dreams is paradigmatic. The process to which the dream narrative is subjected when delivered up to free association is simply a particular case of the fundamental rule which requires the application of the method to everything that comes to mind, whether it is a dream or not; moreover, analysis liberates speech delivered lying down, addressed to a hidden addressee, as I pointed out in 1970.

This helps us to understand how the theory of the frame, which Freud did not elaborate, is merely a technical application of the theory of dreams as described in Chapter VII of *The Interpretation of Dreams* (Freud, 1900). One speaks in analysis as if one were dreaming out loud, or as if one were sharing one's dream with someone who had remained awake. Many theories of language in psychoanalysis do not take this into account and, in particular, Lacan's. In other words, they do not take account of the conditions of the production of speech and language in the "session" of psychoanalysis. That is why we can say that *the frame seeks to transform the psychical apparatus into an apparatus of language*. The model "dream / dream narrative" is what the whole of the first topography is built around. It met with its accomplishment and limits in the *Metapsychology* of 1915. It led to the conclusion that the unconscious is made up of object- or thing-presentations, the only real object-cathexes. As for affect, it was necessary to wait until 1923, when the second chapter of *The Ego and the Id* re-established the rights to existence of unconscious affects. I will come back to this. It follows that the proposition "the unconscious is structured like a language", in spite of the reservations introduced by the relationship of similarity "like", has no substance as a basis for a return to Freud. As such, the "recourse" to Freud, and not the "return", is based on inexistent evidence.

A digression on Lacan

I offered a lengthy critique of Lacan's theses as a whole in my contribution of 1984 and will not return to it here; however, I will add a recent supplementary opinion to what I said then. This opinion was aired by Natalia Avtonomova (1991), a Russian linguist, during the colloquium "Lacan avec les philosophes". She was not at all interested in the quarrels between psychoanalysts, who were ignored in the country where she was living at the time when she was speaking (today it is no longer certain that this is still the case). She pointed out that the assimilation of the unconscious with language entails simultaneously, and I quote, "a hypertrophy of the functions of language as a method and an exhaustion, that is to say an impoverishment, of language as an object, more exactly of the unconscious as language, as something structured like it". Avtonomova thus reproached Lacan for impoverishing symbolism. Moreover, the interpretation that Lacan gives of the signifier is very debatable. She writes: "Lacan builds a *homogenous* space in which language and desire can stand together, and even in a single movement; this is the aspect of the signifier". I want to emphasize the word "homogenous", having myself criticized the question of homogenization. On the other hand, Jean-Claude Milner (1995) in a difficult but very interesting book called *L'oeuvre claire*, was to defend Lacan's theory. Provisionally. But his work, which sheds bright light on many points, suffers from a total misappreciation of the problems raised by clinical psychoanalysis which Lacan treats in a cavalier fashion. Moreover, what are we to think of the inaugural sentences in his book? "It is not my aim to elucidate Lacan's thought" – which he does in a remarkable way – "I have neither the authority nor qualifications for that". This is one more case of the phrase, "I know, but still" (*"je sais bien, mais quand meme"*) that Octave Mannoni (1969) taught us to recognize. I will come back to Milner's conclusions, for they are much more illuminating than he himself thinks.

The representational system

There is a lot that could be said on this, but it would take me too far away from my subject which is the need to include speech and word-presentations within the larger ensemble of Freud's representational system. Am I, in spite of myself, giving way to the temptation of revisiting the theory of the relations between the unconscious and language in Freud's work? No, but it is true that we are obliged to return to certain points in order to clarify them. Between us, although the relationship between thing-presentations and word-presentations is indeed the axis of reflection on the Freudian theory of language, other corollaries must be emphasized. In fact, this question, as I have said, is linked to Freud's first topography, which keeps the drive at a distance from the psychical apparatus because the drive is neither conscious nor unconscious; only its representatives are. I want now to clarify an ambiguity concerning the term ideational representative (*Vorstellung-Repräsentanz*), which is opposed to affect and which I have proposed to call the "affect-representative", in other words: a representative of the quota of affect which only presents quantity from the unconscious point of view and quality from the conscious point of view. This ideational representative is an object- or thing-presentation

(*Dingvorstellung*), for example, the breast. The word-presentation (*Wortvorstellung*) only exists at the level of consciousness. Consciousness associates the thing-presentation and its corresponding word presentation, Freud tells us. One cannot be clearer. Language connotes the representation of the objects of the world. In the unconscious, language does not have its place. In psychosis, words are treated as things and translate the attempt to recathect lost objects. One question arises: what is the origin of object-presentations? Freud's answer is clear: it is perception. Presentations are derived from perceptions. It would be worth quoting here Freud's famous letter to Fliess, dated 6 December, 1896 (see Masson, 1985: 207) on the retranscription as a process of stratification, which defends the idea that memory is present not once but is rearranged several times over. Freud points out that he had postulated a similar rearrangement in his text on aphasia (Freud, 1953 [1891]).

Is that all? Can we satisfy ourselves with this chain: perception (*Wahrnehmung*), indication of perception (*Zeichenwarhrnehmungen*), unconscious, preconscious, the latter being capable of becoming conscious through the processes of thought? No, this picture is incomplete. What is missing is the role played by the drive.

Let me recall, then, that the drive is defined as "the psychical representative of the stimuli originating from within the organism and reaching the mind" (Freud, 1915: 122). This psychic representative that is the drive has three connotations: dynamic (what originates in the organism and reaches the mind); topographical (as a concept on the boundary of the somatic and the psychic); economic (as a "measure of the demand made upon the mind for work in consequence of its connection with the body").

Furthermore, the drive has representatives. *It is a representative and it has representatives.* This is what is to be understood by ideational representative and affect. *In short, for unconscious representation, there is a double system of representation. Originating in the external world, it is the thing and object-presentation, capable of bringing satisfaction. Originating from within the organism, it is the psychical representative of the drive that demands satisfaction.* As long as the coalescence of these two types of registration has not been understood, nothing has been understood of psychoanalysis.

Thus the thing or the object represented is the one that has satisfied the drive, which itself is represented by its psychical representative.

Conclusion: *the unconscious representation is constituted by a mixture, an association, an amalgam formed by the cathexis coming from the psychical representative, that is, originating from within the body, and from the object-representative, that is, originating in the external world.*

This representative montage clearly distinguishes this conception of representation from all those upheld by philosophy. This system would be idealistic if it were not referenced. Psychic reality is familiar to us. It is linked to the unconscious and no longer to the conscious mind, and it possesses a degree of belief which knows neither doubt nor degrees of certainty.

102 *Language within the general theory of representation*

That leaves material or external reality. It was only with reality-testing that it would be introduced in the *Papers on Metapsychology* (Freud, 1957 [1917]), in an article on dreams. But, later on, in his articles of 1924 on psychosis, when Freud speaks of the repression of reality, he brings into play the ideas and judgements which represent reality in the ego. It is

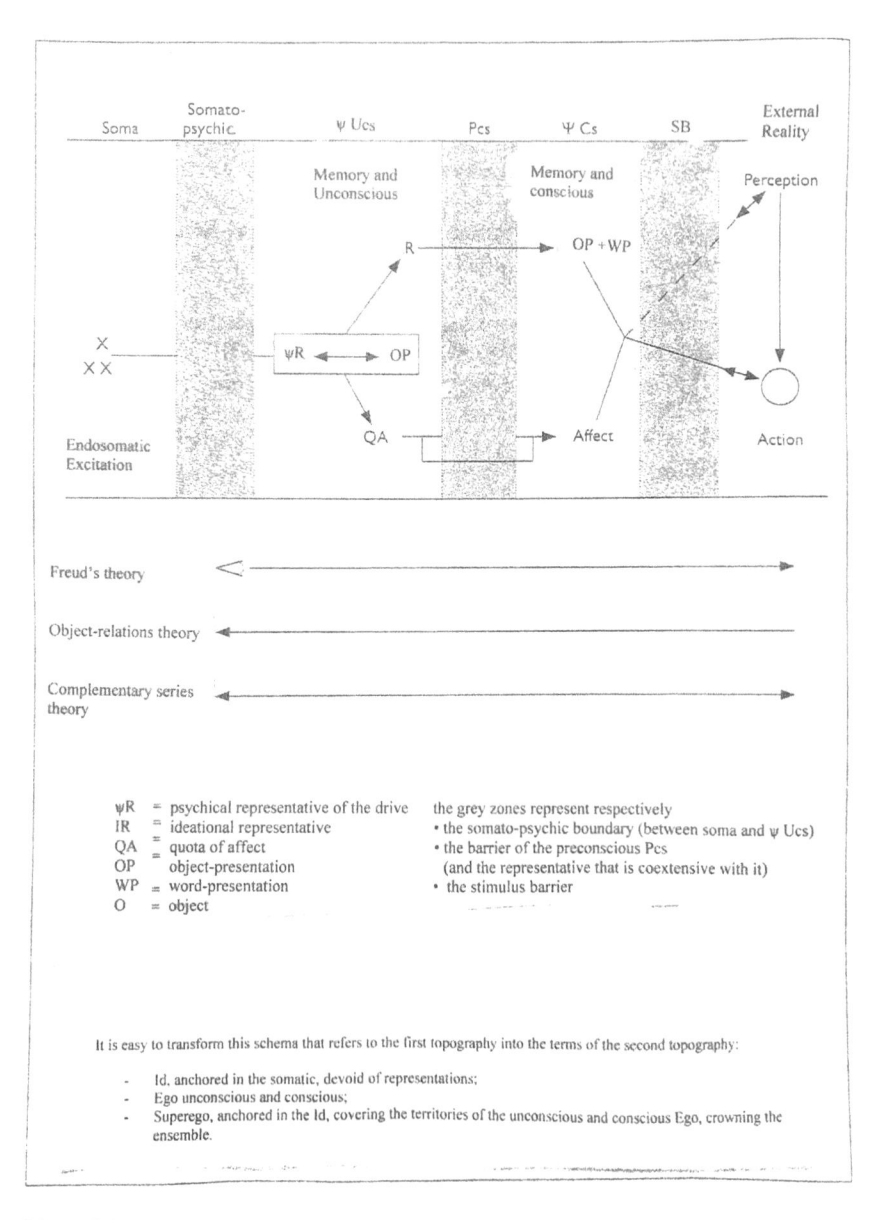

Figure 5.1

interesting to note how much difficulty both Freud and Lacan had in dealing with this problem of external reality. They capitulated, as it were, when faced with the necessity of introducing it; Freud in 1915, and Lacan, I think, around 1970.

Here, then, is the complete picture: psychical representative, ideational representative, thing- or object-presentation (unconscious and conscious), word-presentation, representative of reality. This is summarized in the schema below (see Figure 5.1).

The four territories

You have four territories: the soma, the unconscious mind, the conscious mind and external reality. You can see that the entire psychic formation can be considered *as a medium between soma and external reality*, as if the relation between the soma and external reality were much too dramatic, so that something needed to be inserted in order to metabolize what is happening between them. So the stimuli originate in the soma. These territories are divided into zones that serve as boundaries; hence the need for a theory of boundaries in psychoanalysis. The first boundary is the *somatopsychic* boundary, the second is the boundary created by the *preconscious*, the third is that created by the *stimulus barrier*. Thus the stimuli reach the mind. It is here that we come up against the psychical representatives of the drive, represented by ψR, oR being the trace of the object and of the earlier experience of satisfaction. It is the cathexis of the psychical representative, that is, of the subjective bodily element, on the traces of the object-presentation, which gives birth to desire. From this cell, the internal elaboration of the unconscious succeeds in separating the ideational representative and the quota of affect. The latter will attempt to cross the barrier of the preconscious, each in its own way, at least in the structures of normality. They will give rise to the conscious object-presentation, this time associated with the corresponding word-presentation and with affect as quality, since up to this point Freud has only talked about quantity in this connection. And finally, in the last territory, the relationship between perception and action, with of course the representatives of reality in the ego of which Freud speaks and which show, I think, that when Freud speaks of the repression of reality, he is speaking of negative hallucination, that is to say of the *negativization of perception*.

Lacan or Peirce?

In any case, talking about speech and language by dissociating the elements of this ensemble, or by casting a spell on it, is always possible, but the result no longer has much to do with Freud's psychoanalysis. This diversified view corresponds to the way that Freud theorizes it and stands opposed to the *unifying and homogenizing* conception of the signifier, that which appears and predominates definitively in Lacan's (1960) "Subversion of the subject and dialectics of desire", a paper presented shortly after the Bonneval Days in 1960 on the unconscious, in echo with the contribution of Laplanche and Leclaire (1961 [1960]). There was a sort of radicalization in Lacan's work at that moment. "The signifier is what represents a subject for another signifier", he says. This is a radical definition derived, uncited, from Peirce, as I have shown, which deserves a long and precise commentary. Jean-Claude Milner (1995) did so, but did not make the connection with Peirce.

Certainly, the identification of the conception of the subject is essential here; its nucleus is the idea of the *subject for another*. The signifier represents a subject for another signifier. For there is no subject but for another. But what is important here is the verb *represents*. Representation is reduced here to the relationship between two signifiers, but it cannot be evacuated. In other words, *there is a reference to representation that is not theorized by Lacan himself, even when he includes the verb represent in his definition of the signifier*. Representation is thus reduced here to the relationship between two signifiers. Subject and signifier are linked by a relationship of representation, but one that is reduced to the relationship between two signifiers. In fact, it is the triadic structure of the sign (Peirce, 1998 [1978]), which involves the relationship of a subject with a second called its object for a third called its interpretant, which enables us to make a link with psychoanalysis. Peirce's ideas are much closer to analysis than Lacan's. The relationship determines its interpretant to maintain the same triadic relationship with the same object for some other interpretant. I am now going to give the very difficult definition of the *"representamen"* that I already gave in 1984: a *representamen* is the subject of a triadic relationship with a second called its object for a third called its interpretant. Here it is important to emphasize that an interpretant is not a person. It is both a constitutive element of the sign and a sign itself. This triadic relationship is such that the *representamen* determines its interpretant to maintain the same triadic relationship with the same object for some other interpretant. What does this mean? It means that it is thanks to this that there is analysis, that it is the explanation for the transference. *If there is no possibility of transference on to, for, some other interpretant, everything you say to your analysand happens between you and him; it remains fixed, it does not leave the consulting room, and it has no effect outside it*. And, in fact, it is absolutely essential to understand this transference onto "some other interpretant".

Filiation

This analysis seems to me to clarify certain subsequent positions adopted with regard to those defended by Lacan. For Piera Aulagnier (1964, 1979), who treated psychotics and borderline cases, the Lacanian conception fails to account for them, and so she advanced her hypothesis of the pictogram, which is very close to that of the psychical representative of the drive. Laplanche (1984), on the contrary, who was allergic to the straying biological reference of sexuality in Freud's work, rejected the drive hypothesis and instead defended the introjection of maternal adult sexuality, colonizing the child's psyche, in a theory of generalized seduction generating enigmatic signifiers.

Furthermore, Laplanche defends the idea of a metabola beyond the differences between metaphor and metonymy. It seems to me that this bifurcation is fundamental for psychoanalysis. It is fundamental because we can see how a certain filiation with Lacan's thought, even if it claims to be heterodox, and even heretical in relation to the latter, nonetheless remains in its wake and opens a new direction in psychoanalysis. This model of the first topography to which I have just been referring, bringing together several aspects of the theory of representation, had a long life. It was in this respect that the model *dream – dream narrative – interpretation*, a model that was guided, it may be said, by the key idea of translation, in which Laplanche placed his faith, was to be shattered in 1920. For what has not been sufficiently noticed is that the restricted representational model, that of the first topography, only holds on the condition that it aligns itself with the first drive theory, for which the sexual drive is the only drive model possible, given that the drives of self-preservation play practically no role in it. So the first topography is founded on the sexual drives alone. When the death drives were introduced, it would have been necessary to reflect on what, without Eros, cannot be represented: what we call the unrepresentable; in other words, what exceeds the capacity of any form of representation. With the second topography, where the id replaces the unconscious, Laplanche and Pontalis (1973 [1967]) do not fail to point out that Freud's definition of the id in the *New Introductory Lectures on Psychoanalysis* (1933, p. 73ff) takes up formulas he had already used to define the unconscious, *but no longer makes any reference to representation, that is to say any idea of content is absent from the id*. The contents are pushed back to the level of the ego which, moreover, is to a large extent unconscious. There is no harm in this, I would say. In the id of the life and death drives, the model of *instinctual drives impulses* (discharge in the external world, in the ego, in the body-representation) has supplanted the model of the *dream/dream narrative*. The reference to movement, to what pushes, to what drives towards or for, has been deflected onto representation, outside the id, but this has been connoted by the psychical representative of the drive which is not the ideational representative. The consequences for theories and for language are considerable. The unconscious is no longer either descriptive, dynamic or structural; it is no more than a psychical quality, thereby losing a great deal of its interest. Milner's (1995) book shows that there is a parallel trajectory in Lacan's work, concerning different referents but culminating in the same result. This convergent trajectory is fascinating.

If the unconscious is just a psychical quality, even if it turns out that it can be structured like a language, it remains of limited interest. The id gives pride of place to force in movement, to the instinctual drive impulse in relation to representation. Any idea of a language of the id becomes unthinkable other than in terms of a language of agonistic and antagonistic forces. What does this mean? Finally, the novelty signalled by the introduction of the superego cannot minimize the role of the id, since the latter participates in the constitution of the roots of the superego. Hence the duplicity of the ego and of its moral reference. Lacan was well aware of this and decided to take advantage of it by introducing force into analytic treatment by means of scansion.

And language in all this? It is clear that the disproportion in the relations of force between the instinctual id, the ego and the superego (in part), considered from the point of view of language, casts suspicion over the latter, even when they brandish the word of the Law. "God", Freud reminds us, "is on the side of the big battalions". For me, then, these are the essential aspects of the two stages, of the two models, on which language depends.

After Freud

It remains to be seen what post-Freudian psychoanalysis would contribute to the debate. It has not escaped my notice that this theoretical construction did not remain intact over the course of time. Although I think it is stronger than those that followed it, I am not saying that it should be conserved as such, without criticisms or additions. Even in Freud's time, we can consider that the contributions of Abraham, of Ferenczi, and of Rank stood apart from it. While they did not criticize it, they did not apply it either. Then came Melanie Klein, who defended the model of the object-relationship, while contesting implicitly, even if she still seemed to adhere to it, the drive/representation model. Today, we can say that Kleinism enjoys great success in Great Britain and in South America. As it overlooks the question of language, as does English psychoanalysis generally, moreover, there is little to say about it. On the other side of the Atlantic, the question does not arouse passionate interest either, except for the isolated contribution of von Rosen (1977). We had to wait for Marshall Edelson (1975) and Roy Shafer (1978) to see language attributed with an important role once again. But we are far removed from Freud. I know that these affirmations may be considered excessive. Likewise, more conciliating overviews like those of Anzieu (1974, 1975, 1976, 1987, 1989, 2016 [1985]) did not fail to cite the contributions of Melanie Klein (1975 [1930]) and Hanna Segal (1957) on symbols, those of Alvarez de Toledo (1954) and Arminda Pichon-Rivière (1958), those, in the United States, of Edith Buxbaum (1948) or of Ralph Greenson (1950) on the mother tongue, or alternatively of Howard Shevrin (1972) in the *Nouvelle Revue de Psychanalyse*. A place must be given to David Liberman in

Argentina. There are many others still, who I am unable to cite for lack of space. To my great regret, such pruning is necessary in order to keep the discussion centred.

French psychoanalytic literature has Lacan as its centre. I have already presented and discussed this theorization which goes back to Damourette and Pichon in 1925. They do not forget the links between language and screams – think of Schreber – and give affect its place. I will cite them: "From the outset language has a twofold external value, representative and affective. These two values are in fact inseparable". And they conclude that language is a shared subjective experience, the objective external world does not feature in it. When one thinks that Damourette and Pichon were respected authors for Lacan, one wonders what he did with the positions that I have recalled here.

Whilst the Lacanian cohort meticulously followed the teachings of the Master without answering him, a few voices made themselves heard nonetheless. There were not many, but quality replaced quantity advantageously. I recall a brilliant text by Octave Mannoni (1977), "Isaure et Anaxagore", in *Fictions freudiennes*. He argues that meaning determines the signifier, which is very heretical for Lacan. The aim of analytic interpretation is to make language say what it does not say. The linguist does not care about this and limits himself to what it says. The psychoanalytic interpretation of dreams finds a latent meaning within the manifest meaning, but, Mannoni observes, it has to be the truth. And he concludes that this truth is only noticed within a context of misunderstanding. Mannoni points out that, in chess, meaning cannot refer to what is outside the game, and the game is confined within a closed space. But language is not shut in. Guy Rosolato, the most Lacanian of the non-Lacanians – or rather of those who, having been Lacanian, ceased to be so – continues to adhere to the thesis of the signifier and adds to it the signifiers of demarcation. His thinking, moreover, which develops Lacan's, is very rich. I have already mentioned the views of Jean Laplanche and Piera Aulagnier.

This barely outlined picture needs to be completed with Didier Anzieu's (1976) "sound envelopes of the self" and the ideas of Roland Gori (1978, 1996), who reintroduces the body in the act of speaking. Nevertheless, in Gori we can find links, already postulated by Klein and Bion, between language and the depressive position, and the reminder that the speaking subject is the fruit of the separation from the mother's body, with a marked reference to Winnicott on the transitionality of language. Once again unconscious affect and the perception of thought through language.

As we can see, although Lacan's thought imposed itself in a remarkable way and could not be ignored by many authors, it gave rise to numerous commentaries which relativized some of his points of view that were too radical or to enriching commentaries that augmented it and had to be taken into account subsequently.

Everything that I have just recalled and adumbrated only has meaning when related to the experience of analysis. From Freud's work, I will recall today just one crucial reference, that of the second eponymous chapter in *The Ego and the Id* (1959 [1923]). In this text which marks the turning taken with the adoption of the second topography, Freud returns to the relations between thing-presentations and word-presentations. It is a truly pivotal chapter, as we say. For him, word-presentations, in other words, the form imprinted by the recourse to language, become connected to thing-presentations which are carried out, I quote, "on some material which remains unknown" (p. 20). Here we can identify a formulation of Freud's affirming that the drives are anchored in the somatic but that they are already psychical in a form unknown to us.

Drives in a psychical form, a form unknown to us, thing-presentations that are dependent on a material unrecognized by us: the psychic background against which are our ideas of the world are formed is unknown but, in any case, it is linked to the body.

It is through this connection-transformation that something becomes preconscious/conscious. Thing-presentations and the corresponding word-presentations form a bloc for the preconscious/conscious, whereas thing-presentations alone characterize the unconscious. This is what accounts for the process of analysis, where we speak and, in so doing, reconstitute the preconscious/conscious bloc. But it must not be forgotten that in analysis we speak in a certain way, and this is what makes for the specificity of analytic speech. I have already drawn attention to this. Freud (1959 [1923]) states: "Word-presentations are residues of memories; they were at one time perceptions, and like all mnemic residues they can become conscious again" (p. 20).

We can thus build the schema:

perception-consciousness → mnemic residues → unconscious ideas/analytic speech-word-presentations → perceptions once again conscious thanks to language

(We should speak of *re-perception* to speak of language as perception.) Affect is subject to a different metabolization. The mnemic residues are "directly adjacent to the system *Pcpt.-Cs*" (p. 20). Verbal residues are derived primarily from auditory perceptions, from a special sensory source. I quote: "A word is after all the mnemic residue of a word that has been heard" (p. 21). There exists a form of thinking based on the memory residues of visual impressions, thinking in images. It is very imperfect from the point of view of conscious memory.

What is repressed becomes preconscious by establishing, through analytic work (here we are really in the world of analysis, since theory is derived from analytic treatment), its preconscious intermediate terms. Freud could have concluded: the preconscious is structured like a language, not the unconscious. But he continued and corrected himself: there is another way of becoming conscious; this is the case for the internal sensations of feelings of pleasure and unpleasure. The register of internal sensations behaves like a repressed impulse: "it can exert driving force without the ego noticing the compulsion" (1959 [1923]: 22). Let us not lose sight of the fact that Freud had in mind clinical analytic work. This is what enabled him to make up for his errors and approximations in the papers on metapsychology, about the interpretation of which there was an attempt to lead us astray at Bonneval in 1960, something I was determined to rectify, especially in 1970. Finally, here is the crucial conclusion:

> The part played by word-presentations now becomes perfectly clear. By their interposition internal thought-processes are made into perceptions. It is like a demonstration of the theorem that all knowledge has its origin in external perception. When a hypercathexis of the process of thinking takes place, thoughts are *actually* perceived – as if they came from without – and they are consequently held to be true. (Freud, 1959 [1923]: 23)

Here the whole idea of a purely internal discourse collapses, and he even cites the extreme case of hallucination. Freud then turned his attention towards the ego in order to discuss its anchoring in the soma, the id, a notion borrowed, let us not forget, from the first psychosomatician, Groddeck (1979 [1923]), who was himself inspired by Nietzsche. And he made the following alarming observation:

> We at once realize that almost all the lines of demarcation we have drawn at the instigation of pathology relate only to the superficial strata of the mental apparatus – the only ones known to us. (Freud, 1959 [1923]: 24)

Finally, Freud added that a person's own body, the ground of the ego, receives stimuli both from the outside and from the inside, and it is therein that its interest lies.

What an astonishing trajectory. Word-presentations, language, the result no doubt of evolution, are located in the most superficial strata of the ego. The "cap of hearing" provides a demonstration of this, on the part of the preconscious closest to the system *Pcpt.-Cs*. The knowledge which can thereby be brought to the ego thus only concerns the most superficial aspects of the mental apparatus. And yet these zones, as is shown by the example of dreams, are capable of psychic work. Furthermore, sleep can provide a solution for a complicated problem that has remained without a solution during the waking state. I recognize this. Language has nothing to say about it. *The unconscious is not structured like a language and the*

110 Language within the general theory of representation

id that replaced it even less. In passing, let me make the following remark: Freud and Lacan speak of the relationship between the unconscious and language, the first to establish the core of their difference, the second to affirm their relationship through structure. After a while both realized that their first intuitions were inadequate. They changed direction: Freud, in order to theorize what he called the id, anchored in the somatic and without any reference to representation; Lacan, in order to radicalize his initial views and to step back a little from the signifier, preferring in its stead the matheme and the letter, before finally combining them in the practice of Borromean knots. Both of them reflected on the relations between nature and culture, but in their own way. Freud leaned more towards nature and Lacan towards culture, except right at the end. The real difference is that Freud drew on clinical work, whereas Lacan freed himself from it.

Model

Textual exegesis is not enough; seventy-two years have now passed since *The Ego and the Id*. I propose the model below (Figure 5.2), which represents the essential relations. It is a model that was used by von Foerster (1960), but I am referring to it with a completely different aim. Here we can see the upper chain, which is the chain of language, with its movement back and forth, passing through the cell language-speech. The lower chain is the chain of the primary processes. It passes through the

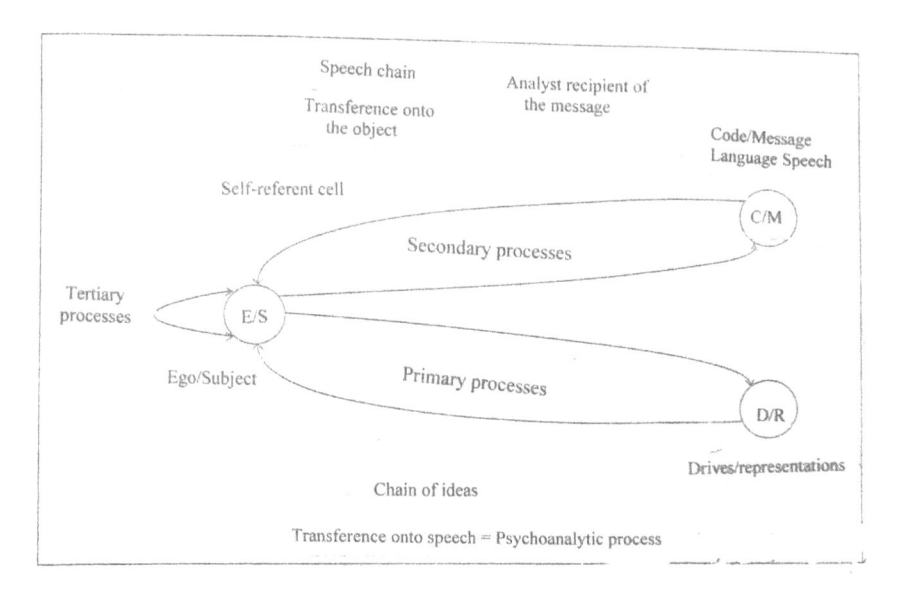

Figure 5.2

cell drive-representation. And both of them culminate in the cell of self-reference; this is how it differs from the two others. It is the *ego-subject cell and the seat of tertiary processes, processes of linking between the two chains.*

The lower chain serves to illustrate transference onto speech; this is what is required by the fundamental rule. The upper chain exemplifies transference onto the object, that is, onto the analyst to whom speech is addressed. The place of the object, which is not indicated here, underlines its intertwining role.

By uniting the two models, we obtain the general figure (Figure 5.3) presented below.

This last schema, which is a synthesis of many contributions, remains congruent with the idea of the indication of analysis. It concerns, then, those cases of analysis that are well indicated and finds its equilibrium in Oedipal and neurotic structures which reveal its intelligibility. But its limits, its deficiencies must also be highlighted. This is a model that works and does not work. And what I am interested in here is the limits of what is analysable, which I discussed in my London Report (Green, 1975). I will therefore pursue my exposition by referring to observations derived from analyses of borderline states and no-neurotic structures.

The work of the negative

In *The Work of the Negative* (Green, 1999 [1993]), I described those situations in analysis when an analyst, reminding an analysand of what he/

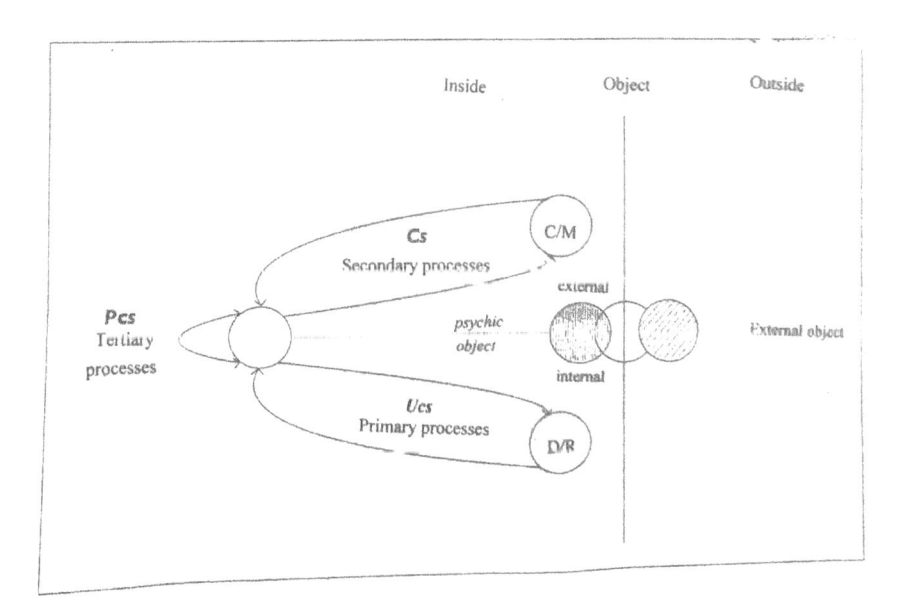

Figure 5.3

she has said previously – and it is not necessary for the analyst to refer to moments in the distant past, the remarks may have been made just a few sessions earlier – hears that the supposed enunciator of these remarks does not recognize them at all, has no recollection of them, any more than he/she recognizes him/herself as their author. You will have noticed just how essential the ideas of *recognition* and *translation* are. Amnesia? Undoubtedly, but were the mnemic residues sufficiently repressed? I had long assumed that they were – until I became aware that a mere instance of forgetting is generally lifted when the details are recalled concerning the content of what has supposedly been "forgotten". So I put forward the hypothesis of a negative hallucination pertaining to the interpretation of words, in other words to the wish to negativize what the words were intended to say, as if it had never occurred. What they signified, in short, had resulted initially in dissociating the words, the signifiers, from their content, the interpreted unconscious meaning, and then later in negativizing the mnemic residues derived from perceptions, that is, in rendering the words unrecognizable. So it is the perception of thought processes during interpretation that had undergone a negative hallucination, confirming Freud's hypothesis that language is a mode of perceiving thought. The residues of acoustic perceptions, what was heard, had been erased, blanked out. From that point on, the associative paths are also cut, and so the associative network as a whole founders in the process. A progressive series of denials are employed to achieve this result. The analyst then has to get round the obstacle and present the patient with another way of approaching the psychic events in question in order to promote new forms of recognition. Let me note in passing that the negative hallucination does not pertain exclusively to word-presentations; it is sometimes affect that is negativized, while language is still preserved in memory. And sometimes the object becomes unrepresentable, disappearing from the stage like certain characters in a dream who are felt to be present but are unidentifiable and even unrepresentable.

Without realizing it, I have in the process touched on the problem of the unrepresentable, the limit of my theorization. This may relate to that which does not have access to representation, thus to the psychical representative of the drive insofar as it is different from the ideational representative, pure cathetic energy, or, on the contrary, to the most abstract forms of thought that must consent to adopt an aspect of representation – trace of language or of writing – in order to be perceived, that is to say communicated, interpreted and exchanged. In analysis, as I have said, the *transferences of representation are the means by which the transference-representations are apprehended*. But since The Work of the Negative I have had the opportunity of enriching these observations. I have highlighted, in subjects presenting forms of negative hallucination pertaining to language, other psychic mechanisms. First and foremost, confusional mechanisms in which indiscernible elements appear, that is to say the incapacity to give language access to the light of day, in other words to make it intelligible for the analyst who understands nothing of the manifest content that is recounted to him. The analyst does not know, for example, if the patient is telling him about an event that has occurred in real life or if he is recounting a dream, or if the patient has passed surreptitiously from one to the other, or if he is speaking about himself or if his remarks are projections onto the analyst. Sometimes, it is the patient himself who will say he takes himself for someone else: "I think I am Dr Green", one patient said to me, whom people easily took for a dead uncle whom he had not known. He bore his first name and his father would make a slip of the tongue by saying "my brother" rather than "my son". As for his mother, she deliberately introduced her son to people in the neighbourhood as her brother or her husband. A heavy legacy.

Identification is thus a mechanism that stands in opposition to representation. This has not been stressed enough. One is not "like" but one *is* the one with whom one identifies, following a distinction made by Winnicott. There is a contraction of time, of the logic of enunciation, in which the locutor and co-locutor are one and the same. Listening more carefully, I understood that this patient was complaining about a cut, a split between word- and thing-presentations. Having drawn attention, for example, to the long delay separating the occurrence of an event that had happened to him and which he was only now reporting in the analysis, I suspected naturally some sort of effect of negative transference or resistance. Then I finally heard what he was saying to me which can be expressed as follows: "I don't have the words to relate what happened or to express what I felt. It's not that I don't want to say anything but that I cannot say anything, not because I am holding back or wish to hide something from you but because I do not have the words at my disposal to communicate it to you". This is a good example of the disconnection between the unconscious and the preconscious: words are lacking. This was already the case in *Studies on Hysteria* (Freud with Breuer, 1895) one hundred years ago; is it true that what his patients told him bore only the mark of repression? This explanation seems insufficient to me. In fact, we can see the importance of what I have described as tertiary processes, processes of linking between unconscious and preconscious representations. It will be the analyst's task to find "the words to say it", as a novelist said. When he proposes in his interpretation a verbalization of the psychic processes by filling in the blanks and re-establishing links, as Bion saw, the patient feels a great sense of recognition (*reconnaissance*), in both senses of the word (recognition and gratitude), towards the analyst.

A last example, to finish with, is that of patients with a psychosomatic structure, those whose affective turbulence is situated in the proximity of the id and not of the ego. Their poverty of language and its stereotyped and operational quality have been emphasized: "That's all", they say, cutting short invitations to associate. A clinical observation by Jacques Press

(1995), on which I made a commentary (Green, 1995) in the *Revue française de psychosomatique*, shows that this poverty is only such when one wants to apply to it the categories of the neuroses which Pierre Marty (1976) calls "mentalized". However, based on a close analysis of their verbal communication and the links that can be revealed in it, I am inclined to suspect an unapparent, invisible and rationalized delusion. But what is that? An unrepresentable pain which takes on the status of a physical condition or illness, in which the subject attacks his body to save his ego, even putting his body in mortal danger in some cases. A question arises here: What is the father doing? What is he thinking about? It will be said: he has other things to do. So it is up to the analyst to think about it so that the patient does not share the same body as his mother, as Joyce McDougall (1985, 1989) has suggested.

Conclusion

In discussion with Laurent Danon-Boileau (1993), a fully-fledged linguist and psychoanalyst, I put the following decisive question to him: "Do you have the impression during a session that you elucidate what you hear by means of linguistic theories? Do you think about it sometimes?" He replied: "Never". And then, after a while, he continued: "Except with children, but afterwards, in order to reconstruct what happened".

I do not have time today to plunge into the enigma of the foundations of language. I would nevertheless like to make a few remarks on the subject by way of conclusion. Language depends on temporal organization. Everyone knows the importance of the order of words, a classical problem in linguistics. This order is sequential, and therefore temporal. We operate, then, on the basis of two propositions: the secondary processes, thus language, are subject to the order of time; the primary processes, thus the unconscious, are unaware of time. These two propositions have been questioned, justifiably, by Anne Denis (1995), who postulates the existence of an archaic and primitive temporality, a temporality that is different from the characteristics of the preconscious-conscious, thus closer to the unconscious. This temporality consists of simultaneity, it is infinite and undefined, and above all it is inseparable from auto-eroticism and constitutive of the first sensations of identity. This last statement is taken from Anne Denis. I translate: what we are dealing with here is a protolinguistic temporality. I would not be surprised if it opened the way to the *deixis* studied by René Thom (1983, 1991) and Laurent Danon-Boileau (1992). Anne Denis links biological or physical rhythms with the metaphorizing – Jean-Luc Donnet says intertwining (*intriquante*) – response of the object. This means that a lack of response can impede structuring. The virtues of silence seem to me here to be very debatable, with all due respect to those who advocate it on the pretext that it is the unconscious that interprets. Chaos sets in, due to a lack of meaning (*faute de sens*). "*Faute de sens*" is to be understood in two ways: what is lacking and what is at fault for lacking. "There follows, as Anne Denis says, an incorporation of a demonic or *caïque*,[3] non-representative object" (Denis, 1995). These deficiencies can be observed in autistic subjects, drug addicts and psychosomatic subjects. The child lacks a "native" language – we also say mother tongue, Anne Denis affirms. This point of view in no way ignores the object-relation, but is nonetheless attached to the intrapsychic perspective of the co-construction of language and temporality. Time obliges me to limit my exposition of Anne Denis' ideas, who will perhaps have the opportunity of speaking herself.

I would like to draw attention to what seems to be a similar way of thinking in an unpublished contribution communicated to me by Marie-Thérèse Montagnier. It is very surprising for me to notice the closeness between the two ways of thinking. She is interested in the temporal organization of the discourse in the style of a patient's way of speaking and emphasizes the negative hallucination of the object that occurs here involving the danger, in the countertransference, of a withdrawal of interest in listening. It is fundamental. The analyst understands nothing, and because he understands nothing, he becomes bored, and because he becomes bored, he ceases to listen.

The non-occurrence of the analytic process and the self-absence that connotes it lead Marie-Thérèse Montagnier to write: "Form and movement prevail here over all content, all depth, all veracity". It is the same way of thinking here that places rhythm more than the phoneme at the origin of protolanguage. These studies, which concern both protolanguage and the constitution of temporality, further earlier investigations. I will confine myself to recalling the studies of Julia Kristeva (1977) on the *chora*, the prelinguistic maternal receptacle, and those of Monique Pinõl-Douriez (1975, 1984, 1989; Pinõl-Douriez et al., 1994) which, for me, unlike many others, have the merit of being convincing. Perhaps it is precisely because the role of representation in the broadest sense is never forgotten.

I think I have said enough to back up my arguments.

Namely,

1. Linguistics and psychoanalysis cross paths without actually meeting.
2. The analysis of Freudian thought is incompatible and irreconcilable with Lacanian discourse.

---

3 Translator's note: *caïque*, term used by André Green taking into account the second topography – thus the id and its "economy" – concerning non-neurotic and/or psychosomatic patients (see "Conclusion" in Pinol-Douriez, 1997).

3. The reference to borderline cases of what is analysable calls for the hypothesis of the characteristics of a protolanguage or of an archaic temporality, which rests on the intertwining and metaphorizing response of the object, based on rhythms that must be metaphorized.
4. There exists a theory of form and movement in analysis, which is complementary to that of what is signified, and which takes the place of the signifier by exploding its linguistic envelope.

References

Alain-Miller, J. (1975). Théorie de la langue. *Ornicar?* 1: 16–34.
Alvarez de Toledo, L. (1954). El análisis de asociar, del interpetar y de las palabras. *Revista de Psicoanálisis*, 11: 267–213.
Anzieu, D. (1974). Le Moi-peau. *Nouvelle Revue de Psychanalyse*, 9: 195–208.
Anzieu, D. (1975). Le transfert paradoxal. *Nouvelle Revue de Psychanalyse*, 12: 49–72.
Anzieu, D. (1976). L'envelope sonore du soi. *Nouvelle Revue de Psychanalyse*, 13: 161–179.
Anzieu, D. (1987). Le signifiants formels et le Moi-peau. In: Anzieu, D., Houzel, D., Missenard, A. et al. (Eds.) *Les enveloppes psychiques*. Paris: Dunod.
Anzieu, D. (1989). *Psychanalyse et langage. Du corps à la parole*. Paris: Dunod.
Anzieu, D. (2016 [1985]). *The Skin-Ego*, trans. N. Segal. London: Karnac.
Arrivé, M. (1994). *Langage et psychanalyse. Linguistique et inconscient. Freud, Saussure, Pichon, Lacan*. Paris: Presses Universitaires de France.
Atlan, H. (1983). L'émergence du nouveau et du sens. In: Dumouchel, P. and Dupuy, J.P. (Eds.) *L'auto-organisation. De la physique au politique*. Paris: Seuil, pp. 115–130.
Aulagnier, P. (1964). Remarques sur la structure psychotique. *La Psychanalyse*, 8: 47–67.
Aulagnier, P. (1979). *Les Destins du Plaisir*. Paris: Presses Universitaires de France.
Austin, J. (1962). *How to Do Things with Words*. Oxford: Clarendon.
Avtonomova, N. (1991). Lacan avec Kant: L'idée du symbolisme. In: *Lacan avec les philosophes*. Paris: Albin Michel, pp. 67–86.
Bally, C. (1913). *Le langage et la vie*. Geneva: Droz.
Bally, C. (1921). *Traité de stylistique française*. Paris: Klincksieck.
Bally, C. (1932). *Linguistique générale et linguistique française*. Bern: Francke Verlag.
Benveniste, E. (1956). Remarques sur la function du langage dans la découverte freudienne. *La Psychanalyse*, 1: 3–16.
Buxbaum, E. (1948). The role of the second language in the formulation of ego and superego. *Psychoanalytic Quarterly*, 17: 279–289.
Chomsky, N. (1975). *Reflections on Language*. London: Random House.
Crick, F. (1989). Neural Edelmanism. *Trends in Neuroscience*, 12: 240–248.
Culioli, A. (1990). *Pour une linguistique de l'énonciation I*. Gap: Orphrys.
Edelman, G. (1992). *Bright Air, Brilliant Fire: On the Matter of Mind*. New York: Basic Books.
Edelson, M. (1975). *Language and Interpretation in Psychoanalysis*. New Haven, CT: Yale University Press.
Foerster, H. von (1960). On self-organizing systems and their environments. In: Yovits, M.C. and Cameron, S. (Eds.) *Self-Organizing Systems*. London: Pergamon Press, pp. 31–50.

Freud, S. with Breuer, J. (1895). *Studies on Hysteria*. S.E., 2. London: Hogarth.
Freud, S. (1900). *The Interpretation of Dreams*. S.E. 4 and 5. London: Hogarth, pp. 1–621.
Freud, S. (1905a). *Jokes and their Relation to the Unconscious*. S.E. 7. London: Hogarth, pp. 9–236.
Freud, S. (1905b). *Three Essays on the Theory of Sexuality*. S.E. 7. London: Hogarth, pp. 123–243.
Freud, S. (1915). *Instincts and their Vicissitudes*. S.E. 14. London: Hogarth, pp. 109–140.
Freud, S. (1933). *New Introductory Lectures on Psychoanalysis*. S.E. 22. London: Hogarth, pp. 1–182.
Freud, S. (1953 [1891]). *On Aphasia: A Critical Study*, trans. E. Stengel. New York: International Universities Press.
Freud, S. (1957 [1917]). *A Metapsychological Supplement to the Theory of Dreams*. S.E. 14. London: Hogarth Press, pp. 217–236.
Freud, S. (1959 [1923]). *The Ego and the Id*. S.E. 19. London: Hogarth Press, pp. 1–66.
Gori, R. (1978). *Le corps et le signe dans l'acte de parole*. Paris: Dunod.
Gori, R. (1996). *La preuve par la parole. Sur la causalité en psychanalyse*. Paris: Presses Universitaires de France.
Green, A. (1966). L'objet (*a*) de J. Lacan, sa logique et la théorie freudienne. *Cahiers pour L'Analyse*, 3: 15–37. Reprinted in Green, A. (1995) *Propédeutique*. Seyssel: Champ Vallon, pp. 159–184.
Green, A. (1973). *Le discours vivant*. Paris: Presses Universitaires de France.
Green, A. (1975). The analyst, symbolization and absence in the analytic setting. *The International Journal of Psychoanalysis*, 56: 1–22. Also published in Green, A. (1986) *On Private Madness*. London: Hogarth, pp. 30–59 (reprinted London: Karnac, 1997).
Green, A. (1979). Psychanalyse, langage: l'ancien et le nouveau. *Critique*, 381: 127–150. Reprinted in Green, A. (1995) *Propédeutique*. Seyssel: Champ Vallon, pp. 125–150.
Green, A. (1995). Commentaire de l'observation de Jacques Press. *Revue française de psychosomatique*, 8: 41–48.
Green, A. (1999 [1993]). *The Work of the Negative*, trans. A. Weller. London: Free Association Books.
Greenson, R. (1950). The mother tongue and the mother. *International Journal of Psychoanalysis*, 31: 18–23.
Groddeck, G. (1979 [1923]). *The Book of the It*. London: Vision Press.
Hagège, C. (1985). *L'homme de paroles. Contribution linguistique aux sciences humaines*. Paris: Gallimard.
Hjelmslev, H. (1970 [1943]). *Prologomena to a Theory of Language*, trans. F.J. Whitfield. Madison, WI: University of Wisconsin.
Jakobson, R. (1962). Why "mama" and "papa"? In: *Roman Jakobson: Selected Writings I: Phonology*. The Hague: Mouton.
Jakobson, R. (1963). *Essais de linguistique générale*, trans. N. Ruyet. Paris: Minuit.
Jakobson, R. (1968 [1941]). *Child Language, Aphasia and Phonetic Universals*, trans. A.R. Keiler. The Hague: Mouton.
Klein, M. (1975 [1930]). The importance of symbol formation in the development of the ego. In: *Love, Guilt and Reparation and Other Essays (1921–1945)*. New York: Delacorte Press, pp. 219–232.

Kristeva, J. (1977). *Polylogue*. Paris: Editions de Seuil.
Lacan, J. (1960). Subversion of the subject and dialectics of desire in the Freudian unconscious. In: *Écrits*, trans. B. Fink. New York: Norton, pp. 671–702.
Lacan, J. (2006 [1953]). The function and field of speech in psychoanalysis. *Écrits*, trans. B. Fink. New York: Norton, pp. 197–268.
Laplanche, J. (1984). La pulsion et son objet-source: Son destin dans le transfert. In: D. Anzieu, R. Dorey, et al. (Eds.) *La pulsion pour quoi faire?* Paris: Association Psychanalytique de France.
Laplanche, J. and Leclaire, S. (1961 [1960]). L'inconscient, une étude psychanalytique. Report presented at the Bonneval Colloquium. *Les Temps Modernes*, 183: 81–129.
Laplanche, J. and Pontalis, J.-B. (1973 [1967]). *The Language of Psychoanalysis*, trans. D. Nicholson-Smith. New York: Norton.
Mannoni, O. (1969). Je sais bien mais comme même. In: *Clefs pour l'imaginaire ou l'autre scène*. Paris: Seuil, pp. 9–33.
Marty, P. (1976). *Mouvements individuels de vie et de mort*. Paris: Payot.
Masson J.M. (Ed.) (1985). *The Complete letters of Sigmund Freud to Wilhelm Fliess, 1887–1904*. Cambridge, MA: Belknap.
McDougall, J. (1985). *Theatres of the Mind*. New York: Basic Books.
McDougall, J. (1989). *Theatres of the Body*. New York: Norton.
Menahem, R. (1986). *Langage et folie*. Paris: Gallimard.
Milner, J.-C. (1995). *L'œuvre claire*. Paris: Seuil.
Peirce, C. (1998 [1978]). *Ecrits sur la signe*, trans. G. Deledalle. Paris: Seuil.
Pichon-Rivière, A. (1958). La dentición, la marcha y el lenguaje en relación con la posición depresiva. *Revista di Psicoanalisis*, 15: 41–48.
Pinõl-Douriez, M. (1975). *La construction de l'espace*. Lausanne: Delachaux et Niestlé.
Pinõl-Douriez, M. (1984). *Bébé agi. Bébé actif*. Paris: Presses Universitaires de France.
Pinõl-Douriez, M. (1989). La genèse de la pensée et des représentations. In: Lebovici, S. and Weil-Hapern, F. (Eds.) *Précis de psychopathologie du bébé*. Paris: Presses Universitaires de France.
Pinõl-Douriez, M. (Ed.) (1997). *Pulsions, représentations, langage*. Lausanne: Delachaux et Niestlé.
Pinol-Douriez, M., Boubli, M., et al. (1994). Naissance de la pensée. In: Kaës, R. (Ed.) *Les voies de la psyche. Hommage à Didier Anzieu*. Paris: Dunod, pp. 237–253.
Press, J. (1995). Une observation clinique. *Revue française de psychosomatique*, 8: 25–40.
Rosen, C.G. von (1977). *Style, Character and Language*. New York: J. Aronson.
Rosolato, G. (1964). *Essais sur la symbolique*. Paris: Gallimard.
Rosolato, G. (1977). Les hallucinations acoustico-verbales et les champs perceptifs du corps. *L'evolution psychiatrique*, 3: 729–741.
Rosolato, G. (1978). *La Relation d'inconnu*. Paris: Gallimard.
Rosolato, G. (1984). Destin du signifiant. *Nouvelle Revue de Psychanalyse*, 30: 139–170.
Rosolato, G. (1985a). *Élements de l'interprétation*. Paris: Gallimard.
Rosolato, G. (1985b). Le significant de la demarcation et la communication non verbale. In: Rosolato (1985a), pp. 63–82.
Rosolato, G. (1989). Le négatif et son lexique. In: Missénard, A. (Ed.) *Le négatif. Figures et modalités*. Paris: Dunod, pp. 9–22.
Saussure, F. de (1972 [1916]). *Cours de linguistique générale*. Paris: Payot.

Searle, J.R. (1969). *Speech Acts: Essays in the Philosophy of Language.* Cambridge: Cambridge University Press.
Segal, H. (1957). Notes on symbol-formation. *International Journal of Psychoanalysis,* 38: 391–397.
Shafer, R. (1978). *Language and Insight.* New Haven, CT: Yale University Press.
Shevrin, H. (1972). Condensation et metaphore. *Nouvelle Revue de Psychanalyse,* 5: 115–130.
Widlöcher, D. (1992). De l'émotion primaire à l'affect differencié. In: Bloch, H., Bloch, S., et al. (Eds.) *Émotions et affects chez le bébé et ses partenaires.* Paris: Eshel, pp. 45–58.

6 The psychoanalytic frame
Its internalization by the analyst and its application in practice[1] (1997)

I would like to say how much I appreciate the courage and the frankness of my Canadian colleagues. They have ventured to choose a theme "The future of a disillusionment", which challenges our identity as analysts and highlights the threats to our practice. We should not be surprised that it gives rise to passionate points of view, and the lively exchanges attest to the depth of our commitment, irrespective of our divergent opinions.

The meetings made possible by this colloquium offer us particularly favourable conditions for a dialogue on "neutral ground" since, as a result of their history, Quebecers, neighbours of the Americans, maintain relations with England and France and are French speaking. Having been exposed to a variety of influences, they are well placed to play a mediating role. This dialogue, of course, cannot be fruitful if no one is prepared to make any compromises.

I. The crisis

For the very first time a president of the International Psychoanalytic Association (IPA) recently recognized, in a speech in Barcelona, the existence of a crisis in psychoanalysis, an examination of which seems to me to be indispensable. However, I do not entirely adhere to the description of the crisis situation, as set out in the text of the invitation to this colloquium. I have noted a number of elements in it that I would like to comment on briefly:

1. The idea of a "reversal of culture", suggesting that public opinion, hitherto favourable to psychoanalysis, has recently changed tack and become hostile.

---

1 This paper was read at the colloquium "L'avenir d'une disillusion", at Val-David, Quebec, August 24, 1997; it was subsequently published in Green et al. (2000). Translated into English by Andrew Weller for this edition.

2. The false "guarantee of lucidity" inherent in the state of being a psychoanalyst. (In reality, the fact of being a psychoanalyst affords no guarantee as to the pertinence of a discourse that reflects the ideas of one's colleagues, quite to the contrary!).
3. Man's "ineradicable need for illusion" which explains the more or less late and inevitable appearance of disillusionment. For me, this inevitable evolution is, from a certain point of view, salutary, for it obliges us to ask ourselves questions about what we think, about what we are doing. This is clearly not without risk, but we have the choice between death and a possibility of rebirth.

Let us note, then:

– the impossibility, in psychoanalysis, of drawing on classical epistemology whose theses seem inappropriate
– the singularity of psychoanalytic clinical experience and its independence with regard to medicine and psychiatry. This singularity calls for clarifications.

I am not certain that the document that we are invited to debate indicates the aspects in which our practice has really proved itself to be decadent and has deviated from its initial aims. For example, when one reads in it that "speech and desire are no longer solicited", one can clearly see the source of such a formulation: a large part of the psychoanalytic field is made up of patients in whom the value of speech or the existence of desire are highly problematic. Can we really speak of "desire" when we are dealing with a borderline case? Can the same function and the same weight be attributed to speech in the case of a phobic neurosis as in that of a narcissistic personality?

Nor can we allege that it is the patients who have changed, obliging their analysts to interest themselves in their needs more than their desires; and it would still be necessary to agree on what is understood by "needs". In turn, I will try to identify the different factors that are contributing to the crisis, both outside and within psychoanalysis. They have their roots in the fragmented and conflictual foundations of the identity of the psychoanalyst, which leads me to suggest a new way of tackling the fundamental questions it raises: Who am I when I define myself as a psychoanalyst? What do I do when I practice psychoanalysis? And what do I think about psychoanalytic theory?

A subversive power

Ever since it came into existence, psychoanalysis has been subjected to attacks of all kinds. I do not think, however, that we should adopt the position of a victim, for it should not be forgotten that psychoanalysis itself represents a virulent attack on the human sciences and the conception of man that they convey. It is precisely because psychoanalysis is subversive that it is rejected; fifty years after Freud's death, we have still not gotten over it! Great ambivalence towards him is still noticeable, in spite of the praises sung to Heinz Hartmann in the United States, to Melanie Klein in England and to Jacques Lacan in France; the infatuation only lasted, moreover, as long as the representatives of the culture thought they could derive benefit from it, after which they rejected this toy and chose another in its stead.

At the present time, it is the turn of neuroscience and cognitive science to have the wind in their sails, for a while; then disillusionment will follow without it being possible to deny their interest entirely.

Quite clearly, the ambient ideology resists the seduction of psychoanalysis and seeks to refute it in various ways. Philosophy as well as morality (and the very structure of society) have felt challenged by it.

The hypothesis of the unconscious dealt a severe blow to philosophical thought. And we continue to ask ourselves how we can evade this difficulty.

As far as morality is concerned, the recognition of infantile sexuality, and more generally of the instinctual drive sources of the superego, brings its weight to bear upon every ethical conception. For sociology, the question raised by *Civilization and its Discontents* (Freud, 1930) seems even more urgent than in Freud's time.

Alternative ideologies

For the last fifty years there has been a desperate search for alternative ideologies through which the outlines of our cultural environment emerge. I will summarize in five points this phenomenon that is reflected in:

1. A reinforcement of philosophical and religious ideologies. Sometimes philosophy ceases to refer to consciousness and turns towards being to avoid the unconscious; sometimes it adopts the point of view of the philosophy of language in which logical positivism does away with the questions posed by psychoanalysis. In the domain of religion, things are no more encouraging. Freud fought against it because it prohibited thinking, but it still rises from its ashes periodically. "Religion is dead!" you will tell me. And yet, in Paris, 500,000 young people still rush to see the Pope! Official statistics suggest that people no longer believe in official religion but continue to believe in life after death or in hidden influences, and flirt with Buddhism or with sects. Psychoanalytic materialism seems unacceptable. Although there is now greater sexual tolerance, the religious superego is still more powerful than one thinks.
2. Nor can we disregard the advent of alternative political ideologies, such as Marxism or faith in revolution, even if they are considerably

weaker than they once were. Is it not surprising to see how young people have turned Che Guevera into a cult figure fifty years after his death? Faith in revolution and in change – a change of society that is supposed to change man – is still present in spite of undeniable signs of losing steam: it is important to continue to dream.

3. On another more subtle, more "elaborate" level, we may also note the advent of structuralism, which ushered in a real upheaval in the human sciences. Although structuralists accepted the existence of the unconscious, they always conceived it as a formal unconscious, without content, without drive, without repressed contents, whether it was the unconscious in which linguistics (Ferdinand de Saussure), anthropology (the Oedipus complex according to Claude Lévi-Strauss) or biology (the genetic code) was interested.

4. The ever increasing importance of medical ideology also plays a part in this demand for alternatives. It is thought that biology will resolve all the problems of the mind. I belong to a generation that saw the birth of chlorpromazine (an antipsychotic introduced in the year that I entered psychiatry). But since 1953 what solutions has chemotherapy really offered, apart from certain limited improvements? Just recipes! But no decisive change in the way we understand the mind. And now there is talk of psychosurgery.

5. A new religion has taken over from former beliefs: intelligent machines, computers and artificial intelligence. Not to mention cognitivism and genetics, the advances of which have reinforced the idea of hereditary fatalism. (I have already discussed, in "Méconnaissance de l'inconscient" (Green, 1991), the relations between the unconscious and science.)

The hotbeds of the crisis

Where are we at today? What are the hotbeds of the crisis?

Scientific criticism

On the theoretical or epistemological level, the rejection by science of the existence of an unconscious mind represents the most formidable threat that we have to face. For example, in certain psychoanalytic circles – even in major research endeavours – they no longer speak of "psychical apparatus" but of "brain", while refusing to admit that there is an ideology of science or that science serves as an endorsement for ideology.

The failure of humanism

At the moral level, we have to face up to the failure of the concept of humanity: humanism is dead; its ideological struggle has failed. We are living in an age that is no longer one of anxiety, but rather one of despair. The development of counter-cultures is now part of the landscape; the notion of evil has become so relative that it no longer serves as a point of reference and everyone manages as best as they can, resorting to tobacco, hashish, heroin or tranquillizers. A genuine drug culture is developing as a way of escaping from social determinisms. The modern concept of the "connected" man is not very favourable either to the development of psychoanalysis. Because it does not have an answer for everything it is deemed to be useless; and where it could contribute answers, its effects are limited because it is too expensive and its results uncertain.

You only have to look beyond the four walls of your consulting room and try to find out what young people think, what people think in general, what affects them, what attracts them, and you will see that these problems are only too real.

The economic situation

On a practical level, we have to ask ourselves whether economic crises will not one day get the better of psychoanalysis. The situation is not exactly the same in France as in the United States, inasmuch as in France, patients have never really counted on a third party payer; the reimbursement by Social Security of the fees paid to analysts has always been quite limited and, in any case, the patient is usually required to make a significant personal contribution. Europeans have accepted more easily that psychoanalysis is not a medical treatment; one cannot be reimbursed for the fees paid to a psychoanalyst in the case of failure as one can, for example, with a surgeon.

Does the crisis situation at the economic level imply that psychoanalysis is henceforth reserved for the better off? Certainly not! A downward revision of our financial ambitions is therefore necessary. We need to get used to the idea that our economic status will continue to deteriorate. We belong to the middle class, the one that is the most exposed irrespective of the political scenario offered. We also need to envisage working as employees in healthcare organizations; I do not think we can go further than that in suppressing psychoanalysis . . . Perhaps this is how psychoanalysis will be able to survive! It will be an opportunity to distinguish between those who are ready to make personal sacrifices in order to be able to continue to practice and those who prefer a more lucrative path.

Fragmentation and disorientation of the psychoanalytic body

Scientific criticism and the economic situation are thus the two greatest dangers facing psychoanalysis currently, especially as the image that the psychoanalytic milieu gives of itself is rather worrying. It comes across increasingly as a divided body, vulnerable and closed in on itself. Psychoanalysts do not know what to think anymore or adhere exclusively to a psychoanalytic sect (Kleinian, Lacanian, Winnicottian, etc.), which only increases the risk of fragmentation.

II. The analytic frame

My remarks will now be concerned with the question of the psychoanalytic frame or, more precisely, its internalization in the analyst and its application in practice. We cannot, however, avoid making a detour via the history of psychoanalysis, with particular reference to experience and its theorization.

Back to experience

Let's take a typical case: a young, intelligent, sensitive and curious young man, suffering from symptoms of inhibition and anxiety or from some other sense of unease that is more difficult to define as it does not involve any major incapacity, and for which other forms of therapy have not been of any help, goes to see an analyst who is well trained, experienced and morally irreproachable. The analysis unfolds in the traditional setting; the basic silence is interspersed with interpretations and the development of the process reveals an analysable transference neurosis, followed by its resolution, resulting in the disappearance of the symptoms and the return of greater psychic freedom. One could not imagine a more misleading situation for the progress of the analysis! Thus all nostalgia for the past is inappropriate. Why? In such a case, it is difficult to call into question the nature of psychoanalytic action due to the very fact of this natural evolution. What action occurred? What was the nature of this action? For lack of an answer, we could appeal to the recognition of the "unconscious", of the "repressed", of "resistance", of the "transference", of the Oedipus complex, etc. For the researcher who is also an analyst, the above questions elicit other questions that aim precisely to circumscribe the nature of what happened: What was involved? Was it a matter of intervening at the level of ideas, or images, or affects, or principles of functioning, or forces? That cannot be decided! A considerable field is therefore left open to speculation, that is, to theoretical constructions that are not based on any experience.

If analysis has to confine itself to the development of an elegant or faultless reasoning, we cannot expect any progress other than "formal"; nor can we expect any pertinent light to be thrown on the nature of what is involved. *No further theoretical progress has resulted from the clinical field of the so-called classical neuroses*. The result of an approach – where one sees the way in which the analyst conceives the analytic undertaking – seems to me to be questionable because it circumvents the obstacles that could have obliged us to examine them. Most analysts tend to keep silent about the failures that ought to call into doubt the theoretical corpus on which they are based, preferring to elaborate a favourite theory or construction that conceals their ignorance. The black hole of the questions that remain unanswered and the intolerable character of the absence of a conception on which to base our action forces us to choose an accessory – the theoretical fetish – that acts by means of aesthetic pleasure, as a substitute for the quest for truth; this artefact functions once again as an infantile sexual theory.

This applies to contrasting approaches – extreme schematizations (allegedly scientific) or bold speculative constructions – which all reflect a splitting of thought that hesitates between recognizing truth and the reassuring power of a theory that we exhibit proudly like the emperor's new clothes. Otherwise, all we have left is the abyss of our ignorance and the intolerable character of certain concepts that are an affront to our narcissism. Alas, with time, we notice that the emperor is naked!

Would it not be better to consider the products of some of our theorizations as "transitional" concepts, whose truth or falseness we cannot prove but which we adopt, until we are more fully informed, for their heuristic resources?

The reader will perhaps find it paradoxical that I am drawing on analyses that unfold without any problems in order to denounce the theorizations that have arisen from them, when it is in connection with difficult cases that they usually seem to be the most conjectural. But we are perfectly aware of the debatable character of our convictions when it is a matter of difficult analyses, whereas we fail to ask ourselves questions when it is "good" cases of analysis that are involved.

Now, in Freud's work, the entire analytic theory is articulated around one and the same aim, as he reaffirms in *Analysis Terminable and Interminable* (Freud, 1937): that of understanding why "it doesn't work" and what we can do or think in order to create more favourable conditions for analysis to work well. Here it is the entire history of psychoanalytic technique and theory that resurfaces. Certain critical moments – which I will only highlight without dwelling on them – punctuate this permanent questioning in Freud's work: first, the analysis of the "Wolfman" (Freud, 1918), as an analysis of an infantile neurosis (which announced an openness to borderline cases and introduced revolutionary changes); then, the contestation of Ferenczi (between 1929 and 1933); and finally, the emergence of the leaders that Melanie Klein, Bion, Winnicott, Hartmann, Kohut and Lacan, among others, have become.

What is analysing? The two postulates of Freud

After the First World War, the IPA met once again for a Congress (Budapest, 1918), and Freud was able to renew contacts with analysts after a long period of separation, which, admittedly, had provided the opportunity for in-depth reflection. He addressed his colleagues in these terms:

> Why "analysis" – which means breaking up or separating out, and suggests an analogy with the work carried out by chemists on substances which they find in nature and bring into their laboratories? Because in an important respect there really is an analogy between the two. The patient's symptoms and pathological manifestations, like all his mental activities, are of a highly composite kind; the elements of this compound are at bottom motives, instinctual impulses. But the patient knows nothing of these elementary motives or not nearly enough. We teach him to understand the way in which these highly complicated mental formations are compounded; we trace the symptoms back to the instinctual impulses which motivate them; we point out to the patient these instinctual motives, which are present in his symptoms and of which he has hitherto been unaware – just as a chemist isolates the fundamental substance, the chemical "element", out of the salt in which it had been combined with other elements and in which it was unrecognizable. In the same way, as regards those of the patient's mental manifestations that were not considered pathological, we show him that he was only to a certain extent conscious of their motivation – that other instinctual impulses of which he had remained in ignorance had cooperated in producing them. (Freud, 1919: 159–160)

I have chosen this text for its provocative value. We can already see the idea emerging of analysis as a laboratory. But Freud's positivism is redeemed by speculative thinking that prompts me to claim that our goal is the same – even if the technique described by Freud is not exactly the same as ours. In rereading this text, we can see that the process of separating out goes together with structural combination and that certain terms appear quite frequently in Freud's text: "elements", "instinctual impulses", "instinctual motives" (what sets in movement), "motivation" (what mobilizes). We can understand that it is necessary to break down or separate out what was initially compounded, according to the sequence: movement-combination-movement-separating out. Reference is made to "forces" (any idea of movement necessarily implies that of forces that animate it) that do not strive towards the same aim as that of psychology; in other words, that do not intervene at the level of the functioning of consciousness in the same way.

The reference to the chemist's approach may seem debatable, but it does not seem alien to the approach we take "genetically" when, rather than going from the simple to the complex, we go from the complex to the simple. The notion of cause is linked here to the notion of movement because it is a question of instinctual impulses. Freud was alluding on the one hand to the conscious and the unconscious and, on the other, to movement, motion; these two components would give birth to different psychoanalytic theories: those centred on the unconscious and those centred on the drives.

In another text, published in the *Encyclopaedia Britannica*, he wrote:

> [From the dynamic standpoint] psychoanalysis derives all mental processes (apart from the reception of external stimuli) from the interplay of forces, which assist or inhibit one another, combine with one another, enter into compromises with one another, etc. All of these forces are originally in the nature of *instincts*; thus they have an organic origin. They are characterized by possessing an immense (somatic) store of power ("the compulsion to repeat"); and they are represented mentally as images or ideas with an affective charge. In psychoanalysis, no less than in other sciences, the theory of the instincts is an obscure subject. (Freud, 1926: 265) (Freud's emphasis)

To sum up:

1. Psychic processes are traced back, as far as their origin is concerned, to forces, and considered as the result of the interplay of these forces.
2. This origin has its source in the body; the notion of psychic delegation – delegation of organic forces that have their source in the body – gives rise to "images or ideas with an affective charge".

Freud adds:

> An empirical analysis leads to the formulation of two groups of instincts: the so-called "ego-instincts", which are directed towards self-preservation, and the "object-instincts", which are concerned with relations to an external object. (ibid.)

The theory of Edith Jacobson, taken up by Otto Kernberg, was subsequently built around these concepts. It is worth noting, however, that Freud does not use the terms "*self*-representation" and "object-representation", but rather that of "instinct" (or drive). Moreover, in his work, he is only concerned with object-representation. He concludes:

> Theoretical speculation leads to the suspicion that there are two fundamental instincts which lie concealed behind the manifest ego-instincts and object-instincts; namely (a) Eros, the instinct which strives for ever closer union, and (b) the instinct of destruction, which leads towards the dissolution of what is living. (ibid.)

Two postulates may be inferred from this: one concerning what lies at the origin, that is, the identification of the psychic material psychoanalysis deals with (the object of psychoanalysis is precisely this psychic material and its transformations); the other concerning the search for what is hidden behind the appearances revealed by observation, which could be discussed at length. These postulates were progressively relativized, and then contested by those who came after Freud.

And yet, in the same text, Freud states that: "The most important conflict with which a small child is faced is his relation to his parents, the 'Oedipus Complex' . . ." (ibid.: 268). Note the contradiction: on the one hand, he proposes a logic that is expressed in terms of forces and, on the other, he favours, in connection with the Oedipus complex, a logic in terms of relations.

The question of origins after Freud

Subsequently, psychoanalysis was to call into question Freud's schema, beginning with the question of the primal, or of origins, which would be formulated roughly in these terms: is it really a matter of somatic, organic forces, of a primitive material that will give rise to psychic representations? – a biologically grounded question. Or is it a matter of relations between persons? – a psychologically grounded question that suggests the idea of an Oedipus complex from the outset (which Freud did not want). These questions call for answers whose consequences at the epistemological level analysts do not always fully appreciate. Psychoanalysis seems to have evolved over the course of time towards a "psychologizing" conception of the primal.

First period: Relativization of the drive

Initially, analysts did not dare touch the drive. They contented themselves with relativizing it, of attaching it to a corresponding term, a complementary factor, which could take on the most varied forms. We thus witnessed the emergence separately of the drive and the ego in Hartmann's work, the drive and the object-relation in Melanie Klein's work, the drive and the signifier in Lacan's work, and the drive and the process of integration and development in Winnicott's work. While the drive was thus relativized, it was not, for all that, rejected.

Second period: Mutation, taking a step back from biology

To counterbalance the disillusionment concerning the hopes Freud had placed in biology – no biological findings back up the hypothesis of the drive as Freud had described it – there was an attempt to redefine the relations between psychoanalysis and biology: some suggested rethinking them in terms of biological determinism and modifying psychoanalytic theory in this way (a current of thought developed in this direction within the IPA). Aware that it was necessary to be able to account for certain aspects of psychic functioning, some analysts distanced themselves from this approach by advancing the hypothesis of biological components that are not confined within the limits of biology (this is what I have called "metabiology").

Third period: The complete repudiation of biology

A more recent current of thought emerged with Heinz Kohut's conception of the *self*, opening the way for the most recent form of this theoretical evolution, namely, the theory of intersubjectivity (illustrated by Robert Stolorow, Ted Jacobs, Owen Renik, etc.), which goes hand in hand with a radical rejection of the metapsychological construction as a whole.

The question of origins thus gave rise to the rejection of the anchoring in the somatic postulated by the instinctual drive theory. Freud's approach was thus dropped in favour of an approach based on a new conception of psychic processes which no longer had anything to do with the notion of force or with an interplay of forces. The relational current of thought then occupied the foreground and manifested itself either in systematic studies (René Spitz, Margaret Mahler, Adolph Stern), or in a reversal of the Freudian hypothesis (take for example the project of Laplanche, who, with his theory of generalized seduction, establishes the source-object in the place of the instinctual drive organic source; this substitution is supposed to transcend the questions raised by Freud's theory, while, in reality, what is involved is a reversal of his hypothesis).

Once the biologizing dimension has been rejected, psychoanalysis is not for all that left without foundations, even though it does not always distinguish itself very clearly from a "psychologizing" process. A great deal of latitude is given to psychology with the precise aim of ensuring that the dimension of meaning in relationships prevails.

The question of the subject arises in a veiled form; I do not think, however, that it is necessarily linked to psychology, as in theories of intersubjectivity, for example. Lacan, for his part, was never restrained in his criticisms concerning the advent of the *homo psychologicus*, which he even considered to be a true catastrophe. He was the first to denounce the error of "psychologizing" approaches. "When will someone show me a signifier without signification?" he asked. This shows that Lacan cannot be classified among the ranks of the subjectivists or of those who, by rejecting the biologizing hypothesis, brought grist to the mill of psychology.

Other conceptions of the unconscious

The developmental approach

A current of thought to which a large number of analysts have rallied focused on a developmental approach – common to Anna Freud and

Melanie Klein, even though the latter's theory of observation could not be more "mythological". From the moment Melanie Klein envisaged the two major positions (paranoid-schizoid and depressive) and suggested the possibility of moving from one to the other – even though she was drawing on a completely different theory of origins – she was placing herself within the framework of the developmental approach. Nevertheless, it seems to me that her hypotheses are interesting, particularly the mechanisms of defence of the paranoid-schizoid position (splitting, projective identification, denial, idealization) and those of the depressive position (reparation).

In the wake of this approach, we saw the birth of movements based on observation – the method of Esther Bick, among others. It is astounding to see how psychoanalysts ask themselves few questions about their impasses! Thus the adepts of "observation" have never looked into the differences between the conceptions and conclusions of Mahler, Stern, Lebovici, Bick and Winnicott, who all practice observation, in their own way.

These methods are based on an ideological hypothesis of the observer. It is clear that abandoning the reference to the drive has not resolved the problem of finding a common meaning around which researchers could rally.

Kleinian theory, for its part, has neglected something important by suggesting that the motor of development is purely negative, because it consists in trying to neutralize archaic anxieties or to overcome destructive tendencies. According to this theory, its dynamism is not a result of the quest for pleasure, of attractions and fixations to the object; consequently, neither sexuality nor pleasure play any role in it. This amounts to saying that there is no motor, or, if there is one, it works without fuel – except when it comes to warding off the monsters of the past.

The advocates of Kleinism claimed to reach greater depths, at archaic levels. If I trust my experience and that of my colleagues – after all, it is the only material of psychoanalytic observation on which we can rely – nothing allows us to assert that people who have undergone a Kleinian analysis behave differently from those who have chosen another way, or that they are less exposed to regressive or pathological forms of behaviour. I have never considered that they show greater lucidity regarding themselves or that their insights seem more profound during shared exchanges. The results of Kleinian analyses are in no case better than those of other forms of analysis; decompensations are just as frequent, and their limitations are just as noticeable as those that can be identified in any other approach.

The reversal of the drive

A very different conception, that of Jean Laplanche, puts the emphasis on interhuman relations, whose specificity, in his view, is not sufficiently elucidated in Freudian theory. For him, the communication of meaning always has a whiff of alienation about it. The Other – a Lacanian concept – takes the place of the drive source. The Other (it is important to appreciate the difference that this concept establishes in comparison with the classical concept of the "object") is above all a vector of meaning, the vector of an enigmatic meaning, first and foremost for itself. It is the enigma that has the function of thrust and that justifies the thrust of development: what the concept of the drive teaches us is ignored. While this results in an enrichment of communication, on the other hand the notion of force is discarded. This criticism of force is generalized under the pretext that force is a simplifying factor of the psyche. In my opinion, quite the opposite is true!

The open, non-metapsychological approach

I am referring here to the creation of a different analytic style, one that is allusive, light, almost ungraspable, corresponding to the image of an unconscious that needs to be approached delicately because it is always elusive and evanescent. According to this approach, the unconscious is only sensitive to work that proceeds by delicate touches, which seems to me to be debatable, and the psychic constructions that it inspires are random. Whether it be the Other or the Stranger, it is nonetheless "an" other; it is not an other in me, but the exact contrary. In reality, we are dealing here with a logic of the preconscious that does without the notion of organization and gives rise to the elaboration of structures associated more with the novel or the story than with a metapsychological vision (J.-B. Pontalis): one moves around a nucleus that is forever inaccessible and keeps the reader in the mystery of what is uncertain. The risk of being mistaken is thus avoided because one is always elsewhere.

Putting theories of representation to the test

Why does the analysis of ideational contents (*représentations*) not suffice in itself? What justification is there for hanging on to this antiquity in the form of the drive? "Psychic delegation gives rise to images or ideas with an affective charge", Freud tells us. So why do we not satisfy ourselves with that? For several reasons:

1. "It is not presuppositions that I defend", Freud writes, "but the latest conclusions of analysis". In other words, it is not hypothetical starting positions (Bion's alpha function, for example), but rather what Freud noticed throughout his long experience and the reflections that arose from them. There is no fundamental difference between his deductions and ours today. For me, we cannot do without the notion of force: without it, a good many psychoanalytic concepts would become unthinkable, in particular, those of fixation, resistance, transference,

repetition and the compulsion to repeat. No theory grounded exclusively in representations can account for it; this ensemble of concepts cannot be reduced to psychology and absolutely calls for the *energetic* and *economic* notion of force[2] as the vector of a signifying potentiality that can be characterized by quantitative power and the capacity for transformation.

2. The theories of representation elaborated by Freud, at the beginning and then throughout the period that covers the field of practice of the first topography, have been put to the test subsequently; borderline cases, narcissistic structures, character neuroses and psychosomatic structures have led to the emergence of a new clinical practice. I am not saying that it is necessary to go down this route – as I am sometimes said to have claimed – but I think that it is indispensable to take it into account when the time comes to elaborate a general theory of the mind, and even more so of psychoanalytic technique. This approach has given birth, among others, to the concept of "void" and of "default trauma" and has made it possible to conceptualize the cathexis of what I have called "negative narcissism", notions that have their roots in Freud even if they were not developed by him.

3. As early as *Mourning and Melancholia*, Freud (1917 [1915]) was reflecting on object- cathexes and conceived of the presence, in mourning, of a mechanism that is not linked solely to the fate of representations. The notion of destructiveness could no longer be considered as contingent or secondary in psychoanalytic theory (Kernberg has placed great emphasis on this point). What interests me more particularly is the effect of destructiveness – not to be confused with aggressiveness – on thought processes and the sphere of representations. Even without drawing on the concept of the death drive, destructiveness must be thought of not as a mere externalized manifestation but as *a destruction of thought processes*. Melanie Klein herself did not throw any light on this; it was necessary to wait for Bion to draw all the consequences of it. This was how psychoanalysis evolved.

4. We cannot fail to take an interest in the phenomenon of the extension of the field of experience constituted by what lies outside psychoanalysis. Even if we are not in the position of experts and, consequently, are not able to respond to it, we cannot abstain from reflecting on the matter. As is suggested in *Civilization and its Discontents* (Freud, 1930), the drive is also active in the social domain; we cannot do without it in psychoanalytic theory, even if the latter is concerned with the intrapsychic. For lack of time, I will simply point out that this calls for a transformation of the theory of representation.

---

2 It seems that biology has just proved the existence of such energy at work in cellular "motors".

The epistemological aporia

In our practice we are faced with the formidable paradox of having to find meaning and of elaborating it on the basis of formations that are *apparently* meaningless. This observation applies, generally speaking, both to the unconscious in its most superficial forms and to the pathological manifestations that resist analysis the most. The methods by which we try to interpret a meaning differ from those that we generally use.

Psychoanalysis cannot base its practice on intuitive meaning and logical meaning; it has to break with ordinary modes of understanding. It is important therefore to define the principles of an adequate method. It is not enough to start from common sense, to make a critique of it and to identify a rational principle in it in terms of unconscious desire – there would be a lot that could be said, moreover, about what was accepted under the dictatorship of reason by Freud himself! Quite clearly, modern theories of complexity no longer allow us to think in this way. We cannot content ourselves, therefore, with following common sense, but must make a detour. We cannot be satisfied with a meaning that originates in the emitter and reaches the recipient intact, as traditional theories of communication claim. We have to find the means to break this spontaneous intelligibility, while at the same time eschewing the elegant paraphrase of theoretical language.

Another logic is therefore necessary. But how is it to be defined? Are we faced here with an aporia at the epistemological level? The domain that is the object of psychoanalysis cannot be approached by the usual instrument of knowledge, namely, by the ego. As the means that the latter has at its disposal are not adapted to knowledge of this hypothetical domain, this domain can only be described through opposition – through the negative, therefore, as Freud indicates in his *New Introductory Lectures on Psychoanalysis*: "What little we know of [the id] is of a negative character and can only be described as a contrast to the ego" (Freud, 1933: 73). It is a matter of thinking the unthinkable, of relinquishing the ego, which requires a sacrifice that is far from easy. I have always admired Freud's lucidity: with simple formulations, he expresses truths of very great significance. In writing this new lecture, Freud knew very well that what he was going to say about the ego and the superego would be much more readily accepted than what he had to say about the id. One cannot seduce with the id but one can get round the difficulty or circumvent it with the ego. "The ego", he writes, "can . . . observe itself, criticize itself, and do Heaven knows what with itself" (ibid.: 58).

The concept of "frame"

The mutation represented, at the theoretical level, by the reference to the "frame" – associated with the names of José Bleger, Donald Winnicott, Jean-Luc Donnet and Willy Baranger – should now appear more clearly, and that is precisely what I am aiming at. Modern epistemology teaches us that the definition of an object depends on how it is divided up. The object is never given as such; its division reveals the reality of which it is the analogon. But if it is only a "commodity", how will we make it appear?

The frame is a field of forces; what does it show? It makes it possible to become aware of the force that manifests itself first in the form of the transference, a non-univocal phenomenon: transference that refers to the past, transference that emerges from the present, *here-and-now perhaps, but transference that is transport*. I have described the transference as a double act in two parts that take place within a single operation: "transference onto speech" and "transference onto the object". The act of verbalization translates all the psychic movements that carry within them something that is not in the nature of speech but that infiltrates it and carves out a path for itself through it. Affect finds a space for expression there. Speech, which is movement, is inhabited by force; thus it cannot be reduced to meaning. In short, this is what I mean when I speak of transference onto speech. As for transference onto the object, everyone knows what is involved. I will therefore not dwell on that.

The particular position of the analyst in the transference reflects several contradictions: he is there and he is not there; he is both present and absent. He offers himself as a paradoxical object that is both seductive – in terms of the offer of seduction evoked by Jean Laplanche – and in the background, refusing to take responsibility for what he has partly created. His role consists in capturing the meaning and in giving it form.

The frame provides a space whose relatively constant characteristics make it possible to observe the effects of this non-encounter – that is to say the inaccessibility of the object of the transference, the impossibility of, or prohibition against, using the analyst to satisfy one's own desires or to serve those of the analyst. The aim consists in impeding the lifting of forces whose only destiny is to become "images or ideas psychically charged with affect". Owing to the obligations (fundamental rule) and prohibitions (prohibition against contact and acting out), this interplay of forces, conceived by Freud, becomes, during certain moments of the transference, noticeable for the analyst, if not for both protagonists; at that moment it is no longer only a hypothesis. The analyst may fail to recognize it, however, if he is prey to a countertransference resistance that isolates him from his patient.

The forces that govern the elaboration of the scenario of projection have an inestimable power of dramatization. The field of forces that the subject is permitted to express through speech, but which he is forbidden to act out, makes it possible to evaluate his capacities for representation and elaboration through verbalization. The frame thus makes it possible for the analysand's "private madness" to manifest itself: it throws light on his capacity to stage his personal dramaturgy. Through an examination of the relations between the images or ideas, it also shows how his intrapsychic and intersubjective relations are intertwined. Finally, it reveals the system of cathexes as well as the different forms of anti-cathexis and decathexis. Better than any other means, it makes it possible to approach the mechanisms furthest away from the ego – those of "private madness". The frame represents, as it were, the device – or the "laboratory", to use Freud's expression – which, thanks to the control that it offers (evaluation of the transference and of the process by the analyst in the constant and limited time of the session), allows for the transitory manifestation of those aspects of the personality over which the ego has least control.

This method obviously implies a judgement on the value of the ideas or images: their more or less communicative function, their force of impact, their energetic charge – close to an explosion of acting out or to a loss of reality-testing, when they take the form of a *passage à l'acte*, hallucination, depersonalization or somatization. The ordeal of the session is facilitated by the reliability of the analyst (guardian of the frame), his tolerance for the analysand's projections, his perception of the danger presented by outbreaks of regressive tendencies for the analytic situation, his appreciation of the moment of interpretation (and of its target) and, finally, his way of responding to its effects.

Throughout this process, force oscillates on the one hand between its representation and its anti-cathexis and, on the other, between its representational elaboration through language and its capacity to engender thought. This cognition, which is never cut off from its instinctual drive and affective sources, tends towards "thirdness", opening out onto both another space and another time, from the here-and-now of the session. This process allows us to consider the analytic situation as a return to oneself via the detour of a similar other; this movement illustrates precisely the trajectory of force tracing the path of representations. The psychoanalyst will have to capture the effects of this force that wants to take possession of the object, to grasp the effects of meaning that emerge from the relationship marked by a double incapacity (impossibility and prohibition) and, finally, to transform the demand for pleasure into the satisfaction of recognizing what determines the demand and what makes it possible to preserve the object differently. The link is maintained and transformation of the relations to the object becomes possible because its "consumption" has been avoided. We can then distinguish between what is representable and what remains unrepresentable, and sift out the relationship between what is knowable and what is unknowable in the psyche through the relationship to the other.

It is a matter of approaching the "psychic delegations" in the form of "images or ideas with an affective charge" thanks to an adequate frame – fundamental rule, free association and evenly suspended attention – in order to go back to their prototypes and to account for everything that a theory of the ego cannot explain. Hence the need for a theory of what is not ego in its most radical form, that which covers the functions of the id on the one hand and of the object on the other. It should not be concluded, however, that these representations are simply the domain of "another" psychology; rather, they are an attempt to account for the latest results of analysis.

Experience teaches us that three majors parameters can favour the disturbance of psychic forces: psychosis (due to hallucination and the effect of fragmentation), psychosomatics (due to the danger of somatization) and psychopathy (due to the *passage à l'acte* and acting out). We can therefore conclude that the frame provides a model that reveals its properties as well as its deficiencies, that is to say its limits.

Psychoanalytic psychotherapies

There are thus situations in which the frame cannot be established, which means that other solutions have to be found. We resort to psychoanalytic psychotherapies, for example, when the frame necessary for analysis cannot be set up; freedom is more limited and the conditions of analysability are modified. If the defences are in danger of collapsing, the detour via the similar other makes the conflict tolerable; it cannot, however, be integrated because meaning cannot be understood through the transference relationship and then reintegrated by the subject. The distance required in order to forget the presence of the other, to put the person of the analyst between parentheses, is lacking; yet such distance is necessary for analysis to gravitate towards classical models.

We are dealing here with a pathology of the encounter, unlike a pathology in which one reproduces unwittingly something that has already taken place. The actuality of the encounter becomes, then, the essential concern of the session of psychotherapy, and psychotherapy, the exercise of the process of internalization in its actuality – or rather, it is the process of internalization that takes place in the session and not work on something that has already been internalized. In the work of psychotherapy, which is at the limits of the analysable, the analyst must first have internalized the frame so that it is always present, even if it cannot be applied; it will serve as a reference in relation to which the analyst will analyse what he is doing (analysis of the analysis and not of the transference or countertransference alone). Once the frame has been internalized, the emergence of what hinders the process of internalization – not only repression or splitting but destructiveness – appears more clearly. The therapeutic work must lead the patient to become aware of the destructiveness that he directs against his own psychic activity.[3] Far from detracting from it, these elaborations seem to me to broaden the significance of Freudian theory.

---

3 I have described, under the term "internalization of the negative", mechanisms of this order (Green, 2011 [2010]).

Face-to-face, shadow-free

The impossibility of establishing an analytic frame with certain patients inevitably favours the construction of a theory of presence, perception and acting out. The experience acquired in the course of sessions with "heavy cases" teaches us that the object can only be apprehended when it is perceived. The analyst's shadow-free presence thus seems necessary. The object is there – it's him and no other – it is not a representative, at least not immediately. Symbolization is thus more restricted.

However, with these patients, the object is never perceived as such but in terms of their own psychic reality, the internal roots of which they are largely unaware. Perception functions like hallucination: between the internal object and the external object, no likeness can be discerned. In other words, the transference is barely interpretable. An adequate apportionment between material reality and psychic reality seems to be lacking. Such a distinction requires acceptance and recognition of the unconscious, that is, a certain form of figurability in relation to the Other, to the object, to the drive, which could be formulated as follows: *from the moment it is in me, it is necessarily also me.*

The presence of the object at the perceptual level implies the possibility of returning to the object in its reality, without any projection, and sometimes permits a reinforcement of the denial of the trace which is inseparable from the principle of negative hallucination and also, perhaps, from that of repression. The failure of the trace becomes that of the corollary failure of psychic reality.

The role of fantasy in these patients seems, moreover, uncertain; they are only interested in what is real and imagination is only stirred in relation to "realizable" references. The detour via the similar other is thus not in the order of the imaginary, but belongs to the confusion of a relationship between communication with the other and communication with oneself (the unknown in oneself has to pass through the perception of the interlocutor, but it is often "objectivized" so as to be neutralized).

Faced with the masochism (infiltrated by perversion, narcissistic injury and the denial of reality) that inhabits these patients, the analytic treatment becomes anti-therapeutic, favouring the onset of the negative therapeutic reaction. Furthermore, the disappearance of the object at the end of the session erases its traces, which cancels out the effect of *insight* that may have occurred. In this case, meaning is not sufficient to create an effect: acts are necessary. The absence of symbolization forces the analyst to repeat himself, acts (verbal) that are sometimes accepted and sometimes rejected by the patient in an impulsive and violent way. The obsession with transformation into acts, in Freud, which is supposed to replace remembering, becomes clearer; the "model of the act" put forward by Bion to explain the failure of verbal thought could be substituted for it advantageously, since here even words become acts.

Following Winnicott, I think that it is necessary to "cease psychoanalytically to be a psychoanalyst" when the circumstances require it. This is not just a joke. This paradox seems to me, on the contrary, to be very important, because it invites us to give up the direct aim of analysis without, however, ceasing to maintain a psychoanalytic relationship. The creation of a "transitional field" requires the analyst to be able to be touched by the patient's gaze, so that the patient in turn can cathect what, within him, can be touched by the analyst.

It has to be admitted that, notwithstanding the object's presence, silence risks provoking the decathexis of the internal object. It remains to be understood what happens when the object – present and yet absent – strives to favour the incorporation of a presence with the aim of potentially being conserved in spite of its absence, during and after the session. This is Winnicott's famous notion of the "capacity to be alone in the presence of the mother". From this point of view, analytic psychotherapy seeks less to track down the trauma upstream than its internalization downstream.

Resistances of the analyst

The force of resistance inherent in any attempt to modify the ego – to which Freud (1937) refers in *Analysis Terminable and Interminable* – turns out to be a resistance to internalization. The internalization of the frame by the analyst is aimed at fending against this insufficiency. The most difficult task for a patient in the analytic situation is to be able to see himself not only as a person or a subject but also as a field of forces, that is, as the point from which the subject will emerge through the creation of psychically cathected representations – which gives meaning a carnal, instinctual drive cathexis.

The analyst's identity depends on his capacity to go back and forth between the various representative modalities, to make the transition between the inside and the outside, what is real and what is fantasy, in order to constitute the symbolic (Lacan). The different responsibilities of the analyst's activity involve a movement back and forth between two parameters: the internalized frame and the current session of face-to-face psychotherapy, in which a process unfolds that facilitates internalization in the here-and-now. I propose an alternation between recentring (analysis in the analytic situation) and decentring (analysis in the context in which the analytic situation cannot be established).

One question remains unresolved: How is the frame internalized? This was a question Freud asked himself in a somewhat ironic fragment of *Analysis Terminable and Interminable*:

> But where and how is the poor wretch to acquire the ideal qualifications which he will need in this profession? The answer is, in the analysis of himself, with which his preparation for his future activity begins. (1937: 248)

This observation retains all its significance today. The only way for the future analyst to internalize the frame is to undergo a very thorough analysis himself in order to be able to appreciate its effects and, eventually, if he feels the need to do so, to renew the experience later on in order to go further or to surmount blockages. The importance of the frame can never be stressed enough: it is the stage that makes it possible to imagine the interplay, the intersubjective relations, the forces and the production of the representative registers that belong to the body, language, the Other, and the work of thought and abstraction. In the end, if analysts want to overcome the crisis in which they find themselves, they will only be able to do so by doing as thorough a personal analysis as possible, with everything that implies in terms of investment, outside institutional life, so that it remains a private adventure. In my view, this is the programme on which we need to reflect. Pathways must be established between the centre of psychoanalysis and the limits of what is analysable, and thinking must be forced to move between contradictory polarities in order to respond to the necessity of forming a picture today of the true nature of analytic practice, while taking into account the full scope of its field and the varieties of situations offered by experience.

References

Freud, S. (1917 [1915]). *Mourning and Melancholia*. S.E. 14. London: Hogarth, pp. 237–260.

Freud, S. (1918). *From the History of an Infantile Neurosis*. S.E. 17. London: Hogarth, pp. 7–122.

Freud, S. (1919). *Lines of Advance in Psycho-Analytic Therapy*. S.E. 17. London: Hogarth, pp. 159–168.

Freud, S. (1926). *Psycho-Analysis*. S.E. 20. London: Hogarth, pp. 263–270.

Freud, S. (1930). *Civilization and its Discontents*. S.E. 21. London: Hogarth, pp. 57–146.

Freud, S. (1933). *New Introductory Lectures on Psychoanalysis*. S.E. 22. London: Hogarth, pp. 1–182.

Freud, S. (1937). *Analysis Terminable and Interminable*. S.E. 23. London: Hogarth, pp. 209–254.

Green, A. (1991). Méconnaissance de l'inconscient: Science and psychanalyse. In: Dorey, R. (Ed.), *L'inconscient et la science*. Paris: Dunod, pp. 140–220.

Green, A. (2011 [2010]). *Illusions and Disillusions of Psychoanalytic Work*, trans. A. Weller. London: Karnac.

Green, A., Kernberg, O., et al. (2000). *L'avenir d'une disillusion*. Paris: Presses Universitaires de France.

7 Dismembering the countertransference

What we have gained and lost with the extension of the countertransference[1] (1997)

Anyone who wants to enter the dark forest of the countertransference must accept that they will go astray before finding their way. At first glance, no notion should be more familiar to the analyst, since it is he himself whom he must question and not the stranger that the analysand remains. It may seem simpler to engage in a subjective analysis, a self-analysis, than to analyse the psychic life of another person. But experience soon teaches us that this is not so. This is more than a paradox, rather a fundamental teaching of our practice. The analysis of the unknown that inhabits us, that we are for ourselves, the analysis of that part of our psyche called the unconscious, is more difficult to gain access to than the unconscious of the patient: the latter, at least, can take the avenues of the transference. Let us say that by exposing itself, the analysand's subjectivity becomes "objectified" for the analyst, because the object that it becomes gives him the opportunity to go out of himself in order to meet it. However, he knows that in order to understand it, he will have to give up his own subjectivity and allow himself to be possessed by the strangeness induced by the analysand that he will have to recognize, while preserving his ability to communicate. We see the extent to which he will be caught between the danger, when he considers the other as a stranger, of leaving intact a singularity from which he wishes to keep his distance, and the reverse danger, of seeing what he thinks he understands of the other in relation to himself, through an abusive appropriation.

This is what makes the analyst's position difficult: analysing two objects at once, the patient's transference and his own countertransference. On this last point, I must admit that nothing authenticates this way of seeing ourselves, which sometimes colludes with what we would like

---

1 This chapter was first presented as a paper at the Palermo Franco-Italian Colloquium in 1997. It was published in J.-J. Baranes, F. Sacco and A. Green (Eds.) (2002). *Inventer en psychanalyse: Construire et interpréter*. Paris: Dunod, pp. 131–161. It also appears in A. Green (2012) *La clinique psychanalytique contemporaine*. Paris: Ithaques, pp. 79–105. Translated into English by Andrew Weller for this edition.

to leave in the shade. Freud himself recognized, as early as 1897, that if self-analysis was possible, ultimately analysis would become superfluous. In that case it would be necessary to rely on analytical practice, in the absence of a second analysis, to obtain a more convincing result. This position has been defended, although it is difficult to accept that analysis of the transference no longer occupies the primary place. Countertransference, unlike other elements, affects the analyst in the most intimate aspects of himself – something that goes beyond his professional identity and can reach to the very roots of his being. Moreover, the literature shows that most of those who had a vocation to contribute to the advancement of our theory approached this subject without reaching a consensus. The difficulty encountered by any analyst in elucidating what the countertransference is for him has provoked such an abundance of writings that it is impossible for me to make an exhaustive review of them here.

Luisa de Urtubey, however, tried to do so in the report presented in 1994, at the Congress of French-speaking psychoanalysts. I can only refer those who wish to study this problem more deeply to that report. They will find in it the essential contributions that have marked the history of this issue.

The theme of the countertransference has, however, been the subject of a recent revival which provides an opportunity for radical questioning. A few years ago, the movement called "intersubjectivity" was born in the United States. The origins of this trend go far back. Intersubjectivity brings together a group of analysts, some of whom are products of Heinz Kohut's *Self* psychology, but who wish to go further. Its principal representatives are Robert Stollorow, James McLaughlin, Judith Fingert Chused, Ted Jacobs and in particular Owen Renik. On the initiative of Davide Lopez (1997), the magazine *Gli Argonauti* published, in a bilingual Italian-American edition, the positions of some representatives of American psychoanalysis who hold these opinions, and these were widely discussed. In this latest development of psychoanalysis across the Atlantic, what is attributed to the countertransference is pushed so far that it seems to eclipse the role of transference.

The intersubjective dispute

When in 1995, at the Amsterdam Congress of the International Psychoanalytical Association, I was asked to discuss a contribution by Theodore J. Jacobs, I did not realize that my critique was addressed to one of the most prominent representatives of a recent analytical movement in the United States. In his presentation, Jacobs showed how, during a session, his own personality resurfaced through his more or less distant affects and memories from childhood, and how, in his positive and negative responses to the patient, his own fantasies and identifications predominated. It was not the first time I had seen these mechanisms described. Some of Thomas

H. Ogden's contributions had focused on similar phenomena. After the event, it seemed to me that my objections focused less on the facts evoked than on their interpretation. Ogden used the phenomena that appeared during the session to show that they belonged to the unconscious owing to their unexpected and surprising emergence, before reintegrating them with the ideas or images evoked by the analysand's discourse and connecting them to a current that had initially been discarded. The difference between his and Jacobs' technique was noticeable but not easy to specify. Everything became clear for me when I understood the interactive perspective to which Ogden subscribed: rightly or wrongly, I was reminded of the interpersonal dimension of mother-child observations. Since then, this impression has been largely confirmed.

The importance given here to the countertransference is not reduced either to the elucidation of disruptive factors in the treatment, nor to the necessity of their being taken into consideration in the session. It is a complete reformulation of the psychoanalytical experience, in which the basic assumptions of the treatment are challenged. One has the feeling that, for the proponents of this approach, the movements of the transference derive less from the patient himself, but rather from the preconscious perception of the countertransference – in fact, from the analyst's transference onto the analysand. No analyst will dispute having encountered similar cases, but most often we interpret them as the result of a difficulty of the analysis in progress. But here, beyond the examples attached to this situation, the conclusions are applied generally to the whole analytical process. The tendency, especially in Great Britain, to only make *here-and-now* transference interpretations leads analysts to advocate listening "for the transference". The whole analysis is offset by this paradigm since the analyst's listening calls in return for the "counter-listening" of the patient,[2] whose material is interpreted in relation to this organizing parameter.

Intersubjectivity conceives of the analytic situation as a psychic field constructed by two reciprocal interpersonal worlds that include the unconscious life and the empathic or containing capacities of the participants: "Each becomes part of the psychic reality of the other" (Fogel, 1997).

This definition fixes the functional identity of the partners; the nature of their exchange is a living relationship between two "real" people, "doing things together that are meaningful". The partners are linked by interpersonal relationships and interact with one another. Knowledge results from interpretation, due to the *insight* which arises from it. Oratorical precautions barely conceal the dilution of the density of the analytic exchange, under cover of a style of thought, which, despite its "intentional" theoretical endorsement, seems to be inherited from a model of what I will call the

---

2 This should not be confused with the thesis of listening to interpretations (Faimberg, 1996), which remains the analysis of the return of the effects of the interpretation.

psychic "behaviour" of the surface effects of speech. The disappearance of the ordinary parameters of analysis (drive impulses, unconscious fantasies, more or less deep anxieties) and, especially, the lack of precision concerning the elements of the representative register, in favour of "enactment", give the impression that there is an idealization of the heuristic value of the model attributing a communicative function to the act. The concept of enactment trivializes former measures of prevention against acting out. Joseph Sandler (1976) had previously described the case of the analysand who pushes the analyst to respond to the analytic situation occasionally by accepting to play a role, which, in English, is called *acting*. In the conception of intersubjectivity, everything is interpreted from this angle as inevitable and even desirable.

Under the influence of the "new Kleinians" (led by Betty Joseph), it has become commonplace to account for material by talking about what the patient "does" to the analyst, implying that the analyst considers thinking as an equivalent of acting; this goes as far as imagining that the analysand seeks through what he communicates to influence the analyst and to dictate to him what he would like to make him think. So we have gone from a figure of speech to a movement in reality: enactment. Giving a satisfactory definition of this term is not very easy. Sometimes, it seems that its use designates what a subject expresses through his actions – which is intelligible not from making deductions from the ideas that are attributed to him, but from what he shows through his behaviour, even to the point of inducing the analyst to play a role. We thus see that this meaning goes beyond "acting out" and bypasses the register of speech. In fact, "enactment" is the result of interactions between two subjects. We perceive implicitly that the role of the interactive model is to place the act in a privileged position in the exchange.

We are faced with a curious mixture of lucidity and naivety: authenticity, the exposure of the analyst's feelings, and the adoption of a "real" role on his part are advocated, all from the analysis of his personal *reactions*. It is almost no longer legitimate to use the term "countertransference", since the reference to the transference has itself taken a back seat. It is a question of contesting – backed up by scientific data – Freud's fundamental hypotheses. We cannot deny the role played by models outside psychoanalysis. Thus, after the impact of the theories of Ferdinand de Saussure and then of Noam Chomsky, which marked Jacques Lacan's thought, it is around linguistic pragmatics (Austin, Searle) that the conceptions of language of certain analysts meet who are not in the Lacanian lineage, since there is talk of "speech acts". The performative becomes a general scenario since "saying is doing". From there, slipping to "making the analyst do" as the neo-Kleinians claim, is easy to imagine.

What becomes of Freud's *Agieren*? It is drowned in the general case. One thing is sure: from this viewpoint, representation is dethroned since it is included in the act. Fantasies are sometimes acted out or, as they say, actualized. Is it the same thing? I do not have time, within the limits of this presentation, to undertake a detailed theoretical examination of this issue.

However, we can mention the contribution of their leader, Owen Renik (1993). According to him, the analyst's subjectivity is not negotiable, he is in the position of an "observer-participant". This status, long recognized in the human sciences, derives from the relationship of uncertainty described by Heisenberg in physics. This is confirmed in analysis, since the parameters identifiable in the analyst are numerous, poorly defined and complex. As we see, Renik disputes the plausibility of a benevolent neutrality and rejects the role that imagination or thought play as prerequisites for action. The analyst, whether he likes it or not, is caught in a system of acts; more precisely, interactions that must be acknowledged and used.

Awareness of countertransference is always retrospective – it comes *after* the countertransference enactment. The tendency to adopt a behavioural model is clearly visible. Awareness, it is claimed, follows the self-perception of a behavioural manifestation. These manifestations may go unnoticed because of their faintness; however, the source of the analysis of the countertransference lies in the sometimes imperceptible outcropping of preconscious acts, which is referred to as "micro-activity". The image of two psychic realities present together is a matter of behaviour, the representation being obscured or posterior to the enacted expression. What grounds this analytical conception is in fact a revision of the theory of the relationship between the mind and thought.

For Renik, thinking is an attempted act of behaviour involving motor activity on a very small scale; an idea that recalls the "philosophies of the mind" based on neuroscience. In fact, these ideas are not so far removed from Freud's theory of small quantities "palpating" the outer world. But, in Freud's case, it is the confrontation of this minimal perceptual activity with the different modes of representation that governs relationships.

On reading them, one sometimes has the impression that the real opponent of the intersubjectivists is Heinz Hartmann; however, their arguments do not spare Freud, to whom they make the same reproaches. Two ideas are at the root of this trend: interaction and interpersonality. This position, in reaction to Freudian solipsism, does not however opt for the theory of object-relations; it prefers to conceive an exchange of actions between two subjects, each of them being inclined to *react* to the other. In fact, they turn away from the idea of interiority, all knowledge of this type being random and marked by the uncertainty hanging over its hypothetical contents. Surface effects are clearly preferred to it, as if the deliberately superficial study of a relationship between two subjectivities presented undeniable advantages over the speculations concerning the "interiority" of one of them. But I suppose that the idea of superficiality will be rejected and that the partisans of this tendency will see themselves as being faithful to the exploration of the depths of the psyche that they will approach from the angle of the exchanges between the partners of the analytical couple; hence the idea of equal levels of competence between the two partners.

What is the purpose of the analyst's personal analysis? According to this perspective, it changes the conception of interpretation. Each of the two protagonists attributes intentions and deeds to the other. All the classic recommendations warning against the subjective shifts of the analyst are therefore ineffective; they cannot be avoided "even for a moment" (Renik, 1993). Ultimately, this *intersubjectivity* or these "interactions" lead to a certain scepticism and the conclusion that an analyst cannot, ultimately, know the point of view of the patient, an analyst can only know his own point of view (Renik, 1993).

Strictly speaking, such an observation should lead to the impossibility of analysis. No argument could save it from the objection: surely this fight against Freud's solipsism has only succeeded in supporting the solipsism of every analyst. This objection will be overcome by implicitly defending the concept of a two-sided reality: the countertransference of one person is the result of the empathy of another, or the countertransference enactment is the correct interpretation given to another person. The criticism of objectivity is not unfounded when one thinks of analysts who have lined up under the banner of *the science of psychoanalysis*, but is radical subjectivism the right answer? The idea of an unconscious determination of the countertransference is reduced to an intention on the analyst's part of not being conscious of it. Is this compatible with the theory of causality based on purely unconscious determinations? The choice of the deliberate abandonment of self-control is not posited here as the precondition for a quest for messages emerging from the deepest parts of consciousness. It is limited to the simple reception of the messages in the direct exchange, being satisfied with listening to the surface psychic phenomena.

It is undeniable that Freud, like some of his successors, can be reproached for a certain analytical authoritarianism. But should we support "equality" between the analyst's and the patient's point of view? This strictly synchronic vision threatens the very heart of the notion of transference, which is linked to a diachronic dimension. This concerns the reliving of affects originating in childhood and resulting from the relationship with the desired or fought against, loved, admired, envied or hated parent owing to the very fact of the gap between the generations, which led to the repression of these forbidden feelings. The erasure of the generation gap leads to the disappearance of repression. What can we say about splitting? I have not forgotten the remarks of Serge Viderman (1970) on the construction of the analytic space, and his insistence on the newness of transference communication. It cannot be said, however, that the idea of equality between the analysand's and the analyst's points of view arises from this.

When advocating the adoption of the patient's point of view or "vantage point" (Schwaber, 1992), and therefore abandoning that of the analyst, the role of the analyst's identification with the analysand in the most classical form of analysis is overlooked. Moreover, no distinction is made between the "point of view" of the analyst as a person and that deduced from the analysis of the transference which is at another level. The analyst is himself an integral part of the analytic function, which requires a subjective decentring away from the conscious thoughts that the situation arouses in him. His receptivity to the transference implies a renunciation of what could alter his "benevolent neutrality". It is therefore wrong to speak of a "point of view of the analyst", because what is involved is something quite different: the communication of the analyst with his own unconscious at work gives rise to a specific mode of thought that is the result of his willingness to abandon a particular point of view and to be surprised by what he did not expect. The identification of unconscious determinations is accompanied by an openness of thought necessary to reveal undetected factors that influence the course of psychic events. Here it seems there is a difficulty in admitting that the specific processes of the analysis are situated far from the conditions of their observation.

Most of these propositions were seeds in Kohut's *Self* psychology, expressing his sympathy for a phenomenological approach. Their subsequent development foreshadowed an orientation of psychoanalytic therapy based on the analyst's approval.

It is not a question of defending either an "analytical democracy" respectful of the "point of view" of the patient, or an autocratic relationship of the "subject who is supposed to know" (Lacan, 1975), but rather a question of basing the rules of analytic technique on a theory defining its object. The goal is always to allow the patient to have better access to his unconscious and to increase his autonomy. But this movement lacks a consistent theory of relations between the intrapsychic and the intersubjective.

To achieve this, it may be necessary to take a step backwards and consider the solutions that other currents of psychoanalysis have tried to bring forward.

Contradictions

Glenn Gabbard (1995), striving to get to grips with the whole question, saw the countertransference as the response to the search for that *common ground* about which Robert S. Wallerstein (1995) had raised questions. However, this desperate rescue effort was only a counter-shot in the United States against the dissemination of theories in which relationists, socio-constructivists, mutualists, relativists, perspectivists and, of course, subjectivists, confronted each other, not to mention the modernists and post-modernists and finally, more recently, positivists. I would be incapable of providing an answer if I were asked what ideas relate to each of these terms. What I think I can say is that North American psychoanalysis, which had long kept itself at a distance from the mainstream of cultural ideas, then largely opened the sluice gates to them, at the risk of being inundated. It seems to me, moreover, that this questioning, as it is posed, is a sign of profound disorientation, the search for a solution that could stop the crisis. Gabbard's article sought to bring together, in an area of intersection – a "common ground" – two separate concepts that belong to opposing theories. Between intersubjectivity, which has promoted enactment as a guiding idea, and projective identification, the pillar of Kleinian theory, finding areas of overlap seems difficult.

Melanie Klein had already shown little enthusiasm for Paula Heimann's key article (1950) which suggested that the analyst should rely on his countertransference responses to decipher the patient's non-verbalized psychic reality, when the latter uses projective identification to convey a message. Since then, more recent Kleinian contributions, and the echo they aroused in Ogden, have facilitated their adoption across the Atlantic and allowed for the discovery of hitherto unknown authors in North American bibliographies.

Enactment refers to the attempt to actualize a transference fantasy which had provoked a countertransference reaction (Chused, 1991). The question arises whether this is the usual, typical mode of analytic communication to the exclusion of all others, as Renik suggests, or whether it is a case of occasional circumstances as some Kleinians think. Be that as it may, the essential idea that arises from these observations that have appeared in analytic fields that are organized very differently is that the process that includes countertransference reactions (variously interpreted) allows us to admit the idea of a joint creation by the analysand and the analyst – implying the inseparability of intrapsychic and intersubjective domains. The essence of the current discussion is to wage war against the idea of a virginal blank screen constituted by the analyst's mind onto which the patient projects his unconscious fantasies. Is that so new for us?

Less than two years after this article on countertransference, Gabbard (1997) published, in the same *International Journal*, a second text returning to the objectivity of the analyst! Should we see in this a "repentance" in the sense given to the word by painters? Still, after examining again the different theoretical systems to which analysts now refer, he conceded, unlike Renik, the existence of a certain *objectivity* in the analyst. Gabbard defended the *difference* between the reality of the analyst and that of the patient where previously he had supported their concordance, their reciprocal resonance, their symmetry and their complementarity. A reality therefore exists independently of the mind that thinks it, according to the classical philosophical tradition. But here, Gabbard makes the analyst play this role. Wholesale subjectivism cannot answer all questions. We then witness the inevitable return of the developmental point of view that describes the transition from subjectivity to objectivity. In analysis, this concerns the difference between the analyst's perspective and that of the patient, which cannot avoid taking into account the externality that escapes the transference/countertransference mutuality. But is it objectivity or *another* subjectivity? Nothing indicates the nuance, which is nonetheless sizeable. One has the impression of a retreat after an imprudent advance: actualization, so evident in Gabbard's previous work, has given way to mentalization (Peter Fonagy's self-induced reflection), bringing the pendulum back to representation. One feels that Gabbard sometimes hesitates between the views of the authors discussed in his previous article and those he quotes in support of the following article. He concludes that there are two poles of separation and oneness used to define each other, the *analytic object* being the product of this co-construction. The analyst is held to be both a reflection of the projections onto him and that of his own subjectivity. Who will sort this out and how? We are back to our departure point. Why do we get the impression – I mention here those of my colleagues with whom I discussed these ideas – that we are witnessing here an unfortunate aberration which risks compromising, this time from the inside, the future of psychoanalysis which is already strongly under threat from the outside?

The report by Luisa de Urtubey (1985) showed that today there is a broad assent bringing together analysts who think that countertransference is an integral part of the analytic treatment. For that, it was not necessary to question the Freudian concepts from the bottom up. The impression that emerges from reading these works is that a drift that began with the rejection of the theory of drives, and then of all Freudian metapsychology (Merton M. Gill, e.g., 1977), was followed by the adoption of a resolutely psychological position (*Ego psychology* and *Self psychology*) before arriving at the discovery of the subject, emerging from intersubjectivity after a temporary interest in the theory of object-relations.

Intersubjectivity seems to have been reborn from the ashes of Harry S. Sullivan's old interpersonal conception; it was renewed by the work of Daniel Stern, based on interactive theory. The change that the concept of countertransference would undergo was to be expected; it was announced in 1950 by the contribution of Heimann. But we did not think it would take this turn. One is struck on reading these studies – especially when clinical examples are cited in support – by the lack of reference to the subject or to intersubjectivity, at least in the sense given to them in Europe. The "subject" is not subject to any rigorous psychoanalytical definition, it is a datum that seems self-evident and does not call for any conceptual analysis. This is certainly not the subject of Jacques Lacan's unconscious, or Raymond Cahn's, or that of philosophy. Everything suggests that this is the subject of empirical, not to say naïve, consciousness. As for intersubjectivity, it is obviously not the classic theme of Husserlian philosophy either. In fact, nothing clearly distinguishes "interpersonality", a term of psychopathology that is related to the notion of person, from "intersubjectivity" that would require a theorization of the subject. In addition, whatever oratorical precautions are taken, this bloodless intersubjectivity appears deprived of any density and *a fortiori* any opacity. If we have such reservations with regard to this presentation of countertransference, it may be necessary to find the reason beyond the picture of it that is proposed to us. For it is perhaps the transference it evokes that we have difficulty recognizing. What we are told about it never gives us the impression that it reflects a process that is only understandable as an echo from afar, *transferred* into space and time, whose obscure intentions we must guess and which must be deciphered by gathering the scattered shreds of meanings that often take on an appearance opposite to what their message reveals. We hear about the meeting of two unconscious minds, but what we sense is rather an intersubjective transparency where the level of analysis of the spontaneous or "enacted" reactions does not exceed the most immediate preconscious. We hardly see the interpretation ripen in the analyst's mind, branching out through associations, coming up against blind spots, letting fantasies emerge, looking for links between elements scattered in the material in order to bring out what is covered by consciousness. And when countertransference confessions are admitted, they appear "hypocritical" because they are linked to superficial ideas. The affirmation of their personal character does not dispel the feeling that the character of the analyst's confidences is scarcely compromising. What ship sailing in the Arctic would set its course based on the visible parts of the icebergs it sees? The recommendation to ask the analyst to make himself, for the occasion, "real", leads us to question what this psychic reality may be that is constantly confused with the idea of the subjective vision of the patient. We are far from the Freudian conception which defines it.

It is as if the idea of a theoretical-practical gap were not even mentioned. The theory is supposed to reflect entirely and completely a practice from which we have erased the asperities, obscurities, tensions and the relationship of the phenomena observed with the problems of the frame. As for denunciation, or even relativization, of objectivity, if one relies on contemporary philosophers to reject it, one cannot say that the examination concerning the concept of truth in Freud, in Bion or Lacan, is for a moment taken into consideration. Most worrying is this adoption of the model of the act as the main theoretical reference. *Interaction, enactment and actualization* are conceived less as "presentifying" (i.e. making present) than as "actioning"; examples of this abound. In fact, the analytic situation has moved from the sphere of representation, that is to say from fantasy, to that of the perception-action pair, action becoming the necessary prelude for perceiving thought retrospectively, without asking whether the channel chosen to hear the communication does not change its meaning.

"Enough of words! Action!" These innovations can be linked to Sandor Ferenczi's research. One cannot pretend that, since the beginning of these controversies, analysis has not evolved – and even changed its point of reference – without however falling into a tendency that results in this denial of itself. What is unfortunate is that this claim to the discovery of a new paradigm is based on epistemological models adopted without discussion, rather than critically examined –like that of the way of thinking emerging from the neurosciences in the new "philosophy of mind". One has the impression that the agreement between intersubjectivists and Kleinians rests on a common approach, which aims at the reversal of the model of the drive into action, a pre-Freudian position. They do not want to hear any more talk of the drives. But it will nevertheless be necessary.

Axiomatic choices and their consequences

It is necessary to distinguish between the progress that the intersubjectivists brought to the conception of the countertransference and the theoretical changes that they propose. It is now accepted that countertransference can no longer be considered as emerging from the analyst alone. It is heuristically more interesting to consider it as a co-construction of the analyst and the patient. We have known this since the 1950s, when the idea of a *two-body psychology* was put forward. The expression is, however, misleading because, if it is indeed a "psychology involving two people", it is about a single person and for him alone. The theorization of the principal authors is underpinned by epistemological criticism of objective knowledge. It would have been more desirable, before applying it a little too quickly to psychoanalysis, to take a step back by first exploring more deeply the peculiarities of the latter. We will have cause to regret, once again, the isolation due to the language barrier depriving the Anglo-Saxon reader of several decades of debate in Europe and, more particularly, in France. They have scarcely argued in favour of the objectivity of psychoanalysis. But even when communication is possible, if there is no linguistic barrier (as there is in the case of English literature), then a barrier of thought prevents it. Psychoanalytic experience refers to an unknown that is even more elusive than that to which the critique of knowledge refers. One may wonder about the deep reasons inviting us to abandon at any price the theorization that continues to place the *source* and the *motor* of the phenomena produced in session on the side of the analysand alone. We must not confuse the certainty that the transference depends on the one who analyses it, and who therefore mingles his own subjectivity with it, with the idealism of intersubjectivist theses. This is an extreme idealism since it includes, in its constructions, the ideas emanating from the other subject who forms part of the picture. Is the patient just the dream of the analyst or is the analyst the patient's dream, like the Lao-Tzu butterfly? I am not disregarding the advantages of the new way of looking at things that do justice to the extent and the depth of the exchanges. On reading their theses, it is difficult to escape the impression that one is dealing with the active avoidance of a real problem, rather than the discovery of a theoretical advance.

It is perhaps because intrapsychic theories seek to circumscribe a hypothetical source material at the limits of what is thinkable, conceived as uncontrollable, that all profitable analytical work can only relate to its more readily available derivatives. Let us refresh our memory.

> What is unsatisfactory in this picture, and I am aware of it as clearly as anyone, is due to our complete ignorance of the dynamic nature of the mental processes. We tell ourselves that what distinguishes a conscious idea from a preconscious one can only be a modification, or perhaps a different distribution, of psychical energy. We talk of cathexes and hypercathexes, but beyond this we are without any knowledge on the subject or even any starting-point for a serviceable working hypothesis. (Freud, 1939: 97)

The conflicting knot of Freud's theory which locates within the mind this unstable internal antagonism between the unconscious and consciousness becomes, in analytic experience, the possible source of a conflict between the analyst's interpretations and the resistances of the patient. It must be said that it is easier to elucidate what is happening in the analytic session by turning to the exchange of relations between the two partners and their search for a consensus than to dwell on the fundamental darkness of the phenomena over which we have only an indirect and partial grasp. Should we pay the price for this change of perspective, moving towards a more superficial understanding of the exchanges? When some authors stress that what happens in the analysis lies beyond the production of an unconscious phantasy of the patient (a position close to that of Bion and Lacan), they mean that the real or potential reverberations of the process spread out away from the producing source. When Lacan argues that the big Other is the one to whom the immediate material must be related, it is certainly not to defend the perspective of interaction. Although the analysand's perception is sufficiently acute to discern, unconsciously, the points on which he can apply his own projections to the analyst, or even lead him to assume certain roles (Sandler, 1976), this does not imply, in my opinion, that this relationship can be defined in terms of interaction. In the same way, enactment cannot constitute an essential parameter; it remains a manifestation of projection. I do not see any convincing reason to modify the place of the system of representations which find, in the analytic situation, their privileged place of expression. The idea of an *actualization* is completely relevant; it was, moreover, formulated by Freud in respect of repetition. It does not acquire more meaning by reducing the process that takes place within it to the act or even enactments. On the other hand, it is better understood as a process whereby a potentiality passes over to a status of efficiency, without it necessarily taking behavioural paths. In all cases, the short-circuit adopted is to be put down to resistance. The actualization is only the result of the part of this ensemble that can find a mode of expression comparable to a chemical precipitation.

In short, actualization does not in any way imply recourse to the model of the act and is nothing other than one of the ways by which all that is not conscious can find a way out in the preconscious-conscious that is likely to attract attention. To actualize is to make actual, probably through activation; it does not necessarily mean making acts happen. We have the proof of this with the idea of "speech acts", which are not actions but rather extend the register of acts to what is not an act, on the side of speech. The same goes for psychoanalysis. One must avoid the confusions that erase Freud's distinctions between symptomatic acts, bungled actions, specific actions and *"acting out"*. In other words, in this conception it is a matter of placing the act as a phenomenological landmark attestable *in praesentia*, in communication, while others regard it as a model for the functioning of the psychotic parts of the personality, even when no act is involved because it may be a matter of fantasies, dreams, or verbal formulas linked to *action as modalities opposed to elaboration*. In the latter case, the model refers to projective identification, distinct from an action, and remains in the order of mental mechanisms. To prefer the model of the act is to include within it the aspects of psychic life that are most foreign to it. The (unconscious) logic is admirable: the rejection of the hypothesis of the drive was initially directed at the extremes that could be opposed to it (the object, the self, the subject) before culminating in its inversion, namely, action, which deprives it of its fruitfulness as an *internal* process, whereas the new line of critical questioning would have been much more appropriate if it had focused on the concept of representation, understood in its specific psychoanalytic sense, that is to say, relating either to the drive or to the object. This reference to the act takes over from the well-known idea of "realization".

Hallucinatory wish-fulfilment is the perfect example of what psychic reality is. Reading the proponents of enactment, one has the impression that the external reality of the session is accentuated. This is a position that seems more accessible to them than structures derived from an unfathomable mind, which is difficult to detect, to authenticate or to attribute with a "psychic" reality that has the particularity of granting a belief "without degree or doubt in relation to certainty" with the unconscious ideas it shapes. Clearly, it is necessary to remove a certain number of ambiguities surrounding the notion of psychical reality. This conception of reality must not be confined within the limits of individuality; on the contrary, look at group ideologies. It is not incompatible with a coupling of subjectivities. For an analysis to be possible patient and analyst must have common structures. As I pointed out in 1975, the analysis leads to the construction of a third element as an analytic object that is based only partially on the intersubjective perspective, related to a dual relationship. This position was taken up and developed by Ogden (1994). But we must ask ourselves if the two-person relationship can create this third element or if we must attribute its origin to the structure of the subject, beyond the relationship between two people. On this point, certain conceptions like those of Charles S. Peirce, whose scope goes beyond analysis, make it possible to conceive of it. It is undoubtedly here that analysts are sent back to their initial presuppositions, beyond the recognition of the mutuality of transference/countertransference relationships. Behind the apparent subject-act pair, a decoupling of representation has in fact occurred. There then slips in, without our realizing it, a new implicit pairing: perception-action. This is the impression that emerges from these presentations, the analyst perceives what is in him (through the enactment) more than he represents what escapes observation.

Going beyond the countertransference in the theory of psychic functioning

The arguments I have developed will have convinced you, I hope, that it is impossible to present a theorization of the countertransference that ignores its relation to the idea of psychic functioning. I will reluctantly forego shedding light on the central phenomenon of countertransference, which has been done extensively in the literature of recent decades, and attempt instead to grasp its different forms and main modalities. It is from this perspective that I will try to understand some disagreements as well. Most of the time, the alternative theorizations do not include the considerations on which the opposing positions are based.

Do I have to apologize for going back to Freud? We know how intransigent he was about the somatic anchoring of the mind; this obliges us to admit that, at the foundations of the edifice, a power endowed with energy connects *physis* and psyche. I avoid using the word "drive", so as not to favour premature associations, which happens when one thinks one knows too far in advance what the ideas involve that one intends to elaborate.

I will bring to the fore the idea of force. This Freudian hypothesis is systematically minimized, if not totally rejected, by all analysts who advocate a more or less psychological or philosophical point of view, according to the theoretical contexts that are derived from it. What is primary, according to the terminologies, is the relation of "motivation" or "intentionality"; the epithet of the unconscious then applies to the guiding concepts without modifying the type of reference to meaning, variously interpreted depending on the theoretical contexts that arise from it. Freud's positions were part of his naturalistic ideology whose ancient roots have never completely disappeared. Freud defended himself by stating that his affirmations found their source in the latest results of psychoanalytic experience. One can, of course, consider that the limitations of his analytical technique were themselves determined by the conception of the mind on which he relied. However, it seems to me difficult to conceal the transference components highlighted by the concept of force. Furthermore, I do not see how to account for resistance, as manifested in the treatment, if we do not refer to it, with regard to both the analysand and the patient. Likewise, for the notions of fixation or inhibition to continue to be meaningful, the explanation given by the explicit or implicit participation of force cannot be suppressed. Moreover, one cannot dispense with recourse to it when explaining repetition and, *a fortiori*, the compulsion to repeat. That this force does not exist in the pure state, without being entangled with other paradigms, is indeed certain. A force dissociated from meaning could not belong to the psychic domain. If I am obliged to isolate it somewhat, it is because the idea of meaning purified of all force has been defended in recent years by certain authors. Going back to the 1950s, there was virulent criticism of the concept of energy that was held to be unsuitable for theorizing the psyche.[3] In truth, what was lost in the process of this dusting down of the theory is precisely the originality of the Freudian conception of causality. The connection of force and meaning makes them together a primary organization of the psyche.

Force is none other than that of the internal movement towards a source of external satisfaction. The psychic space in which it originates is variable according to the case. This force is not totally blind; but nor can it be said that it possesses a quality of consciousness allowing us to attribute to it the properties of intentionality. Certainly, the model of returning to the traces of an earlier experience of satisfaction helps us to think about it, but what Freud calls "wish" (*désir*) is the movement that drives the repetition of the experience, rather than consciousness of its aim. It is a force that responds to a state of internal tension that can be of somatic or psychic origin but which, in any case, remains linked to its roots in the body, and therefore, is not aware of itself. The most difficult thing to conceive

---

3 These criticisms stemmed above all from contributions in favour of Ego psychology, determined to free psychoanalysis of all traces of Freud's hypothetical biologism. I am speaking less of Hartmann – even though he stated that his aim was to build a general psychology – than of his contemporaries, allies and sometimes adversaries, who felt that he did not go far enough in this direction. This tendency is not confined to the United States.

is undoubtedly that, once set in motion, it progresses, most often through an object, towards a goal of which it has only a vague knowledge and which will only emerge when it is in the vicinity of the object. In this time or place – do we know what to call it? – a crossroads of production and exchanges is established. The first mode of production anticipates contact with the object through the creation of what psychic activity expects (Winnicott); the second, a two-way relationship between anticipation and the realization of contact with the object from whom satisfaction is expected. By inscribing and superimposing itself on these two activities, the object's response modifies the original versions, or even negativizes them, or proceeds with reversals, turning round into the contrary, displacements, condensations, etc. But the essential conclusion to be drawn is that the genesis, activation and modulation of representative activity puts heterogeneous forms into circulation and to work, giving birth to a space to be maintained and to be protected by defences.

I am not unaware of the objections raised by this way of seeing things; I adopt it only because it seems to me the best, in the light of the lessons of experience. But this requires the sacrifice of many requirements of thought. It can be argued, following Freud, with Winnicott, *that meaning is linked to anticipation in the vicinity of the object, along the trajectory that carries anticipation towards it, through the maintenance and transformation of the operative force that creates what it expects* (Winnicott's subjective object). Of course, the proximity of the object during this anticipation helps meaning to be born, to be constituted. But in any case, we cannot do without a conception of movement, in search of *both satisfaction and object* (to obtain it). Everything was complicated by Freud's need to accept, at a certain moment, the idea of a "beyond" the pleasure principle. This revision of his theory did not prevent him from preserving, even in this beyond, the requirement of binding sustained by cathexis which he conceived as the expression of the drive. And even if we refute the theory of drives, we can continue to rely on the concepts of movement, cathexis and binding, all of which can be understood as developments of the concept of force. Force is a basic assumption about the nature of the mind, but it is an abstraction. For no one has ever been able to demonstrate a force in analytic experience, except in an intuitive mode. On the other hand, the assumption is enhanced in the form of a concept that is better elaborated with the drive as a demand for work – here the dynamic register is articulated with the economic register.

Drive theory is so often rejected that we need, even if we continue to support it, to find other formulations to express what it relates to. We will draw them from the vocabulary of clinical analysis or from that which reflects the facts of experience in the theory. Sometimes, a direct intuition connects the notion and the phenomenon; sometimes we have to deduce it from the notion alone. Thus Freud spoke of the *attraction* (of the unconscious, then of the transference); attraction and *wish* – we can add *cathexis* (a reference that is above all topographical, but which requires us to recall the forcible occupation of a territory). *Resistance* echoes this. The series is extended by the terms "fixation" or "attachment", recalling that of "relationship" (a force that keeps the terms in relation to each other), of linking and even, ultimately, of "transformation" (because something must preserve the terms that undergo the changes and the result of this process). We thus detect the presence of this hypothetical force, under the most diverse appearances that allow us to sense its presence, which gives it a serious chance of referring to a reality. Force is therefore the result of an induction upstream, capable of making us grasp intuitively what the basis of the familiar notions is, but to which we must attribute the relations that exist between them. The same approach should be applied to the phenomena of the transference, the countertransference and their manifestations.

In many cases, for reasons that are mostly ideological, the concept of force is refuted. It is reproached for bringing theory closer to mechanics, of which dynamics are a part. It was the moving bodies of physics that were associated with it originally, but Freud's application of it to the human body, and to the "living forces" that inhabit it, seems to me legitimate. If one prefers to distance oneself from this orientation, one will focus on products derived from force (wish, cathexis, attachment, etc.). It can even be reintroduced (force of attraction, see Pontalis) and located in the object. One naturally thinks here of the illusions of the state of being in love – is it the object that attracts from outside or am I pushed from within towards it? As G.-A. Goldschmidt (1988: 91) noted, a drawer (*tiroir*) is a *poussoir*[4] (*Schieblade*) in German. Is it a question of point of view, or a desire to avoid a troublesome solution?

A priori, nothing prevents the coupling of force with the act. In doing so, internal psychic work is bypassed. Let us go back to Freud's original formulations, concerning the dynamic point of view in psychoanalysis:

> [Psychoanalysis] derives all mental processes – apart from the reception of external stimuli – from the interplay of forces which assists or inhibit one another, combine with one another, enter into compromises with one another, etc. All of these forces are originally in the nature of *instincts*; thus they have an organic origin. They are characterized by possessing an immense (somatic) store of power ("*the compulsion to repeat*"), and they are represented mentally as images or ideas with an affective charge. (Freud, 1926: 265) (Freud's emphasis)

So that is the force-idea, if I may put it that way, with both its levels. The first, hypothetical, organic, whose image is *constructed*, because it cannot

---

4 "Pusher" as opposed to "drawer".

be otherwise; the second is ascertainable by experience, whose image, subject to revision, is that of mental representation, of ideas or images with an affective charge. The ensemble forms, in Freud, an inseparable bloc. Mental representation has its source in the organicity of force (physical): it emanates from it. As organicity unfolds, it makes force representable. It was this bloc that would be broken by the moderns with their rejection of drive theory and the search for another theory that would be based on mental representation alone, whose nature nonetheless remains random. What are mental representations (ideas or images) with an affective charge related to? To the object relation, to the *self*, to the *self*-object interaction, to intersubjectivity? We can see that the uprooting of the Freudian psyche, far from remedying a stumbling-block, leads to a crossroads of uncertainties as heavy as those to which they were supposed to respond. In these new options, we have lost the original status of representations – not just any, but those which "have an affective charge" – as well as the hypothesis of the transformation of the interplay of forces into "mental representation". Other translators propose the idea of psyche as an emanation or delegation. Now, all alternative solutions implicitly place this representation in relation to the object, as an activity of the self or the subject, without mentioning its relationship to the body. Freud is the only one to do so. Amongst his successors, mental representation is the representation of the psychic by the psychic. Obviously, I do not underestimate the obscurities of this transition from the organic to the psychic. But, on the other hand, to explain all the derivatives of this force, as if one could consider them without invoking this sponsorship, does not seem to me to be worthy of what cathexis, attraction, fixation, resistance, repetition compulsion, etc., actually are.

I therefore propose to consider that the manifestation of force is most often invisible because mental representation (which cannot do without the more or less direct relation to the object) transforms it and makes it pass partly into the elaboration of representation and partly into the relations of the links between the different types of representations. Force has not only participated in the creation of meaning but also in its links in extension and "intension". However, in certain circumstances, a regression can call into question these networks within representative systems (this is topographical regression) or its relation to representation (dynamic regression) or its position as a mediator between representatives of the body and of the outside world.

To return to the question of countertransference: can we not suppose that its ordinary expression, an integral part of analytic treatment, is situated within the framework of the affectively cathected ideas or images between the partners of the analytic couple, while the forms taken by the countertransference in the acceptance that Freud gives it are linked to this "immense (somatic) store of power (*'the compulsion to repeat'*)"?

Of course, what is problematic in Freud's formulation is this parenthesis: somatic. It is difficult to interpret, as if it were the mark of a magnitude which, for Freud, had its *raison d'être* in the link with the organic. This is what I call the "metabiological hypothesis", which takes on the appearance here of the compulsion to repeat. Some people prefer another interpretation, to escape the return of the drive which is "the source of everything bad".

The inaccessibility of the object of the transference in the analytic situation pushes on the one hand towards the regressive deployment towards force and, on the other hand, towards the reactivation and actualization of the process of representation. The movement in search of meaning toward the object turns round on itself, unable to obtain what it expects from the object, returning to the situation of helplessness that no reassurance can overcome. The situation is then that of an inverse power, possibly opposing the work of representation, which results in the revelation of the (internal) object in a more or less figurable form, and which at the same time reveals, via reflection, the work of the emerging subject. Movement, waiting, the quest for meaning, as well as the echo evoked by the reversal that wards off a threatening state of distress, may impose the most paradoxical and resistant forms of the work of the negative on elaboration. It is necessary to differentiate between the analytic experience of non-neurotic structures and that of classical indications: the latter can lead the analyst to dispense with this notion of force in the name of other parameters that are sufficient for the analysis of "images or ideas with an affective charge". It should also be emphasized that by drawing on the study of the first relations between mother and child, interpretations in terms of relationships are favoured. Having rejected all the aspects logically linked to force, because of the obscurity of this notion, we have kept to the representation-affect pair, slipping towards the conception resulting from the data of the perception of the mother-child couple and of the externalized affects that are exchanged in it.

In fact, the analytic situation is a means of capturing the forces that are always present behind the affectively charged ideas or images that offer the structures of meaning a permanent source of elaboration. However, these can never exhaust the power of psychic energy which is constantly renewed and pushes for the creation of the scenario dramatizing projections. This is what, in some extreme cases, allows us to bring to light what I have called the analysand's "private madness" (Green, 1986).

The psychoanalytic frame is thus a device favouring the manifestation of force. Thanks to the cover it offers and the proximity of the analyst, it aims to convert force into intelligibility structured by the reference to the values of representation of the analyst-object. The eventual failure of this more or less temporary device brings us back to the return of what has been concealed. The analyst's presence and the paradox, formed by the offer he proposes while at the same time removing himself from the patient's view, testify to a complementary orientation towards the patient's quest for force. This orientation obliges the analyst, in certain cases, to use the force of the adversary by allowing himself to be inhabited by it. But all of this takes on a broader meaning if one supposes something beyond present intersubjective relations.

The transcendental dimension in Lacan, and also in Jean Laplanche, who both emphasize the indefinite referral of the process, the transferences of transference to which it gives rise, plead against reducing analysis to the two partners. A necessary condition – even if it is not sufficient – of the analysability of this psychical reality places analytic thinking at the heart of a fictional (transitional) existence that gives its specificity to the atmosphere in which the session takes place. To speak of a fictional reality does not in any way diminish the influence of its power and its ability to master the whole of psychic activity. I cannot refrain from referring to another dimension beyond the present relationship, that which designates the inaccessible sources of the psychical activity constantly feeding its flow, the very psychic activity, in short, that animates the vitality of the individual. The countertransference, although it appears to be part of analytic work, is therefore a return to oneself via the detour of the similar other, as I have suggested. But it will be on the condition that we consider the possible intersections of force and meaning, their potential imbalance which can be responsible for the deepest intuitions of the analyst as well as for the distortion of the responses caused by the analysand's transference. In this case, I would see it as the consequence of force being carried along by force, in a situation of mutual hypnotic fascination where the trap of otherness will close in on the capture of the same by the same. Anyway this trap is permanently present, implicitly. Manichaeism is excluded; analysis cannot circumvent the risk inherent in its practice, hence the need for the permanent analysis of the countertransference.

Dismemberment

From its first appearance in Freud's writings to the latest formulations proposed by the intersubjectivists, the countertransference has constantly transformed the meanings that it illuminates. It is not simply an enrichment of the notion, a complexification made necessary to better reflect what experience has taught us; we must ask ourselves what, in the semantics of such a concept, results in a term expressing the exact opposite of its primary meaning. Indeed, passing from the idea of countertransference as a derailment of analysis – akin to an intragenic disease of analysis subjecting the analyst to constant pressure due to the analysand's entreaties, session after session, and driving him to react by acting out – to the idea that the act, in itself, is the permanent basis of the analytic exchange, is a conceptual mutation that considers the ordinary act of psychoanalysis as a mystery. However, at the centre of reflections on the countertransference, one acquisition seems irreversible: the countertransference is inseparable from the transference, it is

Dismembering the countertransference 161

the result of the work of analysis, at each meeting. The analytic process does not exist outside this entanglement, which can take different forms depending on whether it is neurotic or non-neurotic structures that are involved. Even the idea of complementarity requires nuances: the analyst must keep a certain distance in order to analyse what is happening in it, while the analysand is asked to give such distance up so that he can express his transference. But such distance does not mean a flight from the transference. We would have a better idea of it by evoking the free circulation of thoughts, ideas and affects of the analyst in the various registers induced by the prohibition of the act. So the countertransference is a concept that must be dismembered.

Countertransference includes a conception that refers to the analyst's entire mind, encompassing his view of analysis, the role he intends to give to the frame, and what he expects from the analytic experience in general, and in particular before the beginning of each analysis. At this point, his personal analysis (its gains, but also what has remained unanalysed), his professional experience (successes and failures), his analytical convictions, where theoretical benchmarks play their role, and perhaps also his institutional integration, all converge. All this will form the bedrock of his singular, typical and future countertransference *in the strict sense* of the word. I call this ensemble "ante-analytic" (Michel Neyraut's precession of the countertransference, Jean-Luc Donnet's transference onto the frame), the disposition of the countertransference to expose itself to the emerging transference.

Quite different, and specifically characteristic, is the countertransference at work. This specificity emerges from the latency of the general disposition and is actually embodied in the relationship to a singular transference marked by the conjunction of the forbidden and the impossible. However, this singularity cannot completely escape the previous disposition towards the transference. But it can happen, in a true revelation of the analytic experience, that the latter allows one to go beyond the usual limits. I am not referring to a situation of transgression but to a countertransference experience that surprises the analyst's own expectations, enabling him to gain access to an unknown dimension produced by analytic experience. I am reluctant to use the expression "transference-countertransference exchange". While the mutual relationship is necessary for the progression of the analysis, the motor for the latter remains the transference. The analyst's desire cannot be a substitute for it. The exchange reveals the "difference of potential" between the two partners, which, it must be said, does not confer on the analyst an interpretative authority but rather imposes on him the duty to analyse the analysand's transference and its echo in himself. The analyst knows, during the analysis, the anxiety of uncertainty, the pain of thinking aside, the depressing effects of interpretative inefficacy. He does not escape affliction and distress. Fortunately, he can get out of it, and sometimes he has the great joy of snatching a fragment from the unknown, and is always enlightened by reflecting on it. The analyst's essential tool, interpretation, is always formed from the countertransference, which must not be confused with an unmediated reaction to the patient's transference. The place of the countertransference and (analytic) thinking imply the mobility of the registers and the activation of tertiary processes.

The double register of the processes favours the tertiary thinking that results from the operations of reunion and separation, in relation to the interaction between modes of thought that open up the possibility of emerging from dual impasses. It is found both in the external and internal relationships that give rise to phenomena and transitional objects within a space "on the boundary". To these two possibilities is added, in the context of the analytic situation between analysand and analyst, at the intersection of the exchanges of the transference and countertransference, this "third" analytic object, common to both partners. The applications of what I have called "thirdness" go beyond the confinements of the opposition between subjectivity and objectivity, just like those of psychic reality *versus* material reality, by adopting a way of thinking that uses, in order to have access to a truthful approximation, a found-created fictional construction, to use Winnicott's formula. This means neither imaginary nor real – but rather putting the resonance with the unknown, which we call "unconscious", or "id", or "primordial mind", to the test. This test serves as a mediator for us, for theoretical construction, beyond the transference and countertransference. Here we are at the heart of the paradox between a subjective object and an objectively perceived object that Winnicott recommends we should not seek to resolve, or between the operations of a subjectifying subject and those of an objectifying subject retroactively conceived. They have the advantage of both showing us the insurmountable nature of the hiatus, and of leading to the idea of a quest that always needs more than one object related to the activity of a transmutable subject. Of course, the question of its origins will then be raised. Opposed here are the essentialist interpretations that postulate its existence as being "always already there" and those that assign it a genesis, of which Bion gave the most radical interpretation with his notion of the transformation of beta elements into alpha elements, thanks to the detour by the mother's capacity for reverie.

The most ordinary analytical journey can sometimes encounter bad weather: squalls, thunderstorms or even cyclones. The main thing is to find a new equilibrium thanks to the analysis. The after-effects of these shipwrecks which the analytic couple have survived, and their evolution in the analysis, will have to be evaluated subsequently. It is not unusual for the situation to be less compromised than previously thought. Recovery depends not only on the analytic capacity of the analyst, but also on his absolute sincerity towards himself and his relationship to truth.

Analytical courage – a function of the superego – has a real, necessary existence, and not only in the analysand, even if sometimes it is not sufficient. For it is here that the infinitely cunning resources of the analytic *false self* are fully revealed.

There remains, finally, the countertransference understood as being coupled with the transference or as a meshed countertransference, where the work of thinking is paralysed by a hypnotic relationship of mutual fascination, under the influence of the transference force reverberated in the analyst who mirrors it, without realizing it. It is here that the temptation to act out gives way to the common desire, most often unconscious, to destroy the analysis, or to the preconscious desire in the analyst to end it at any price. This eventuality is not limited to the vicissitudes of transference love. This is what could be called the "reflected or tuned negative therapeutic reaction". I have kept to the broad outlines so as not to complicate even further the most impossible question of this impossible profession.

References

Chused, J. F. (1991) The evocative power of enactments. *Journal of the American Psychoanalytic Association*, 39: 615–639.
de Urtubey, L. (1985) Fondamentale métapsychologie inévitable polyglottisme. *Revue Française de Psychanalyse*, 49: 1497–1521.
Faimberg, H. (1996). Listening to listening. *The International Journal of Psychoanalysis*, 77(4): 667–677.
Fogel, G. (1997). After the paradigm wars: New consensus and integration in American psychoanalysis. *Gli argonauti*, 73: 147–153.
Freud, S. (1926). *Psycho-Analysis. S.E.* 20. London: Hogarth, pp. 263–270.
Freud, S. (1939). *Moses and Monotheism. S.E.* 23. London: Hogarth, pp. 7–137.
Gabbard, G. (1995). Countertransference: The emerging common ground. *The International Journal of Psychoanalysis*, 76(3): 475–485.
Gabbard, G. (1997). A reconsideration of objectivity in the analyst. *The International Journal of Psychoanalysis*, 78(1): 15–26.
Gill, M.M. (1977) Psychic energy reconsidered: Discussion. *Journal of the American Psychoanalytic Association*, 25: 581–597.
Goldschmidt, G.-A. (1988). *Quand Freud voit la mer*. Paris: Buchet/Chastel.
Green, A. (1986). *On Private Madness*. London: Hogarth Press and The Institute of Psychoanalysis.
Heimann, P. (1950). On countertransference. *The International Journal of Psychoanalysis*, 31(1–2): 81–84.
Lacan, J. (1975) *Les écrits techniques de Freud*. Paris: Editions du Seuil.
Lopez, D. (1997). Dialogue on the present status and the prospect of American psychoanalysis: Introduction. *Gli Argonauti*, 19(73): 105–186.
Ogden, T. (1994). *Subjects of Analysis*. Northvale, NJ: Jason Aronson.
Renik, O. (1993). Analytic interaction: Conceptualizing technique in the light of the analyst's irreducible subjectivity. *Psychoanalytic Quarterly*, 62(4): 553–571.

Sandler, J. (1976). Countertransference and role-responsiveness. *International Review of Psychoanalysis*, 3: 43–47.
Schwaber, E.A. (1992) Countertransference: The analyst's retreat from the patient's vantage point. *International Journal of Psychoanalysis*, 73: 349–362.
Viderman, S. (1970). *La construction de l'espace analytique*. Paris: Denoël.
Wallerstein, R. (1995). The common ground of psychoanalysis. *Journal of the American Psychoanalytical Association*, 43(2): 591–594.

Index

Note: italic page numbers indicate figures; page numbers followed by n refer to footnotes.

Abraham, Karl 31, 106
abstraction 38, 39–40
act, the 2, 3, 138
acting out/enactment 59, 135, 136, 137, 138; and countertransference 144–145, 146, 148, 153, 154, 160
actualization 139, 145, 148, 149, 150, 153
adaptation 2, 58, 59
Aeschylus 89–90
affect/emotions 3, 4–5, 7, 12, 39, 58, 83; and countertransference 142, 146; and language 97; and representation *see under* language and representation; and reverie 78; transformation of facts/sensations into 10
aggression 24, 41, 43
Alain-Miller, Jacques 91
alpha elements 77, 80
Alvarez de Toledo, L. 106
anality 31–32
Analysis Terminable and Interminable (Freud) 11, 27, 60, 62, 126, 139
analytic frame 9, 11–12, 26, 31, 60, 79, 97, 125–140; and dreams 61–62, 63, 99; and drives 128, 129, 130, 131; and epistemological aporia 134; failure to establish 137–139; and force *see* force; as laboratory 127–128, 136; and psychic delegation 128, 132, 136–137; and psychoanalytic psychotherapies 137; and representation 132–133, 136, 137; and resistances of analyst 139–140; and silence of analyst 9, 55, 56, 59, 63–64, 69, 70; and success/failure in therapy 125–126; and thinking 38–39, 40, 41
analytic listening 8, 53, 65, 71, 79, 83–84, 143n2; and imaginarization 84, 86
analytic situation 5–6, 125–126; and anality 31–32; and analyst's silence *see* silence of analyst; and the archaic 16, 17, 29, 31; and benevolent neutrality of analyst 81, 82, 145, 147; and borderline cases 31; and borders 41, 42; and boredom of analyst 31, 59, 115; collusion in 58; and compliance-pride conflict 31–32, 33; and countertransference *see* countertransference; and direct observation 17, 84, 131; distance in 71, 79–80, 81, 137; equality in 146, 147; and free association 58, 75–76, 81; and Freud *see* Freud and analytic situation; fusional 44; history of, analyst as custodian of 84–85, 86; and intrusion/separation 44–45; and language 10, 11, 80, 82; and reference myth 80, 81, 84, 86–90; and representation 38–39; and reverie 77–78, 79–80, 80; and speech *see* speech; and thinking *see* thinking/thought, *see also* analytic frame
angst/anguish 3–4
anxieties 44–45, 71, 87–88, 125; archaic 28, 80, 131; castration 19, 26
Anzieu, Didier 106, 107
aphasia 61, 95
après coup 7, 21–7, 61, 84, 85

archaeology, psychic 16, 21
archaic, the 6–7, 15–35; and anality 31–32; *après coup* reading of 7, 21–27; and borderline cases 28, 29, 30, 31, 34; and castration 19–20, 26; and compliance-pride conflict 24–25, 27, 31–32, 33; and drives 24–25, 27; and Ego, three sequential states of 25–26; inaccessibility of 16, 24; and Klein 16, 17; and omnipotence 32–33; and power/potency 30–32; and *Prima/Summa* opposition 15–18, 19, 32n15; and psychosis 17, 18, 21, 28, 29, 32, 34; and psychotic/neurotic structures 28–29; and repression 16, 17; repression 16, 17, 19–20; and sexuality 19, 20; and Superego 20, 27; and Superego-Ego Ideal 22–24, 25, 32, 35
Aristotle 63
Arrivé, Michel 96
artificial intelligence 123
associations 9, 11, 21n8, 48, 88; and silence of analyst 53, 57, 58, 65, 71, 73
Atlan, H. 95
attachment 155–156
Aulagnier, Piera 104–105, 107
Austin, John 92, 95, 96, 144
Avtonomova, Natalia 99–100

Bally, Charles 91, 94
Baranger, Willy 134
Benveniste, Emile 93
beta elements 3n4, 4, 76, 77, 80, 162
Beyond the Pleasure Principle (Freud) 2, 62
Bick, Esther 131
binding/re-binding 7, 22, 39, 49, 70–71, 155
biology 20, 21, 94, 123, 129–130; meta- 130, 159
Bion, Wilfred 2, 3n4, 6, 12, 21n8, 29, 63, 82, 107, 113, 126, 133, 138, 152, 162; and alpha/beta elements 3n4, 4, 76, 77, 80, 162; and emotions 4–5; and linking *see* linking; and Love/Knowledge 78, 83; and psychotic patients 76, 77–78, 80; and reverie 75, 76–80, 84, 86, 87; and silence of analyst 8, 53, 57, 59; and theory of thinking 9–10, 37, 44, 51
blank 30, 47–48, 58, 64, 112, 113; dream 41, 63; psychosis 38

Bleger, José 55n2, 134
Bonneval Colloquium 91, 95, 104, 109
borderline states 1, 3, 13, 85; and the archaic 28, 29, 30, 31, 34; and language/representation 38n6, 92, 104–105, 111, 116; and silence of analyst 55, 64, 69, 71; and thinking 38n5, 44, 47–48
borders/limits 38, 40, 41–42, 43, 44–46, 49, 50, 52; double 45, *see also* boundaries
borders/limits/boundaries 101, 103; and intrusion/separation 44–45
Braunschweig, Denise 63
breast 18n2, 28, 80, 101; good 10, 76, 77; psychic 77
Breuer, J. 92
Britain (UK) 58, 106, 120, 122, 143
Buxbaum, Edith 106

Cahn, Raymond 149
Canada 120
cas limites, les see borderline states
castration 19–20, 26, 28, 48, 67, 69, 71, 89
cathexis 5, 11, 19, 83, 101, 139, 155, 156, 158; anti- 136; counter- 45; de- 5, 30, 139; hyper- 109, 152; object- 99, 133
censorship 61, 70, 95
central nervous system 60
children 16–17, 129; perversity of 98; and psychosis/borderline cases 51–52, 58, 105
child–parent relationship 63; and Superego-Ego Ideal 23–24, 25, *see also* mother-child dyad
chlorpromazine 123
Choephori (Aeschylus) 89–90
Chomsky, Noam 15, 96, 97, 144
Christianity 34
Chused, Judith Fingert 142
Civilization and its Discontents (Freud) 122, 133
classical civilizations 15, 16, 18, 28
claustrophobia 87–88
closure 41, 93, *see also* foreclosure
compliance-pride conflict 24–25, 27, 31–32, 33
condensation 73, 89, 99, 156
Conscious-Preconscious and Unconscious systems (Cs-Pcs-Ucs) 2, 7, 38, 41, 50
consciousness 6, 61, 95, 101, 127–128
Constructions in the Analysis (Freud) 60, 82

container/containment 3, 44
cosmogonic myths 18, 25
counter-interpretation 56, 66, 67
countertransference 12–13, 43, 58, 59, 68, 82, 83, 115, 141–163; and actualization 139, 145, 148, 149, 150, 153; and American psychoanalysis 142, 147–148; awareness of 145; co-construction of 151; and dismemberment 160–163; and enactment/acting out 144–145, 146, 148; and force 154–156, 157–158, 159; and interactive model 143, 144, 149; and intersubjectivity 142–147, 148, 149–150, and object/object relations 141, 145, 149, 153, 156, 158, 159; and objectivity 146, 148–149, 150, 151–152, 162; and psychic functioning 154–160; and psychic reality 143, 145, 148, 150, 153 154; and representation 144, 149, 152–153, 158, 159; and self-analysis 141, 142, 146; and splitting 146–147; and subjectivity/objectivity 148–149; and thirdness 154, 162
crisis in psychoanalysis 1, 120–125; and alternative ideologies 122–123; and economic crises 124; and end of humanism 123–124; and fragmentation of discipline 124–125; and theory of unconscious 122, 123; three elements of 120–121
Culioli, Antoine 92, 94–95, 96

Danon-Boileau, Laurent 94, 114
de Urtubey, Luisa 142, 149
de-cathexis 5, 30
death 17, 121; and thinking 44, 45, 48, 49
death drive 2, 62, 78, 133
decathexis 5, 30, 139
decentring 61, 80, 139, 147
defence mechanisms 19–20, 28, 29, 62, 70, *see also* repression; splitting
delusions 43, 47, 49, 51–52, 75, 82, 95
denial 19, 32, 42, 68, 138
Denis, Anne 114, 115
depression 30, 43, 59, 65
depressive position 131
Descartes, René 34–35
desire 32, 67, 96; and crisis in psychoanalysis 121; and drives 3–4
destruction drives 63, 69, 70, 71
digestive model 76–77, 86

discours vivant, Le (Green) 91
dismemberment 160–163
displacement 73, 98, 99, 156
distance 71, 79–80, 81, 137
Donnet, Jean-Luc 38, 55n2, 114, 134, 161
double limit 7
dreams/dreamwork 2, 10–11, 40–41, 56, 70, 75, 78; and analytic frame 61–62, 63, 99; of father 79; and language/representation 98–99, 105, 107; manifest content of 10, 65; narrative of 94; and other psychic night activities 41, 63; and thing-/word presentations 10–11, 99; and transference 62; and wish fulfilment 72
drives/drive theory 1, 2–4, 7, 60–61, 151, 155; and abstraction 39–40; and action schemes 96; and the archaic 24–25, 27; and decentring of psyche 61; of destruction 63, 69, 70, 71; as force 11, 12, 13; and Id 5; and language/representation 92, 94, 96, 97, 100, 101, 103, 105, 108; and object 11, 22; and origins 128, 129, 130, 131; partial, regression of 69–70; relativization of 129; reversal of 131–132; and thought 37, 39–40, 50, *see also* death drive; impulse; instincts
drugs 123, 124
Dumézil, George 15

"écarts du discours, Les" (Green) 91–92
Edelman, Gerard 95
Edelson, Marshall 91, 106
Ego 2, 5, 26, 48, 63, 102, 103, 134, 136–137; archaism of 27; and borders 40, 41, 42, 43, 45–46; disruption/fragmentation of 8; excitation of 7, 25, 31, 33–34, 42, 46; fragmentation of 8, 65, 69, 70, 137; and language/representation 102, 103, 105, 106; narcissization of 69, 70, 71; and object 23, 24, 25; pleasure-/reality- 25, 45–46; splitting of 59; and Superego 22–24, 32; three sequential states of 25–26; and three types of identification 23
Ego and the Id, The (Freud) 62, 99, 108, 110
Ego Ideal 23, 23n9; and Superego 22–24, 25, 32, 35
Ego psychology 2, 6, 149, 155n3

168 Index

emotions *see* affect/emotions
enactment *see* acting out/enactment
energy, psychic *see* force
enunciation 58, 93, 94, 96, 97
epistemology 5, 6, 11, 17, 94, 121, 129, 134, 135, 151
excorporation 44
experience, emotional/psychic 4–5

Fain, Michael 63
false self 8, 33, 42, 163
fantasies 18, 66, 67, 75, 83, 84, 87, 88, 138, 144–145, 148, 152; of origin 17, 18; primary 16, 20, 28
father 63, 68, 78–79, 89; dead 34; dreams of 79
femininity 28
Ferenczi, Sándor 62, 82, 83, 106, 126, 151
fetishism 26
filiation 104–106
fixation 11
Fogel, G. 143
force 3, 7, 30, 125, 127, 132–133, 135, 136, 139; and countertransference 154–156, 157–158, 159–160; death 49; and drives 2–3, 13, 128; economic notion of 11, 133; Freud's abandonment of 130, 132; and language 12, 106, 109
foreclosure 5, 26, 38, 39, 68
forgetting 112
Formulations on the Two Principles of Mental Functioning (Freud) 36, 77
fragmentation 8, 65, 69, 70, 137
frame, analytic *see* analytic frame
France 122, 124, 151
free association 58, 75–76, 81, 96, 99
Freud, Anna 16–17, 55, 59n4, 62–63, 85, 130–131
Freud, Sigmund: *Analysis Terminable and Interminable* 11, 27, 60, 62, 126, 139; and the archaic 6–7, 15, 16, 17, 18–21, 22, 25–27, 30; *Beyond the Pleasure Principle* 2, 62; *Civilization and its Discontents* 122, 133; *Constructions in the Analysis* 60, 82; and countertransference 144, 145, 146, 150, 152, 154, 155, 157–159, 160; and crisis in psychoanalysis 122; and dreams 40, 60; and drives 2–3, 11, 105; and ego 134; *Ego and the Id, The* 62, 99, 108, 110; and first topography 99, 100, 105, 133; and force *see* force; *Formulations on the Two Principles of Mental Functioning* 36, 77; four periods of 60–62; free association 75, 81; and Id 5, 105, 134; *Interpretation of Dreams* 60, 61–62, 72, 98, 99; and jokes 98; *Jokes and their Relation to the Unconscious* 60; and Lacan 15, 16; and language/representation 4, 10, 100–103, 105, 106, 108–109, 110; limits of 1; and maternal eroticism 79; *Metapsychology* 25, 99, 102; *Mourning and Melancholia* 133; "Negation" 25, 25n10, 26, 39n8, 45, 48–49, 80; and neurosis 2, 29; *Neurosis and Psychosis* 59; *New Introductory Lectures on Psychoanalysis* 105, 134; *On Aphasia* 92; and origins 128–129; *Outline of Psychoanalysis, An* 36, 62; and perception 3n4; *Project for a Scientific Psychology* 46, 60, 61, 73, 86; and psychosis 36, 62; and reference myth 80, 81; and representation 132, 133; and Schreber case 32, 36, 52, 96–97; and second topography 2–3, 62, 105, 108; and self-analysis 142; and silence of analyst 54, 56, 62; *Studies on Hysteria* 92, 113; *Theme of the Three Caskets, The* 54; theoretical standpoint of 27–28; and theory of thinking 36–37, 45–47, 48–49, 50, 51, 52, 82–83; *Three Essays on the Theory of Sexuality* 60, 98; *Uncanny, The* 54; and unconscious 15, 16, 67; and Wolfman case 26, 41n10, 47, 51, 85, 126
Freud and analytic situation 6, 8, 11, 54, 60, 66, 81–83, 126–129; and countertransference 12–13; and forces 13, 127, 130, 132, 135, 154–155, 157; and historicity 84, 85; and laboratory analogy 127–128; and resistances of analyst 139–140; triple characterization of 81
fundamental rule 97

Gabbard, Glenn 147, 148, 149
genitality 69, 79
God 15, 32, 34, 35
Goldschmidt, G.-A. 157
Gori, Roland 107
grammar 93

Greece, ancient 28
Greenson, Ralph 106
Groddeck, G. 109
guilt 2, 24

Hagège, Claude 92–93, 94, 96
hainamoration/hatenamoration 34
Halliday, Michael 92, 95, 96
hallucination 109, 136, 137; negative 5, 40, 47, 49–50, 51, 63, 103, 112, 138
Hartmann, Heinz 16, 17, 62, 122, 126, 129, 145, 155n3
Hegel, Georg Wilhelm Friedrich 6, 15
Heimann, Paula 82, 148, 149
Heraclitus 63
history of the analysis 85, 86
Hjelmslev, H. 96
humanism 123–124
Husserl, Edmund 6, 150
hypercathexis 109, 152
hypnosis 75
hysteria 23, 65

Id 5, 22, 23, 47, 137, 162; and language/representation 102, 105, 106, 109, 110
ideational representative 100–101, 103, 112
identification 23, 23n9, 24, 67, 68; projective 30
identity 8, 41–42
ideologies 122–123
imaginarization 84, 86
imago 34, 42, 67
impotence 30, 32
impulse 2, 3
incest 27, 34, 48, 79
infant development 1, 9–10
infantile sexuality 19, 60, 62
instincts 3, 5, 127, 128, *see also* drive/drive theory
"Instincts and their vicissitudes" (Freud) 25
intellect 73
interactive model 143, 144, 149
interpretant 93, 104
Interpretation of Dreams (Freud) 60, 61–62, 72, 98, 99
intersubjectivity 12, 50, 77, 130, 136, 140; and countertransference 142–147, 148, 149–150, 151; and interpersonality 150; and intrasubjective processes 7, 38

intrapsychic 9, 12, 30, 50, 77, 115, 133, 136, 147
IPA (International Psychoanalytic Association) 120, 126–127, 129, 142

Jacobs, Theodore J. 142, 143
Jacobson, Edith 128
Jakobson, R. 96, 97
jokes 98
Jokes and their Relation to the Unconscious (Freud) 60
Joseph, Betty 144
Jouvet, Michel 94
Judaism 34

Kafka, Franz 73–74
Kant, Immanuel 6
Kardiner, A. 8, 54
Kernberg, Otto 128
Klein, Melanie/Kleinian analysis 1, 10, 37, 49, 55, 58, 62–63, 122, 125, 126; and the archaic 16, 17, 28–29; and Bion 76, 77, 78, 80, 87; and countertransference 144, 148, 151; and desire 3; and object relations 129; and play 62; and projective identification 148; and representation 83, 106, 107, 133; and symbolization 39; and two positions 131
Kohut, Heinz 126, 130, 142, 147
Kristeva, Julia 115

Lacan, Jacques 1, 2, 10, 37, 51, 63, 66, 80, 83, 122, 126, 147, 149, 160; and the archaic 15–16, 19, 21, 23–24, 29; and Bion 21n8, 78; and drives 129; and foreclosure 18n2, 38; and language/representation 91, 92, 97, 99–100, 103, 104, 105, 106, 107, 110; and matheme 21, 83; and Oedipus complex 63; and Other 71, 132, 152; and silence of analyst 54, 56, 59, 71; and symbolization 39
"langage dans la psychanalyse, Le" (Green) 91
language 4 5, 6, 7, 37, 60, 61, 62, 66; and analytic situation 10, 11, 80, 82, 89, 136; and the archaic 16, 21, 35; philosophy of 94, 122; and silence 54; and thinking 37, 44, 47, 48–49, 51, 95; and transference 12, 97, *see also* linguistics; speech

language and representation 10–11, 47, 91–116; and affect 91, 94, 95, 97, 99, 100, 101, 103, 107, 108, 112, 113; and borderline states 38n6, 92, 104–105, 111, 116; and boundaries 101, 103; and drives *see under* drives/drive theory; and ego 102, 103, 105, 106; and filiation 104–106; and four territories 103; and frame/fundamental rule 97; and Freud 10, 99, 100–103, 105, 106, 108–109, 110; and id 105, 106, 109, 110; and ideational representative 100–101, 103; and Lacan *see under* Lacan, Jacques; and linguistics *see* linguistics; and logic/philosophy 93–94; and object-presentations 101, 103; and post-Freudian analysis 106–110; and preconscious 101, 103, 108–109; and psychical representative 11, 101, 103; and psychosomatic structure 11–14; and reality 102–103; schemata of *102*, 103, 110–111, *110*, *111*; and signifiers 93, 103–104, 105, 112; and soma 103, 109; and thing-presentations *see* thing-presentations; and transference 97, 104, 111; and unconscious *see under* unconscious; and word-presentations *see* word-presentations; and work of the negative 111–114
Laplanche, J. 91, 94, 104, 105, 107, 130, 135, 160
Leclaire, S. 91, 104
Lévi-Strauss, Claude 15
Lewin, B. 63, 72
Liberman, David 106–107
libido 19, 22, 32n15, 69
limits *see* borders/limits
linguistics 10, 15, 20, 21, 92–97, 98–99, 114, 144; and the body 95–96; and consciousness 95; and enunciation 58, 93, 94, 96, 97; and interpretation 94; and logic 93–94; and neuroscience/genetics 95; and poetics 96; and referenciation 94; and six classes of language 93; six classes of language in 93; and translation 95; and unconscious 123
linking 42, 50, 65, 77, 78, 85–86; and clinging, compared 79
logic 93–94

London Report (Green) 111
Lopez, David 142
love 78–79, 81, 82, 83, 87

McLaughlin, James 142
Mahler, Margaret 17, 130, 131
Mannoni, Octave 100, 107
Marty, Pierre 114
masochism 26, 68, 138
materialism 21
mathematics 6
matheme 21, 83
maundering 75
melancholia 62
memory 82, 83, 85, 101, *102*, 108; and forgetting 112
Menahem, Ruth 95
metabiology 130, 159
metaphor 9, 56, 59, 105
metapsychology 1, 6, 11, 25, 46, 83, 109, 130, 149; clinical 13; and silence of analyst 8, 53, 55–59; of thinking mind 7
Metapsychology (Freud) 25, 99, 102
middle class 124
Milner, Jean-Claude 100, 104, 105
Montagnier, Marie-Thérèse 115
morality 122
morphosyntaxic language 93
mother 9–10, 88–89; analyst as 28, 31, 54, 56, 75, 78, 79, 86; dead iii, *see also* blank; negative hallucination of 47; and object relations 42; omnipotence of 33–34; phallic 67
mother-child dyad 33–34, 63; and countertransference 143, 159; and erogeneity 79; and reverie 9, 10, 76–80
motor activity 61
mourning 133
Mourning and Melancholia (Freud) 133
Mutterkomplex 28
myths 9, 16, 89–90, 97; origin 18, 25, 45; reference 80, 81, 84, 86–90

Nacht, Sacha 54
narcissism 2, 23, 23n9, 24, 121; and Ego 69, 70; negative 133; and silence of analyst 55; and thinking/thought 41, 43, 45
negation 25, 26, 39; double 42–43
"Negation" (Freud) 25, 25n10, 26, 39n8, 45, 48–49, 80

negative hallucination 5, 40, 47, 49–50, 51, 63, 103, 112
negative therapeutic reactions 2, 33
negative, work of the 4, 5, 12, 13, 39, 111–114
neo-Kleinians 62–63, 144
neural Darwinism 95
neuroscience 1, 94, 151
neurosis 2, 3, 28, 50, 69, 121; and the archaic 29, 30; and desire 4; and history 85; infant/adult/ transference 7, 59; obsessional 31; and perversion 69–70; and psychosis, relations between 63; transference 125
Neurosis and Psychosis (Freud) 59
New Introductory Lectures on Psychoanalysis (Freud) 105, 134
Nietzsche, Friedrich 23, 27, 109
nightmares 62, 63, 70
non-neurotic states 1, 4, 7, 9–10, 69; and psychic voids 10; resistance to analysis of 69, 70; and thinking 40, 41, 50, *see also* borderline states

object-cathexis 99, 133
object-presentation 101, 103
object/object relations 8, 26, 69, 70, 128, 137, 138; and anality 32; and borders 41–42; and countertransference 141, 145, 149, 153, 156, 158, 159; and distance 71; and good/bad objects 80; and identification 23, 23n9
objectivity 146, 148–149, 150, 151–152, 162
obsessional states 48
Oedipus complex 16, 18, 19, 23, 26, 28, 32–35, 48, 89, 90; and omnipotence of mother 33–34; and origins 129; and silence 63, 67, 69; and unconscious 123
Ogden, Thomas H. 142–143, 154
omnipotence 29, 30, 31, 32–34, 35; of mother 33–34; of thought 40, 44
On Aphasia (Freud) 92
oral fixation 18
orgasm 48, 57n3
Other, the 43, 71, 85, 132, 152
Outline of Psychoanalysis, An (Freud) 36, 62

paranoia 65
paranoid-schizoid position 131

parapraxis 98
parricide 27, 34
Pascal, Blaise 15, 34–35
Peirce, Charles Sanders 104, 154
penetration 71, 89
penis/phallus 19, 48, 69, 79
penis envy 28, 87
Pensées (Pascal) 15, 34–35
perception 3, 4, 61, 101, 138; and representation 42, 45–46, 103, 108, 112
perceptual pole 61
performative utterances 95–96
perversion 69–70, 98, 138
Peyrefitte, Roger 69
phallic stage 19
phallus *see* penis/phallus
phenomenology 147, 153
philosophy 34–35, 101, 122, 149; of language 94, 122; logic 93–94, *see also* epistemology
phobic states 48, 121
Piaget, Jean 15
Pichon-Rivière, A. 106, 107
Pinõl-Douriez, Monique 115
play 62
playful subject 97
pleasure principle 19, 85
pleasure-Ego 25, 45, 46
poetry 96, 97
poles, receptor/effector/perceptual/motor 61
political ideologies 122–123
polysemy 9, 66, 67
Pontalis, J.-P. 33, 105, 132, 157
positivism 6, 122, 127, 148
power/potency 30–32
pre-verbal stage 8, 10, 54
preconscious 9, 17, 38n6, 46, 50, 58, 71, 132; and countertransference 143; and language/representation 101, 103, 108–109; and reverie 85, 86
Press, Jacques 113–114
pride 24, 25–26, 27, 32, 33, 34, 35
Prima/Summa opposition 15–18, 19, 32n15
primal scene 20, 48
primary objects 24, 33
primary processes 8, 32, 45, 75, 110, *110*
primordial mind 3, 7
private madness 59, 68–69, 135–136, 159
Project for a Scientific Psychology (Freud) 46, 60, 61, 73, 86

projection/projective identification 26, 30, 38, 43, 57, 58, 131; and countertransference 148, 152, 153; and reverie 76, 77, 80
"Psychanalyse, langage: L'ancien et le nouveau" (Green) 91
psyche: optical model of 38
psychic apparatus 22, 25, 39, 51, 60, 66, 86; rejection of 123
psychic delegation 128, 132, 136–137
psychic functioning 1, 10, 43, 130, 154–160
psychic life 4, 16, 17, 18, 22
psychic reality 33, 85, 97, 101, 138; and countertransference 143, 145, 148, 150, 153–160; and force 154–156
psychic structures 1, 18, 22
psychic voids 10
psychic vomiting 49
psychic work 3, 3n4, 7, 8, 10; and language 4–5
psychical representative 11, 101, 103
psychoanalysis 6, 9, 11–12; crisis in *see* crisis in psychoanalysis; financial cost of 124; and linguistics 97–98; and origins 128–130; subversiveness of 121–122; and theory of thinking *see* thinking/thought; theory/ practice in 60, 62, 63, 126, 132, 150–151
psychoanalytic frame *see* analytic frame
psychoanalytic psychotherapies 137
psychology 96, 127, 130, 137, 149
psychosis 3, 17, 18, 21, 28, 29, 32, 34, 62, 85, 137; and antipsychotic drugs 123; blank 38; and language 101, 102, 104–105; and neurosis, relations between 63; and reverie 76, 77–78, 80; and silence of analyst 58–59; and theory of thinking 36, 37, 47, 48–49, 50
psychosomatic states 18, 30, 50, 113–114, 137

Rank, Otto 62, 106
reality principle 50, 85
reference (linguistic) 93, 97
reference myth 80, 81, 84, 86–90
referenciation 94
regression 20, 69–70; Oedipal 32; psychotic 17
Reik, T. 57
religion 27, 34, 122

Renik, Owen 142, 145, 146, 148
repetition 11, 13, 27, 37, 153
representation 2, 7, 10–11, 13, 78, 144, 149, 152–153, 158; and abstraction 38, 40; and analytic frame 132–133, 136, 137; and countertransference 144, 149, 152–153, 158, 159; and destructiveness 133; and drive 101; and language *see* language and representation; and negative hallucination 47; and perception 45–46; and silence of analyst 56, 57, 64, 72; thing- 38, 62, 83, 100; and thinking 38–39, 44, 45–47, 50, 51
represented states 3, 4
repression 16, 17, 25, 46, 48, 67, 68, 70, 71, 72, 138; and castration 19–20; and language/representation 96, 102, 103, 108
resistance 11, 37, 73, 113, 155, 156
reverie 75–80; of analyst 75, 77, 78, 84, 85, 86, 88–90; and free association 75–76; maternal 9, 10, 76–80, 162; and phantasmatic interaction 84, 87; and reference myth 80, 81, 84, 86–90
Rome Report (Lacan) 91, 94
Rosolato, Guy 91, 107

sadism/sado-masochism 68, 69, 70
Sandler, Joseph 144
Sartre, Jean-Paul 6, 15
Saussure, Ferdinand de 16, 21n7, 92, 94, 96, 97, 123, 144
schizophrenia 26, 65
Schreber case 32, 36, 52, 96–97, 107
science 6, 20, 21
Searle, J.R. 95, 144
second topography 2, 62, *102*, 105, 108
secondary processes 45, 50, 73, 99, *110*
Segal, Hanna 106
Self psychology 1, 142, 147, 149
self, sense of 10
self-analysis 139–140, 141, 142, 146
semantico-referential language 93
semantics 93
sensory perception 3n4, 6
sexuality 4, 20, 27, 41, 63, 92, 105; infantile 19, 60, 62, 64, 122, 126
Shafer, Roy 91, 106
shame 24
Shevrin, Howard 106
signifier/signifying system 21, 54, 61, 65, 72, 89, 129; and language/ representation 93, 103–104, 105, 112

silence of analyst 8–9, 44, 53–74, 139; and analysand as analyst 54; and analytic frame 9, 55, 56, 59, 63–64; and analytic listening 53, 65; and associations 53, 57, 58, 65, 71, 73; and borderline patients 55, 59, 64; and boredom 59; and death drive 62; and empty speech 56, 59; and genitality 69; and inner discourse of analyst 65; and interpretation 9, 54, 56–57, 58, 66–67, 73; meaningful 9; and metapsychology 8, 53, 55–59; and psychosis 58–59; quality/function of 64; and representation 56, 57, 64, 72; and reverberation 67, 68; and Sirens 73–74; structuring function of 58; and void/verbal abstinence 53
socio-biological perspective 20–21
sociology 96, 122
soma 30, 103, 109
speech 4, 6, 43, 48, 65–66, 70–71, 144; acts 95–96, 144, 153; associative 61, 70, 71; in borderline cases 64; and crisis in psychoanalysis 121; empty 56, 59; and enunciation 58, 93, 94, 96; and forces 135; gaps in *see* silence of analyst; linearity of 51, 71; manifest content of 43, 56, 67, 73; transference onto 12, *see also* language and representation
Spitz, René 17, 130
splitting 26, 30, 41n10, 62, 68, 70, 71, 146–147
Stern, Daniel 149
Stollorow, Robert 142
Structural Theory *see* second topography
structuralism 15, 21, 39, 123
Studies on Hysteria (Freud/Breuer) 92, 113
sublimation 17, 27, 41, 45, 98
Sullivan, Harry S. 149
Superego 20, 26, 27, 95, 102, 106, 134, 163; and Ego Ideal 22–24, 25, 32, 35; religious 122
symbolic matrix 9, 56
symbolization 22, 29, 39, 68, 71, 138
syntax 93, 97

tertiary processes 50, 111, 113, 162; *see also* thirdness
Theme of the Three Caskets, The (Freud) 54

thing-presentations 49, 98, 99, 100–101, 108, 110, 113
thinking/thought 7–8, 10, 36–52, 82–83, 145; and abstraction 38, 39–40; autonomy of 8, 41–42, 43; and binding 39; Bion on 9–10, 37, 44, 51; blank of 47–48; and borders *see* borders/limits; and death 44, 45, 48, 49; and double negation 42–43; and dreams 40–41; and drives 37; Freud on 36–37, 45–47, 48–49, 50, 51, 52; and language 37, 44, 47, 48–49, 51, 95; and narcissism 41, 43, 45; and negative hallucination 40, 47, 49–50, 51; and object relations 41 42, 44; omnipotence of 40, 44; proto-/inchoate 51–52; and psychosis 36, 37, 47, 48–49, 50; and representation 38–39, 44, 45–47, 50, 51; and subjective/objective 45 46; unconscious 47, 47n11, 50n18; unthought 41
thirdness 79, 103, 104, 136, 154, 162; *see also* tertiary processes
Three Essays on the Theory of Sexuality (Freud) 60, 98
transference 7, 11, 28, 30, 39, 42, 81, 84, 125, 138, 141; and dreams 62; and forces 135; here-and-now 135, 143; and language 12, 97, 104, 111, 113; maternal 54; and psychosis 58–59; and silence 61, 68, 70, 71, *see also* countertransference
transference neurosis 7, 59
transitional field 71, 139
trauma 2, 62, 89; default 133
two-body psychology 151

Uncanny, The (Freud) 54
unconscious 15, 66, 71, 72, 127–128, 130–132; and the archaic 18; and countertransference 143, 146, 147, 152; Kleinian 28–29; and language/representation 93, 96, 97, 99, 100, 103, 106, 108, 109–110; reverberation of 9, 67; and structuralism 123; as subversive concept 122; timelessness of 67
United States (US) 1, 106, 124, 142, 147–148
unrepresented states 2n3, 3, 4

vagina 69, 70, 79
Verwerfung 26

Viderman, Serge 146
von Foerster, H. 110
voyeurism 17–18

Wallerstein, Robert S. 147
whale fantasy 88
Widlöcher, Daniel 96
Winnicott, Donald 1, 2, 5, 9, 31, 37, 63, 72, 97, 107, 113, 126, 162; and analyst-analysand collusion 58; and analytic frame 55n2, 56, 134, 139; and the archaic 16, 17, 18, 29; and borderline cases 33; and drives 129; and observation 131; and reverie 76, 77, 78, 87; and silence of analyst 8, 54, 57, 71; and subjective object 155, 162; and symbolization 39
wish-fulfilmant 153
Wolfman case 26, 41n10, 47, 51, 85, 126
word-presentations 10–11, 49, 98–99, 100, 101, 103, 108, 109, 112
Work of the Negative (Green) 111–112